Marion Tooley

June 2007

AFTER DIANA

AFTER DIANA

WILLIAM, HARRY, CHARLES,
AND THE
ROYAL HOUSE OF WINDSOR

Christopher Andersen

NEW YORK

Grateful acknowledgment is made
to the following for permission to reprint
the photographs in this book:

Alpha/Globe Photos: 1, 2, 3, 5, 6, 7, 8, 9, 10, 11, 12, 13, 14, 15,
16, 17, 18, 19, 20, 21, 22, 23, 25, 26, 27, 28, 29, 30, 32, 33, 34, 35, 36,
37, 38, 39, 40, 41, 42, 43, 44, 45, 47, 48, 49, 51, 54

AP/Wide World: 4, 24, 31, 50

Gareth Gay/Alpha/Globe Photos: 46

Photorazzi: 52, 53

ISBN: 1-4013-0360-9
ISBN-13: 978-1-4013-0360-0

Design by Jo Anne Metsch

For my mother,
Jeanette Andersen

All my hopes are on William now.

It's too late for the rest of the family.

But William, I think he has it.

—*Diana*

PREFACE

She was the hardest act to follow: the most beloved, psycho-analyzed, written-about, and gossiped-about figure of her time—one of the most celebrated women who ever lived. In the pre-9/11 era, Princess Diana's death in 1997 at age thirty-six seemed unimaginable, surreal—so singularly shocking that none of us would forget where we were and what we were doing the moment we heard the news.

Nearly as stunning was the unprecedented outpouring of grief that followed, as an estimated 2.5 billion people around the world watched Diana's funeral on television. The images of that day—of a million tearful mourners clogging the streets, of Prince Harry and Prince William walking solemnly behind the horse-drawn caisson that bore their mother's body, of the Royal Family sitting in Westminster Abbey while Diana's brother berated them for being cold and unfeeling—were burned indelibly into the minds of a generation.

Now, a full decade later, Diana continues to exert a powerful hold over our imaginations. With good reason. In life, she was a Gordian knot of contradictions: impossibly glamorous yet disarmingly self-effacing, bold yet riddled with self-doubt, worldly yet naive. As high-strung as she was highborn, Diana was also the very definition of the word *mercurial*. She could by turns be sullen, petulant, and Machiavellian, manipulating the press while at the same time claiming to be its victim. She coped with infidelity, divorce, bulimia, suicidal depression, and failed love affairs of her own—and shared the heartbreaking details with a sympathetic world. In return, the Princess used her magic to touch the lives of the afflicted in a way no one else of her social rank and global fame ever had.

More than any other figure, Diana has continued to reshape and redefine the monarchy in death as she did in life. Faced with a dramatically altered landscape, a chastened Queen was forced to bow—literally—to her headstrong ex-daughter-in-law. Things would never be the same, although the intrigue and scandal that had been the hallmark of Diana's sixteen years as a member of the Royal Family would persist.

As the Royal Family grappled with the changes Diana had forced upon them, there were those who sought to neutralize her influence by attacking the person she was. In memoir after self-serving memoir, she would be unfairly portrayed as wildly promiscuous, narcissistic, emotionally unstable, and mentally unhinged. It was something she predicted, along with her own death. "They want me out of the picture," Diana said, "and then they want to erase me from the history books."

The motives for deconstructing Diana are many and varied. Diana had waged a one-woman war against the shadowy "Men in

Gray," those palace officials who actually run the monarchy. They clearly reveled in seeing her portrayed as the proverbial loose cannon. For his part, the terminally stuffy, unapologetically aloof Prince Charles continued to be blamed for Diana's emotional unraveling prior to her death. As details of her extramarital affairs surfaced, Charles could take some solace in appearing to be slightly less of a cad.

Then there was Camilla, blamed by some for Diana's demise and by all for Diana's unhappiness. England's—and quite possibly the world's—most hated woman in the immediate aftermath of the Princess's death, Charles's indefatigable mistress would spend eight painstaking years struggling to earn the public's acceptance, if not its affection. In a startling reversal of fortune, Camilla would replace Diana as Princess of Wales—a title she shrewdly eschewed, for fear of offending Diana loyalists. By the time the world marked the tenth anniversary of her rival's death, nothing stood in the way of Camilla's becoming Queen.

Regardless of who next wore the crown, William and Harry were the true heirs to Diana's unique legacy of charisma blended with compassion. For them, it has been the most difficult—and the most inspiring—journey of all. In the ten years since Diana left Paris in a windowed casket, her sons have grown from schoolboys to men. Along the way, they coped with soul-wrenching grief, depression, palace intrigue, gossip, scandal, internecine rivalry, betrayal, and expectations of greatness—all under the unblinking gaze of a ravenous press. The young Princes have also watched Papa wed the woman who destroyed their parents' marriage, and then learned to accept her as their stepmother—just as they found loves of their own.

Diana had always worried that, as they grew to adulthood,

William and Harry would be indoctrinated in the foxhunting, polo-playing ways of the Royal Family—that they, like the rest of the Windsor men, would have no real knowledge of, or connection to, the outside world.

Over the years, the boys have indeed been thoroughly Windsorized: William and Harry became devoted to their father's side of the family, even as they grew apart from Diana's Spencer clan. Hewing to tradition and country pursuits of the sort their mother abhorred, the young Princes were in some ways virtually indistinguishable from previous generations of royals.

Yet they were Windsor men with a difference. Diana had taken her sons to McDonald's and to Disney World to sample the joys of life beyond palace walls—and to homeless centers, AIDS clinics, and children's hospitals to show them its hardships. William and Harry ("the Heir and the Spare") had never forgotten these lessons their mother taught them. Inheriting her effortless grace and infectious sense of fun, the Princes picked up where Diana left off. They carried on in support of her charities and became passionate advocates for causes of their own.

For the Queen, William clearly represents the last best hope for the monarchy. When she assumed the throne on the death of her father, George VI, Elizabeth II was only twenty-five—William's age today. She wore the crown the night before her coronation so that, she explained, "I could get used to its weight." The crown must never have seemed heavier than it did on that August day in 1997 as she struggled with the momentous change Diana's death demanded.

Diana lived and died in superlatives. She was the bride at history's most famous wedding. She became the world's most famous woman—admired for her style and beauty, but even more for her humanity. She died in history's most famous car crash, and her funeral was viewed on television by more people on the planet than any other live event. Yet the true measure of her life would be in the sons who are fulfilling her legacy, in her lasting impact on the family that spurned her, and in the sense of wonder that she inspires even now—ten years After Diana.

AFTER DIANA

From Day One, I always knew
I'd never be the next Queen.
No one ever said that to me,
I just knew it.

—*Diana*

Sometimes I think they just
want to forget about her.
It's almost as if she never
existed.

—*Diana's friend Wayne Sleep,*
on the Royal Family

1

Sunday, August 31, 1997
5:35 P.M.

He took a few steps toward the body, gasped, then reeled back as if struck by an unseen hand. Beatrice Humbert, the diminutive head nurse at Paris's Pitié-Salpêtrière Hospital, began to reach out to steady Prince Charles but stopped herself as he regained his composure. "He was absolutely white," she recalled, "as if he could not believe what he was seeing."

Humbert understood too well. Ever since Princess Diana had been brought in from the operating room where surgeons had tried in vain to save her, nearly everyone who walked into the second-floor room with its bright, freshly painted robin's egg blue walls struggled to keep from fainting. "It was just too much to take in," Humbert said, "too much, too much. . . ." Charles was "crushed," said another nurse on the scene, Jeanne Lecorcher.

"I had always thought of him and all the royals as very cold and unfeeling, and like everyone else I knew that he really loved Camilla. So I was very impressed by how emotional the Prince became. Very impressed."

No one was more surprised by this reaction than Charles. He thought he had had ample time to rebound from the initial shock. After all, it had been thirteen hours since he was awakened at Balmoral Castle in Scotland with the shocking news that his ex-wife had been injured and her lover, Dodi Fayed, killed in a Paris car crash. The first person Charles called was not the Queen, who was also at Balmoral enjoying the summer holiday with her children and grandchildren, but his longtime mistress, Camilla Parker Bowles. As she had done so many times over the years, Camilla reassured Charles that all would be fine. Diana was a young woman, Camilla pointed out, and they both agreed that she was in the best physical shape of her life; whatever her injuries, she was bound to pull through.

But she didn't. "My God, Charles," Camilla said, weeping, when he called back with the terrible news. "The boys!" She then grabbed a pack of cigarettes off the nightstand, lit up, and puffed away nervously as her lover sobbed over the phone. It was to be expected that Charles would be devastated over the loss of his sons' mother. They agreed that it would do no good to wake William and Harry now; best to let them get their last good night's sleep before hearing the news.

Charles and Camilla were also weeping for another, less selfless reason. "My darling," Charles asked her through his tears, "what is going to happen to us now?"

In the nearly five years since then-Prime Minister John Major announced before the House of Commons that the Prince and Princess of Wales were officially separating, the public had shown signs of finally warming to the long-despised Camilla. Just a few weeks earlier, in the wake of a highly publicized fiftieth birthday party Charles threw for Camilla, surveys showed that 68 percent of Britons thought it was time for the couple to marry.

With Diana and her new Egyptian-born boyfriend grabbing headlines that summer, Charles was more confident than ever that the tide was about to turn in Camilla's favor. On September 13, Camilla was to keep up the momentum by cohosting a celebrity-packed charity ball to benefit the National Osteoporosis Society. It was to be their debut as a couple at a major public event.

The ball was immediately canceled on news of Diana's death, as were the couple's plans to vacation at Balmoral in late September. In a single stroke, the chances of their ever marrying were obliterated. "If Charles intended at some future time to marry the woman who has been his mistress for twenty-five years," the *Daily Mail* wasted no time editorializing, "he knows, and Camilla knows, that this must now be put off to a date so far in the distance that some of their circle are actually using the word 'forever.'"

Once again Camilla, who finally divorced her husband Andrew Parker Bowles in 1995, had become the most hated woman in the realm. After all, it was Camilla who had destroyed the Prince of Wales's marriage and driven the much-admired Diana to suicidal despair. "They've got to blame *someone*," Camilla told one of her neighbors in Wiltshire, where she lived at Raymill, a converted mill house. "That someone is going to be me, I'm afraid."

Raymill, which Camilla had purchased for $1.3 million after her divorce, was conveniently situated just sixteen miles from High-grove, the Prince's country residence outside of London. "If Camilla's car is seen near Highgrove for the next six months," said veteran journalist Judy Wade, "it could be the end of them. The public simply won't tolerate it." Toward that end, Charles and Camilla made a pact not to be seen together in public for the fore-seeable future.

Camilla would indeed be held accountable for ruining Diana's marriage and causing the Princess untold heartache. But blame for the crash would initially—and falsely—be laid at the feet of overzealous paparazzi who pursued Dodi and Diana into the Alma Tunnel.

Camilla was not entirely convinced. "Are they certain it was just an accident, Charles?" Camilla asked him point-blank. "Could it have been intentional?"

"Whatever are you talking about?" Charles shot back. "Those bloody reporters are responsible."

While Camilla would never raise the issue again, Dodi's father was determined to. The flamboyant tycoon Mohamed Al Fayed, who counted among his trophy properties Harrods Department Store in London and Paris's Ritz Hotel, had long been at odds with Britain's establishment. The moment he received word of the crash at his palatial country house in Oxted, Surrey, Al Fayed echoed Camilla's sentiments: "Accident? Do you really think it was an accident?"

In the Arab world, this theory soon gained traction. Predictably, Libyan leader Muammar Gadhafi wasted no time pointing a fin-ger at both the English and the French for "arranging" the acci-dent. But even respected journalists like Anis Mansour cried conspiracy. "The British intelligence service killed them," Mansour wrote. "They could not have let the mother of the future king marry a Muslim Arab."

Diana herself would have found it hard to believe. As a long-time thorn in the side of the monarchy and more recently the world's most visible crusader against the deployment of land mines, the Princess had made enemies of entire governments including, it was suggested, her own. She had always numbered among her sworn enemies the faceless "Men in Gray" who wielded immense power behind the scenes at Buckingham Palace. But even more troubling, Diana had been warned that there were also rogue elements inside Britain's domestic and foreign intelligence agencies—MI5 and MI6—who deeply resented the idea of a future king's mother being romantically involved with a Muslim.

In 1995, after dismissing her royal bodyguards, Diana was driving alone through London behind the wheel of her green Audi convertible when she approached a traffic light. She put her foot on the brake, but nothing happened. Frantic, she kept slamming the brakes as the car rolled into the intersection. Unharmed, she jumped out of the car and took a cab back to Kensington Palace. Then she dashed off a note to her friends Elsa Bowker, Lucia Flecha de Lima, Simone Simmons, and Lady Annabel Goldsmith. "The brakes of my car have been tampered with," Diana wrote. "If something does happen to me it will be MI5 or MI6."

Just ten months before she arrived in Paris with Dodi, Diana predicted the circumstances surrounding her own demise with uncanny accuracy—in writing. "I am sitting here at my desk today in October," she wrote, "longing for someone to hug me and encourage me to keep strong and hold my head high. This particular phase in my life is the most dangerous. My husband is planning

an accident in my car, brake failure and serious head injury in order to make the path clear for Charles to marry."

Incredibly, the woman Diana believed Charles was ready to
commit murder for—the woman Scotland Yard would later confirm Diana identified in the letter—was not Camilla Parker
Bowles. At the time, Diana was reportedly convinced that her husband had fallen in love with and intended to marry someone much
younger and more attractive than Camilla—someone who had not
only grown extremely close to Charles, but to William and Harry
as well: the boys' nanny, Alexandra "Tiggy" Legge-Bourke. To accomplish this, Diana believed there was a conspiracy to remove
both Charles's wife and his mistress from the scene. "Camilla is in
danger," Diana told her lawyer, Lord Mishcon. "They are going
to have to get rid of us both."

In her October 1996 letter, Diana decried what she viewed as
sixteen years of mistreatment at the hands of the Men in Gray.
"I have been battered, bruised, and abused mentally by a system
for years now," she wrote, "but I feel no resentment, I carry no
hatred. I am strong inside and maybe that is a problem for my
enemies."

The Princess made it clear how she felt about her ex-husband.
"Thank you Charles," Diana went on, "for putting me through
such hell and for giving me the opportunity to learn from the cruel
things you have done to me. I have gone forward fast and have
cried more than anyone will ever know. The anguish nearly killed
me, but my inner strength has never let me down. . . ."

Diana signed the letter, put it in an envelope, and sealed it before
handing it to her butler and confidant, Paul Burrell. "I want you to
keep it," she told him, "just in case."

A few months later, Diana would offer a different scenario for her demise. "One day I'm going to go up in a helicopter," she said, "and it'll just blow up. The MI6 will do away with me." (Diana was convinced that MI6 had already done away with her devoted Royal Protection officer Barry Mannakee when it was suspected he might be having an affair with the Princess. He was killed in 1987, when a Ford Fiesta swerved from a side street and struck his Suzuki motorcycle. "It [the affair] was all found out," Diana told her voice coach Peter Settelen in 1992, "and he was chucked out. And then he was killed. And I think he was bumped off. But there we are. I don't . . . we'll never know. He was the greatest fella I've ever had.")

This sad day in Paris, Mohamed Al Fayed knew nothing of Diana's prescient letter. Yet there was no doubt in his mind that Dodi and the Princess had been targets of an assassination plot. Flying his Sikorsky S-76 to Paris, Al Fayed arrived at Pitié-Salpêtrière Hospital at 3:50 on the morning of August 31 and was told his son had already been taken to the morgue. Ten minutes later, Diana was pronounced dead. On Al Fayed's orders, Diana's belongings were gathered up and shipped back to Surrey with Dodi's.

Even as Al Fayed's helicopter whisked Dodi's body off to be buried before sunset in accordance with Islamic law, Diana, whose son would someday head the Church of England, was given the last rites by the only cleric on duty at the hospital—a Roman Catholic priest.

In another odd twist, British Consul-General Keith Moss would give the nod for Diana's body to be "partially embalmed"—preserved from the waist up. The process was ostensibly done for cosmetic purposes. Given the lack of adequate air-conditioning inside the hospital and the nature of the Princess's injuries, French embalmer Jean Monceau told Moss that the body would soon be in no condition for viewing by the family unless action was taken. "It seemed," Moss later said, "the right thing to do under the circumstances."

Charles had, in fact, taken a keen interest in his ex-wife's appearance even before he left for Paris. At one point, he called Nurse Humbert at Pitié-Salpêtrière Hospital to tell her the Princess "would want to look her best" for the dignitaries coming to pay their respects that day.

Whether or not Charles's intentions were entirely innocent, the go-ahead for a partial embalming—made with the full approval of St. James's Palace—would add fuel to the conspiracy bonfires. The procedure makes a full autopsy impossible, since the formaldehyde used in embalming corrupts many toxicological tests. Specifically, it would be impossible to determine if, as was widely rumored, Diana may have been pregnant at the time of her death.

"We did nothing wrong," insisted Dominique Lecomte, one of the pathologists who did the embalming. But because of the procedure, Lecomte and fellow forensic pathologist Andre Lienhart were only able to confirm Diana's injuries instead of performing a full autopsy.

Since Prince Charles had seemed genuinely concerned about helping the Princess maintain her glamorous look even in death ("He was so sweet, he surprised me"), Nurse Humbert thought nothing of it when, over the phone from Balmoral, he asked if Diana was wearing her favorite gold earrings.

"But there was only one earring, on her left ear, Your Highness," she replied. "We cannot find the other." (The missing ear-

ring would eventually be found—eight weeks later, when forensics experts dug it out of the dashboard of the black Mercedes
S280 in which she had been riding.)

"And there was no other jewelry—no bracelets? No necklaces?"

"No, Your Highness. No jewelry at all."

In asking the question—albeit in a far more diplomatic manner—Charles was eliciting the same information the Queen had
already sought. Earlier that day, the Queen had placed her first call
to Paris, but not to ask for medical details or about what might
have caused the accident. She wanted to know if any of the major pieces of state jewelry that Diana sometimes traveled with
were in her possession. "Where are the jewels?" an official from
the British Consul's office had demanded of Humbert. "Madame,"
he repeated, "the Queen is worried about the jewelry. We must
find the jewelry quickly! The Queen wants to know, 'Where are
the jewels?'"

"The Queen had every right to ask that question," Charles told
Camilla, still holed up at her home in Wiltshire. Diana still possessed several pieces of jewelry that belonged to the Crown, as well
as Windsor pieces he had given her over the years, worth millions.
"We can't," Charles said, making a none-too-subtle reference to
the Fayeds, "have them fall into the wrong hands."

The Prince reported his findings to the Queen. Indeed, there
were no items of Windsor jewelry on Diana at the time of her
death—no rings, no necklaces, no bracelets. He then hugged his
grief-stricken sons before leaving to board the Queen's Flight BAe
146 that would take him to Paris along with Diana's Spencer sisters Lady Sarah McCorquodale and Lady Jane Fellowes.

It was not a trip the Queen had wanted her son to make. Her
Majesty had once been fond of Diana; tellingly, the Queen's

warmly worded letters of encouragement to her daughter-in-law were invariably signed "Mama." But in recent years, the Queen had come to regard Diana more and more as a reckless, self-centered threat to the monarchy. Since the Queen had stripped the Princess of her royal status when the divorce was finalized the previous year, Diana had no official rank, no status. Therefore Her Majesty deemed it "inappropriate" for any member of the Royal Family to make the trip to claim the body. "The Spencers are her family, Charles," she told him. "They should be the ones to bring Diana back."

But Charles, who had spent years waging a public relations war against the media-savvy Diana, overruled the monarch. Appreciating full well the intensity of his countrymen's feelings toward Diana, Charles ignored his mother's objections and went ahead with plans to accompany the Princess's body back to England. "We must show Diana the respect she is due," he told his mother. "If we don't we will all be terribly sorry, I'm afraid."

By way of damage control, Charles would be taking along only one senior member of his staff: his deputy private secretary and media Svengali, Mark Bolland. A former director of Britain's Press Complaints Commission who maintained warm relations with most of Fleet Street's most powerful editors, Bolland had been hired the year before to boost Charles's standing in the public eye. An equally important part of Bolland's job was to remake Camilla's image.

"The press has been terribly cruel to her," Charles told his new spin doctor at a meeting in August 1996. "I want you to make people see Mrs. Parker Bowles through my eyes, let them see the marvelous woman I see. Once they do, I know they will love her the way I love her." To accomplish his daunting assignment, Bolland hatched a top-secret plan that would be known behind the walls of St. James's Palace as "Operation PB" (Operation Parker Bowles).

Behind the scenes, Camilla had played a key role in implementing Operation Parker Bowles. Just three months earlier, in late May 1997, she had asked Bolland to arrange a secret lunch at Highgrove with Prime Minister Tony Blair's chief image consultant, Peter Mandelson. With Camilla, Charles, and Bolland in attendance, Mandelson mapped out a strategy for the Prince of Wales to win back the hearts and minds of his people—and for Camilla to make herself acceptable to them as Diana's replacement.

Within an hour of Diana's death, Charles was on the phone with Bolland again—this time seeking advice on how to steer public opinion his way in the wake of the tragedy. Although Diana rightly viewed St. James's as "the enemy camp" where Charles's minions actively plotted against her, Bolland was now among those urging the Prince to make a public display of respect for the dead Princess.

"Diana was right about one thing," said a former junior staff member at St. James's Palace, "everyone around Prince Charles hated her. The rest of the world may have seen her as a saint, but at St. James's the Princess was thought of as scheming, selfish—a borderline psychotic. It was considered disloyal to say anything remotely nice about her."

Now, as the royal jet took off across the English Channel, Charles phoned Camilla for the words of comfort and support he would never get from his mother. His voice broke on several occasions during the conversation, and at one point he pulled a handkerchief from his breast pocket to wipe his eyes. Once he finished the conversation by telling Camilla how much he loved her, Charles huddled with Bolland in the rear of the aircraft to hammer out a public relations strategy for the day. It was, without doubt, going to be an emotionally taxing journey for the Prince of Wales. But the two men agreed it was also going to be a pivotal time in the monarchy's history—a defining moment in which Charles might win the hearts of his countrymen and, in the process, their blessing to marry Camilla.

Once the plane touched down in Paris, Charles and Diana's sisters were whisked in a silver Jaguar limousine to Pitié-Salpêtrière Hospital, where French President Jacques Chirac waited outside to greet them. Then they made their way through the maze of narrow corridors to Diana's small room on the second floor.

In the hours since learning of Diana's death, Charles had steeled himself for the sight of her lifeless body lying beneath a crisp white hospital sheet. Instead, Charles was, he would later confess, "completely unprepared" for the grim tableau that awaited him. Diana was already lying in her coffin, clad in a black shawl-collared cocktail dress and matching pumps borrowed from Sylvia Jay, wife of Britain's ambassador to France, Sir Michael Jay. The Princess's hair and makeup had been done to resemble a recent photo of her in *Paris Match*, and in one hand she held one of her most treasured possessions—the rosary Mother Teresa had given her just two months earlier.

The lid of the bizarre-looking gray metal casket, which had a window in it so that the deceased's face could be viewed by French customs officials at the airport, was propped open. The smell of fresh paint and formaldehyde mingled with the scent of roses and lilies—roses from the Chiracs and lilies from Charles. Oddly, no one else had sent flowers to the hospital.

Struggling to keep from fainting, Charles gasped when Diana's hair rustled in the breeze from the air-conditioning. Then he turned to comfort Diana's sisters, who by now had both dissolved in tears. The trio of mourners sat on chairs that had been brought into the room, hung their heads, and followed a newly arrived Anglican priest in reciting the Lord's Prayer.

When they were done, Charles made a point of meeting with the doctors and nurses who had treated Diana. He thanked them all in flawless French but appeared to grow tongue-tied when he met the two cardiovascular surgeons who had worked frantically to revive Diana by massaging her heart. "Congratulations!" he blurted out to the confused-looking physicians, who might well have interpreted the remark as sarcasm. Startled at his mistake, Charles hastily assured the medical team that he realized they had done all they could. While he chatted with hospital staffers in a room down the hall, Charles was spared the sight of pallbearers from a funeral home jostling Diana as they struggled to lift the gray metal coffin and place it in a large oak casket for the flight to England.

Once back on the plane bound for Northolt Air Base in North London, members of Diana's staff who had come to Paris to assist with the transfer of her body were shocked to see Mark Bolland, a general in Charles's media war of attrition with the Princess. "I wondered," one recalled, "what on *earth* he was doing on the plane."

Throughout the brief flight, Charles was on the phone to Camilla, this time sobbing to her about the "bloody awful" sight of Diana lying in her coffin. "It was so shocking seeing her like that," he said. "It was so . . . final." He allowed that the corpse looked beautiful, but then fixated on the fact that Diana was not wearing her favorite gold earrings. "The nurse told me that when they brought her in, she was only wearing one earring . . . ," Charles told Camilla, his voice trailing off. "They never found the other earring. It's sad, really. . . . That she only had the one earring . . ."

Prime Minister Tony Blair was among the dignitaries waiting on the tarmac when the RAF jet bearing Diana's body in the cargo hold arrived back on British soil. The coffin, covered in the harps and lions of the red, white, purple, and gold royal standard, was then lifted out of the belly of the plane by an RAF honor guard and slowly walked to a waiting hearse.

While Charles headed back to Balmoral to be with his sons, the hearse drove to the Hammersmith and Fulham Mortuary in West London for a second postmortem by John Burton, who was then Coroner of the Queen's Household, and his deputy Michael Burgess—this one conducted according to British law. Diana's personal physician was also there to observe. "I have to attend an autopsy now," he told Diana's sisters, "and it's not going to be easy."

The results of the second autopsy would again raise eyebrows among conspiracy theorists. After they were shown the top-secret English autopsy report, Dominique Lecomte and Andre Lienhart—the French pathologists who had done the partial embalming of Diana in Paris—wrote a memo critical of the coroner's findings. A decade later, the potentially explosive memo and the autopsy report—either or both of which might prove a cover-up—remained under lock and key.

Neither Charles nor the Queen would ever question the circumstances surrounding the crash itself, why ninety minutes had passed before the ambulance carrying Diana arrived at a hospital just 3.8 miles from the crash site, or what either of the autopsies may have revealed. "It is not in their nature to ask difficult questions," a longtime courtier conceded. "They are simply not interested in much more than horses, dogs, and foxhunting. They prefer to keep their heads buried in the sand."

Such was the case in the days leading up to Diana's funeral. Even as a sea of flowers lapped at the palace gates and hundreds of thousands of mourners poured into central London, the Queen refused to interrupt her holiday at Balmoral. Nor would she agree to fly the flag over Buckingham Palace at half-mast, something traditionally done only on the occasion of the sovereign's death. "We did not fly the flag at half-staff for Sir Winston Churchill," she huffed. "We are certainly not going to fly it at half-staff for *her*."

The public's growing resentment was echoed on the front pages of Britain's newspapers. LET THE FLAG FLY AT HALF MAST, trumpeted the *Daily Mail*. The *Mirror* pleaded SPEAK TO US MA'AM—YOUR PEOPLE ARE SUFFERING, while the *Sun* simply asked WHERE IS THE QUEEN WHEN THE COUNTRY NEEDS HER? WHERE IS HER FLAG? and the *Daily Express* demanded SHOW US YOU CARE.

Polls showed that 66 percent of Britons now believed the monarchy was doomed. Fifty-eight percent wanted William, not Charles, to be their next King. "The monarchy must bow its head," warned constitutional expert Anthony Barrett, "or it will be broken."

Britons might have felt even more strongly had they known that the Queen had nixed initial plans to have Diana buried on the grounds of Windsor Castle (as Dr. John Burton, Coroner to the Queen, had been led to believe) and was even resisting Charles's plea for a large public funeral. Her Majesty wanted the Spencers to go ahead with their original plans for a small private service. Again Elizabeth pointed out that, despite her phenomenal popularity, Diana did not qualify for either a state funeral or a royal one. There was simply no precedent for it.

"The Firm," as the Royal Family called itself, seemed oblivious to the people's pain; the public's anger over the monarch's icy indifference was mounting with each passing day. Prime Minister Blair urged Charles to pressure his mother into returning to London immediately to deal with the growing hostility toward the Crown. But how? "She simply will not budge," Charles complained at one point to Camilla. "I don't know what else I can do to make her understand."

Ironically, behind the scenes, Camilla—now unquestionably the most reviled woman in the land—played a role similar to Tony Blair's. Charles had always been reluctant to defy his mother, and now, in a series of intense phone conversations, it was Camilla who gave her prince some much-needed backbone. She urged him to give the Queen an ultimatum: either she would return to London and address the people on television—or he would. "The Queen must be made to understand," she told him bluntly. "You must do this, Charles. The monarchy may come down if you don't." Camilla was not alone in this assessment.

At long last the Queen grudgingly relented on all fronts. She approved plans for a televised public service at Westminster Abbey befitting the young woman Britons now called their "Queen of Hearts." She would return to London and order that the flag over Buckingham Palace be lowered to half-mast. And she would address her people. The Queen's televised speech, in which she paid tribute to Diana "as an exceptional and gifted human being," was the performance of a lifetime. When it was over, Charles phoned Camilla yet again and asked what she thought.

"It seemed," Camilla replied, "very heartfelt."

Whether or not the Queen had been entirely candid scarcely mattered. The important question was whether *the people* believed she had meant what she said. And even if they believed the sincerity of Her Majesty's words, was it enough?

Charles was not convinced. Again, he sought Camilla's counsel. What more could the Queen do to show that she is sorry? he asked her over the phone. What gesture could she possibly make that might quell the firestorm that raged outside the palace gates? "Perhaps Mama could bow," he thought out loud.

"Bow?" asked Camilla, dumbfounded.

"Yes," Charles explained. "She could bow to the coffin. It would send a powerful message, I suppose."

Charles bounced it off his spin doctor, Mark Bolland. Such a gesture could erase much of the ill will now directed at the Royal Family. It could also, Charles added hopefully, help get Operation PB—and his hopes of ever wedding Camilla—back on track.

The Queen, however, had some ideas of her own. She suggested to her son that now would be a good time to make a formal announcement that he was severing his relationship with Mrs. Parker Bowles. Incensed, Charles invoked the word he often used to describe the depth of his commitment to Camilla. "You already know," he told the Queen, "that she is nonnegotiable."

For the time being, the mood on the street was still tense as hundreds of thousands of Britons streamed into London for Diana's funeral. Things could easily turn ugly. Charles warned his mother that, Queen or no, she faced the very real possibility that she might be booed or even physically attacked.

Charles was also worried about Camilla's safety. Since Diana's death, she had received scores of death threats over the phone and in the mail. She could no longer venture outside; when she attempted to do her daily errands, people on the street shouted epithets at her or simply stopped to glare and shake their heads in disgust. At the local supermarket, customers called Camilla "whore" and pelted her with bread.

For years Camilla had managed to shrug off the withering stares and could find humor in some of the most devastating remarks made about her. When it was revealed that Diana had taken to calling her "The Rottweiler," Camilla began answering the telephone "Rottweiler here!" (Charles's mistress also had a nickname for the willowy blond Princess: "Barbie.")

Now, however, Camilla admitted that for the first time in her life she feared for her own safety. The Prince immediately ordered that four Royal Protection officers armed with Glock 9 mm automatic pistols be added to the regular detail that was already guarding his mistress's house.

For all the animosity directed at Camilla and the Queen, the Prince of Wales knew that he too was a likely target. In fact, he was convinced that he was going to be gunned down as he marched in Diana's funeral procession. Just as Diana had done when she predicted her own death, Charles sat down and wrote four letters—one to William, one to Harry, another to Camilla, and the last to the British people.

Writing to William, Charles praised him for his maturity and predicted that he would make a great King. Charles urged the Spare to support the Heir but to never allow himself to be eclipsed by him. In his letter to Camilla, Charles professed his undying love and pledged that he would have made good his promise to one day make her Queen. His letter to the British people was succinct. Despite obvious missteps over the years, Charles wrote, he had always tried to do his duty as Prince of Wales. Now he was sorry that he would not have the opportunity to serve his country as King.

Charles signed the letters and then sealed them in small red envelopes bearing the three-feathered seal of the Prince of Wales.

They were left on the desk of his study at St. James's Palace, to be delivered "in the event of my death."

The next day, 2.5 billion people—the largest number ever to witness a single live event—watched as Diana's funeral cortege made its way from Kensington Palace to Westminster Abbey. Despite the fact that 1.5 million people had poured into the city to pay their respects, the streets were eerily silent as Prince Philip, Charles, William, Harry, and Diana's brother, Earl Spencer, walked solemnly behind the caisson bearing the Princess's body. "It was the most harrowing experience of my life," Spencer later recalled. "There was a clear feeling of high emotion around you of the most sad and confused sort, all hammering in on you. It was a tunnel of grief."

Most spectators averted their eyes when the boys passed by—it was, many later recalled, simply too painful to look at them. Particularly moving was the message on a card tucked among the spray of white lilies atop Diana's casket. Written on the card in Harry's hand was a single word: MUMMY.

Earl Spencer would later reveal that he had been "tricked" into letting William and Harry march behind their mother's coffin. Spencer protested that the experience would be too painful. "I genuinely felt that Diana would not have wanted them to have done it." But royal officials persuaded Spencer that the boys wanted to do it. When he realized halfway through the ordeal that neither William nor Harry had asked to take part in the grim procession, Spencer became angry. "I thought that was where tradition and duty went too far against human nature," he said. This was the incident, Spencer claimed, that would later lead him to make a scathing attack on the Royal Family during his eulogy for Diana.

The Queen was standing outside with other members of the Royal Family when the gun wagon bearing Diana's flag-draped casket approached Buckingham Palace. As it passed by, the sovereign bowed her head and paused for a moment.

Camilla, glued to her television with family members in Wiltshire, shook her head in disbelief. "My God," she murmured and took another drag on her ever-present cigarette.

Once inside the abbey itself, Earl Spencer, still seething over Charles's insistence that the boys walk behind Diana's coffin, fired a broadside aimed squarely at the Royal Family. While Elizabeth sat stoically only a few seats away, Queen Victoria's saucer-size diamond brooch sparkling on her lapel, Spencer praised Diana as someone who "needed no royal title to continue to generate her particular brand of magic." Then he promised that the boys' "blood family"—though it was hard to imagine how the Windsors were any less "blood" than the Spencers—would see to it that the young Princes' "souls are not simply immersed by duty and tradition but can sing openly as you planned."

Camilla, squinting at the telly, took an extra puff on her cigarette. "My word," she said as she listened to Earl Spencer eviscerate the royals. "That bastard!"

When it was over, the Queen returned to Buckingham Palace. A photograph she had seen that morning in the *Times* of London showed a banner spread across the grass in front of Kensington Palace. It read: NO ONE CAN HURT YOU NOW. Perhaps, but the Queen wondered if the reverse was true. In death, Diana was already proving to be an even more formidable threat than she had been in life.

Of one thing, however, Elizabeth II had no doubt. "Poor Mrs. Parker Bowles," she told the Queen Mother over gin and tonics in her drawing room. "There is no way Charles will ever be able to marry her now."

The Queen Mother nodded. "Pity," she said.

Does this mean that Charles is going
to remarry?

>—*Princess Diana in 1996,*
>   *after agreeing to divorce Charles*

I think that very unlikely.

>—*The Queen*

She squinted down at the program resting in her lap, sighed, then lifted her gaze straight ahead. For this occasion, the Queen of England wore a white suit and matching broad-brimmed hat, black gloves, and an expression that would be variously described in the press as "sour," "sullen," and "cross." On her lapel glittered the Australian wattle brooch, made up of 150 yellow and blue white diamonds—a significant piece, but not as historically important as the immense Queen Victoria diamond bow brooch Elizabeth wore to Diana's funeral.

To the 750 people assembled in St. George's Chapel—spiritual home of the Order of the Garter and burial place of ten kings, including Henry VIII—Elizabeth II, seated to the right of the altar with the rest of the Royal Family, made no attempt to conceal her displeasure. With good reason. Only a few yards away, in the nave of St. George's Chapel at Windsor, Charles and his new bride, Camilla—whom the Queen had routinely referred to simply as "That Wicked Woman"—stood at separate lecterns, reading passages from the Gospel aloud. Leading this "service of prayer and dedication" was Rowan Williams, the Archbishop of Canterbury.

At least the sovereign had not been among the thirty friends and family members who attended the marriage ceremony itself. Initially, Camilla and Charles had planned to be married at Windsor Castle, but that was impossible, because the castle was not deemed a legal site for weddings. When the venue for the civil service was switched to the Windsor Guildhall, the Queen declined to attend.

The official explanation for the obvious royal snub—that Her Majesty did not want to overshadow the happy couple at their decidedly low-key nuptials—fooled no one. "The Queen believes Camilla is a scheming, predatory woman," said one senior courtier. "She blames Camilla for pursuing her son to the ends of the earth, ruining his marriage, driving Princess Diana mad, and nearly pulling down the monarchy in the process."

The Queen was not alone in her distaste for the union. Diana's friend Joan Berry publicly called for the Queen to cancel the wedding "even at this late stage." Another friend of the late Princess, Vivienne Parry, insisted "there is only one Princess of Wales in people's minds. And only when Prince William gets married, perhaps many years from now, will it be time for another one."

A Sunday *Times* poll conducted the week before the wedding showed that 73 percent of Britons did not want Camilla to be Queen, and that 58 percent wanted Prince William, not Charles, to succeed the current monarch. The news from the *Daily Telegraph* was even worse: their poll showed that 69 percent of Britons did not want Charles as their next King and that most believed his marriage to Camilla would weaken the monarchy.

Notwithstanding widespread public opposition, only one person's opinion ever really mattered. England's beloved Queen Mother—for decades the most popular member of the Royal Family hands down—had considered Diana to be a spoiled neurotic. After 1991, she forbade anyone from mentioning the Princess of Wales's name in her house. As much as she resented Diana, the Queen Mother (below-stairs staff called her "the Old Queen" and Elizabeth II "the Young Queen") actively loathed Camilla. Mrs. Parker Bowles reminded the Queen Mum of another divorced Mrs.—one Wallis Warfield Simpson, who brought about the abdication of Edward VIII and left her emotionally and physically fragile husband to assume the throne as George VI. It was the crushing burden of reigning over England during World War II, the Queen Mother was convinced, that led to her husband's death at age fifty-six.

"Honestly," the Queen Mother blurted whenever the subject of Mrs. Parker Bowles came up, "I cannot bear that woman! The sheer *gall*."

The Queen Mother held "a certain power over the Queen," Harold Brooks-Baker, Publishing Director of *Burke's Peerage,* observed. "She may have looked sweet and grandmotherly, but she had a wicked wit and she could hold a grudge forever. She made the Queen promise that she would not permit Charles to marry Camilla."

As long as her mother was alive, the Queen kept her promise. The last impediment to the marriage was removed by the Queen Mother's death in March 2002 at age 101. It had been long expected, but Charles, who had always been close to his grandmother despite her abiding dislike of Camilla, wasted no time phoning his mistress with the news. "Let's just say," said a former staff member at St. James's, "that when it came to the death of the Queen Mother, their reaction was . . . mixed."

Events moved swiftly. Shortly after the Prince of Wales and his brothers, Andrew and Edward, paid tribute to the Queen Mother by standing ceremonial guard beside her coffin as she lay in state, the Church of England rescinded its ban on second marriages for divorced couples. With Operation PB ratcheted into high gear, it would be just two months before Camilla was seated directly behind the Queen at the Buckingham Palace ceremony marking the monarch's Golden Jubilee.

Now that the biggest moment of all had arrived, Camilla looked "terrified," said a friend. "She was shaking terribly. For a moment I thought she was going to collapse." Indeed, the day before she had had an inexplicable 103-degree fever—aggravated, doctors said, by stress. Although the groom and the bride never kissed, William as well as Camilla's son, Tom Parker Bowles, were satisfied that it had all gone off without a hitch. "Well, I'm happy with that," William said to his new stepbrother as they stood on the Guildhall steps. "Yup," replied Tom. "Me too." Neither seemed to notice the banner across the road that read ILLEGAL, IMMORAL, SHAMEFUL, or to hear the scattered "boos" emanating from the crowd.

Camilla struck a more glamorous figure at Windsor, where she wore a sweeping, embroidered porcelain blue dress, a hand-painted silk shantung coat, and a feathered gold headdress that re-

sembled crystal-tipped shafts of wheat. Standing at their lecterns
before the Archbishop of Canterbury, they had one more hurdle
to jump through.

As a condition of his conducting the forty-five-minute Service
of Prayer and Dedication, the Archbishop had insisted Charles and
Camilla make some act of contrition—an admission of and apology for their rampantly adulterous behavior. Together, they read
from the seventeenth-century Book of Common Prayer:

"We acknowledge and bewail our manifold sins and wickedness,
which we, from time to time, most grievously have committed,
by thought, word, and deed against thy Divine Majesty, provok-
ing most justly thy wrath and indignation against us.

"We do earnestly repent and are utterly sorry for these our mis-
doings. The remembrance of them is grievous unto us. The burden of them intolerable."

Then the Archbishop asked the couple—first Charles and then
Camilla—to be faithful to each other in their marriage, to understand the covenant of marriage, and to take each other "for richer
for poorer, for better or worse . . . till parted by death."

To drive home the point, the Archbishop asked if they had resolved to be "faithful" and to "forsake all others" as long as they
lived.

"That is my resolve," each replied separately and sheepishly,
"with the help of God." Then they touched hands, and Archbishop Williams intoned, "Let the rings"—they were wearing simple bands made of gold mined in North Wales—"be symbols of
your faithfulness."

This public confession was only one of the many concessions
the couple made, not the least of which was Charles's repeated insistence that if he became King he would not press to have Camilla

crowned Queen. Instead of becoming the new Princess of Wales—or following one suggestion at St. James's that she be simply called "Camilla Windsor"—Charles's second wife had settled for a lesser title that had also been held by Diana: Duchess of Cornwall.

Nothing, of course, could have been further from the truth. By law and tradition, Camilla was already Princess of Wales—among all women in the realm, second only to the Queen herself in rank. If and when Charles becomes King, Camilla automatically becomes Queen. The only exception to the rule would require Charles and Camilla entering into a "morganatic" marriage—one in which Camilla would explicitly be prohibited from becoming Queen. When pressed on the issue, the Prince's office specifically rejected the morganatic approach.

To prevent Camilla from becoming Queen, then, Parliament would have to change the law. And since the English monarch is also head of state in sixteen of the British Commonwealth's fifty-four member nations, laws in those countries would also have to be changed—something that was not likely to happen. Accusing the Prince of Wales of being "less than frank with the country," Member of Parliament Andrew McKinlay echoed the sentiments of many who doubted Charles's true intentions.

Publicly Charles continued to insist that his new wife would be content to remain Duchess of Cornwall until he assumed the throne, when she would then take the title of Princess Consort. Behind closed doors, however, he made it clear to his staff that the ultimate goal of Operation PB was to make Camilla Queen. "We can say what we have to now," he stated flatly. "But Camilla is going to be my wife and she is going to be Queen."

It was something that Camilla now wanted as much for herself, though for years many of her closest friends thought otherwise. "She was marginalized for so long," her friend Harold Brooks-Baker said, "that now she believes she has every right to be Queen." Over dinner at Highgrove shortly before the wedding, Charles startled guests when he laughingly referred to his new bride as "my queen." The new Duchess of Cornwall winced, but cracked back, "Yes, well, let's not get carried away. . . ."

In that, the current Queen could not have agreed more em phatically—although not long after the death of her mother, the monarch had seriously considered stepping aside. For the first time, she broached the idea of abdicating in favor of Charles with the prime minister. Realizing that she might be fortunate enough to follow in her mother's footsteps and live another twenty-five years, the Queen shuddered at the thought of her son ascending to the throne at the age of seventy-eight.

Now that he was married to Camilla, the Queen put any such plans on hold. Regardless of the aging heir apparent, Elizabeth was not yet ready to see Camilla wear the crown. More impor-tant, she was convinced that her people weren't ready either. "Charles may love her, and I'm sure he does very deeply," the Queen told her husband. "But I cannot bear the thought of 'Queen Camilla.'"

The service at St. George's ended with the crowd standing to sing "God Save the Queen"—everyone except the sovereign, who never sings the song in praise of herself. Instead, Her Majesty stood staring straight ahead, her face as expressionless as an Inca mask.

The deed finally done, the Prince of Wales and the Duchess of Cornwall walked out of the chapel arm in arm. Elizabeth, Prince Philip, and the rest of the family fell in behind them. As she made her way down the aisle, the Queen prepared herself for the moment she had long dreaded: for the first time in public, she would be forced to appear alongside "That Wicked Woman."

Stepping outside, the newlyweds beamed as the crowd that had lined the street for hours burst into applause. Camilla's hand flew up to her elaborate hat to keep it from being swept off in the wind.

"Well, here we are then," Charles muttered to Camilla.

"I was rather nervous," she replied.

"Well, we're married now," Charles shot back. "Right, to the plan now," he continued. "Look over at all the well-wishers, lovely isn't it?"

"Oh yes," Camilla said, still holding on to her headdress. "This hat is no good in the wind." Then, looking around anxiously, Camilla asked, "Where's the Queen?"

"They'll be along soon," he reassured her. "She'll be having a good old chat."

Once she did appear behind them on the steps outside, the Queen matter-of-factly remarked to her son, "That all went rather well."

"Yes," Charles said flatly.

"We're leaving now," she told her son.

"Oh, I really want a picture of us all," Charles pleaded. But it was too late; the Queen had already bolted for the Rolls-Royce that would take her and Prince Philip back up Castle Hill to Windsor's opulent state apartments. There she would host a "tea and finger-food" reception for the bride and groom and eight hundred of their friends, including Tony and Cherie Blair, King Constantine and Queen Anne-Marie of Greece, King Hamad of Bahrain, Crown Prince Haakon of Norway, rock star Phil Collins, the designer Valentino, Sir David Frost, longtime pal Joan Rivers, and Andrew Parker Bowles with his new wife, Rosemary.

Since the legendary Grand National steeplechase had taken place the same day, the horse-loving Queen incorporated several sly references to the sport of kings in her speech. "I have two important announcements to make. The first is that Hedgehunter has won the Grand National! The other is that my son is home and dry with the woman he loves. They have been over difficult jumps—Bechers Brook and the Chair—and all kinds of other terrible obstacles. And now," she concluded with just the slightest hint of sarcasm, "they're in the winners enclosure."

Charles then thanked Camilla for "taking on the task of being married to me" before heading out the door. The groom never kissed the bride, but Harry and William both made up for that by bussing Camilla on both cheeks as they left the reception. "It was a real moment," said Camilla's friend Santa Sebag Montefiore. "It wasn't for the cameras." Like the Queen, who posed with the happy couple during the reception, Diana's boys were also photographed next to Camilla for the first time.

"The two boys were in fantastic form," said Harry's godfather, Gerald Ward. "They were both very happy." They had actually spent much of the reception decorating the newlyweds' Bentley with Mylar balloons and graffiti reading C+C and JUST MARRIED. Across the windshield, Harry had scrawled PRINCE+DUCHESS. William, who also shoved a potato in the exhaust pipe of the Bentley in hopes of making it backfire, was disappointed when the gag didn't work.

The young Princes threw confetti as the happy couple climbed into the Bentley, bound for a two-week honeymoon of fly-fishing, hiking, and painting at Balmoral. More specifically, Charles and his bride—who now also assumed Diana's Scottish title of Duchess of Rothesay—would be staying at Birkhall, their newly redesigned residence on the grounds of Balmoral. It was no small irony that Birkhall had previously been the residence of the one person most responsible for keeping Camilla out of the Royal Family—the Queen Mother.

As their car pulled away from the castle, the boys ran after it. Waving their arms wildly, they shouted the line Camilla and Charles had recited robotically throughout the day: "Thanks for coming!"

Once the dust had settled, the normally abstemious Queen allowed herself a glass of sherry with a few straggling family members. "It's been how long? Eight years since Diana's death?" she asked rhetorically. "Eight years. Remarkable, really. Back then I never could have imagined. . . ."

They've got to blame *someone*.

—*Camilla*

2

September 7, 1997
The Day after Diana's Funeral

"I'm very worried about Harry," William told his nanny, Alexandra "Tiggy" Legge-Bourke. Preparing to begin his third year at Eton, the fifteen-year-old heir to the throne was concerned that his brother was not yet strong enough to resume his old routine at Ludgrove, the elite boarding school Harry attended in Berkshire. "I don't," William pleaded, "want to go away from him now. He needs me."

Tiggy reassured Wills that Harry would continue to be well looked-after by Ludgrove headmaster Gerald Barber and his wife, Janet. For the years the two boys had spent there together, the Barbers had served as a major source of emotional support, shielding the Princes from the torrent of lurid tabloid stories about their parents. Moreover, Harry was encouraged to phone his brother at Eton whenever he liked.

In Tiggy, the pretty, tomboyish nanny Charles had hired after his separation from Diana, the boys had a surrogate older sister—someone they could tease and play with, but also rely on for advice and comfort. From the start, Diana had resented Legge-Bourke's presence; Mummy saw the high-spirited, fun-loving nanny as a rival for her sons' affections and on numerous occasions questioned why Charles required assistance from a nanny at all, given the fact that William and Harry spent the vast majority of their time with their mother. Noting that she didn't need a "substitute father" for the boys when they were with her, Diana asked, "Why does Charles need a substitute mother when they are with him?"

Adding fuel to the fire was Diana's growing conviction that Charles had been having an affair with the nanny. Four years younger than Diana, Legge-Bourke was the daughter of a merchant banker and a Welsh aristocrat—Tiggy's mother was a lady-in-waiting to Princess Anne—and had grown up on Glanusk Park, the family's six-thousand-acre estate in the Welsh mountains.

Tiggy was just six years old when she first met the Prince of Wales, and she grew up in the same social circles as the Windsors and the Spencers. She was enrolled in an exclusive school for girls run by Lady Tryon, mother-in-law of Charles's longtime lover Dale "Kanga" Tryon, and eventually went on to the same Swiss boarding school Diana had attended, the Institute Alpin Videmanette. Diana had found fulfillment teaching kindergarten classes in London, and Tiggy ran her own nursery school there.

There the similarities ended. Unlike the cosmopolitan, city-loving Diana, Tiggy shared the Windsors' avowed passion for the outdoors. "She is one of the only women I know," said her friend

Santa Palmer-Tomkinson, "who can skin a rabbit or gut a stag." For over two years, Diana seethed at newspaper snapshots of Tiggy chasing the boys across a muddy polo field, tousling William's hair as they left church, and tossing snowballs at one another as they vacationed together in the Swiss ski resort of Klosters. According to Richard Kay, a *Daily Mail* columnist who was also a friend of the Princess, Diana "raged that Tiggy always seemed to be having fun with the boys." It didn't help that by now "she had convinced herself something was going on between Charles and the nanny."

Diana's animosity toward Tiggy boiled over at the annual Christmas lunch the Prince and Princess of Wales threw for their staff in 1995. Walking up behind Legge-Bourke and catching her off guard, Diana blurted, "So sorry to hear about the baby"—a line others in the room took to imply that Tiggy had had an abortion, and that the baby was presumably Charles's. The spiteful comment was without any basis in fact, but it yielded the desired results. Tiggy broke down sobbing and the next day ordered her solicitor to demand an apology from the Princess of Wales for the "false allegations."

Diana finally succeeded in easing Tiggy out of the picture in March 1997, after the nanny drafted a guest list for William's confirmation at Windsor that omitted several Spencer relatives. Diana was not informed when Charles invited Legge-Bourke to join him and the boys for riding, fishing, and shooting at Balmoral that August.

Regardless of how she resented Tiggy in life, even Diana's staunchest allies believed she would have been grateful for the role Legge-Bourke now played in easing the young Princes' pain. Harry, in particular, required the kind of tactile affection that his mother had always provided. Despite his outgoing, rambunctious nature, a streak of insecurity had always run through Harry; a chronic thumb sucker until the age of eleven, he clung to Diana in a way William never had. During those first weeks after his mother's death, when Harry periodically burst into tears without warning, Tiggy would cradle him in her arms and rock him to sleep.

Just sixteen days after his mother's death, both sides of the family gathered at Highgrove to celebrate Harry's thirteenth birthday. Lady Sarah McCorquodale brought what would be Harry's most treasured gift that day—the Sony PlayStation Diana was planning to bring back with her from Paris. "Happy Birthday, Harry," read the card. It was signed, "Love, Mummy."

For his part, William appeared to rebound quickly, immersing himself in his familiar life at Eton. Staying at the school seven days a week, William was supported by lifelong pals that included Nicholas Knatchbull, a grandson of the late Lord Mountbatten and a distant cousin of William's, and Lord "Freddie" Windsor, son of Prince and Princess Michael of Kent. For counsel and for comfort, William was also able to turn to his housemaster Andrew Gailey, as well as Gailey's wife, Shauna, and housemother Elizabeth Heathcote, "Dame" (matron) of William's residence hall, Manor House.

In the absence of his mother, no woman would have greater influence over the future King's life than the current Queen. This was no accident. Determined to indoctrinate him in the ways of the Windsors, Her Majesty had pushed for William to attend the school that had been preparing the sons of Europe's most powerful families to take their rightful place in the world for 558 years. Borrowing from the Duke of Wellington's famous quote about the

Battle of Waterloo, it was often said that history was "decided on the playing fields of Eton."

Beyond its unparalleled reputation, Eton provided another advantage: situated just across the Thames from Windsor Castle, it afforded Elizabeth a bird's-eye view of those legendary playing fields. Periodically, William would pause during a game of cricket or soccer to wave in Granny's direction—a stunt that had the desired effect of putting his competitors more than a little off balance.

On Sundays Will—always flanked by at least two plainclothes guards armed with automatic pistols—made the seven-minute journey on foot to Windsor Castle. He would walk down High Street, across the bridge that connected Eton to the village of Windsor, and up the hill to Granny's house. On those occasions when he was picked up and driven to the castle, the trip took less than a minute.

These weekly teas with the Queen—during which William shared the details of his life at school and she shared the details of what it was like to be a modern monarch—had actually begun at Buckingham Palace shortly after he turned five. Now that his mother was gone, "William of Wales," as he was officially known at Eton, would look forward to these chats with Granny (Prince Philip was "Grandpapa") more than ever before. While she might pull out an interesting prop to illustrate some bit of history—a letter from Disraeli to Queen Victoria, the draft of a speech in Winston Churchill's own hand—the Queen was careful not to veer too far from the role of doting grandmother.

"Prince William seemed eager to learn everything," said a former footman at Windsor who witnessed dozens of these encounters. "He especially wanted to know about the royal boxes that she is always working on—the blue ones from the Foreign Office and

the red ones with all the boring paperwork about her schedule."
But Her Majesty "spent just as much time listening to him talk
about his water polo and his rugby matches. She always managed
to look as if she really cared, asking lots of questions, always filled
with enthusiasm for what he was doing."

William would need all the sympathy he could get from
Granny; most of the boys at school were told not to mention the
boys' tragic loss and to behave, in the words of one of the other
students' fathers, "as if nothing has happened." The same approach
was taken at Ludgrove, where students and faculty members alike
were cautioned not to mention Diana's death or show any overt
signs of sympathy that might "upset" the younger Prince. The result was predictable: during those first few weeks back at school,
Harry's upbeat, happy-go-lucky nature was punctuated with black
moods and even the periodic crying jag.

Fortunately, Harry was not required to spend the entire school
year grappling with his grief behind the iron gates and brick walls
of Ludgrove. Unlike his older brother, he was allowed to spend
eight weekends a term with their father and Tiggy, usually at
Highgrove. Then, less than eight weeks after Diana's funeral,
Harry was invited to join Papa on the Prince of Wales's long-
planned official trip to South Africa.

It would have been hard to plan a more distracting vacation,
particularly for a thirteen-year-old boy. A safari in Botswana with
Tiggy was followed by a Spice Girls concert in Johannesburg and
then a visit to a Zulu village where bare-breasted women .per-
formed native dances especially for them. "My," gulped the Prince
of Wales while Harry looked on, "what amazing energy."

Complying with new rules set by the Press Complaints Commission in the wake of Princess Diana's death, Fleet Street had

agreed not to publish photographs of the boys in private situations. Now they were giving the British public its first carefully orchestrated look at what appeared to be the affectionate, easy bond between Charles and one of his sons post-Diana.

Back home in London, where positive portrayals of Charles were few and far between, the trip to South Africa was viewed as a public relations triumph for the Prince of Wales. "We were all used to seeing Diana laughing with the boys at amusement parks and that sort of thing," said Peter Archer, longtime royal correspondent for the British Press Association. "Most people assumed William and Harry were not as close to their father, yet there Harry was, clearly thrilled just to be with Dad."

None were more delighted than those aides who had devoted so much time and energy to make Operation Parker Bowles a success. "It was the first chink in Diana's armor," said one. "It was becoming more obvious that she was not the only compassionate one in the family, and that she had just been more adept at manipulating the press to sell that misconception."

William and Harry—"Ma boys!" as Diana used to call them in an exaggerated Scarlett O'Hara accent—had, in fact, forged a new, more intimate relationship with their father virtually overnight. Yet it was, even Charles would concede, less intense than what they had known with their mother.

"I don't keep secrets from ma boys," Diana liked to say. That was particularly true of William, who served as his mother's confidant, protector, comforter, soul mate. "Diana felt in many ways," said her friend Richard Greene, "that William was a male version of her."

Toward that end, Diana's older son was called upon to provide solace when Diana's visits to AIDS clinics, homeless shelters, and hospices became too overwhelming. After cradling a baby dying of cancer, visiting the victims of domestic violence in a battered women's shelter, or holding the hand of an AIDS victim—she had made headlines with this simple gesture of kindness alone—the Princess would often call William and break down.

Another friend she relied on, Rosa Monckton, remembered that she would sometimes pick up the phone and there would be nothing but the sound of the Princess weeping on the other end. "She would simply cry," Monckton said, "totally drained and exhausted." (It was Diana who came to Monckton's emotional rescue when, in April 1995, she allowed Monckton's stillborn daughter, Natalia, to be secretly buried on the grounds of Kensington Palace.) Monckton said that William "was the one person she most counted on. She expected a great deal from Prince William, and he did not hesitate to give it."

Still, Diana worried that she was putting too much responsibility on her son's slender shoulders. "William is an incredibly sensitive soul," she told Greene. "He needs to be protected."

That did not stop her, however, from exposing both boys to the larger world outside the walls of "The Big House," as she referred to Buckingham Palace. She took them to homeless shelters, AIDS clinics, and schools for the mentally retarded. But she also exposed them to the kinds of simple everyday pleasures that had long been denied the royals—trips to amusement parks, go-cart tracks, and fast-food outlets like McDonald's and Kentucky Fried Chicken (the Princess's favorite). "Diana wanted William and Harry to be royals, but with a difference," said Greene. "She wanted them to be warm, caring, involved people—not cold fish."

Accordingly, she freely confided in William about her grandest hopes and deepest fears, and even shared with the boy some of the details about her extramarital affairs. "Diana told William anything and everything that popped into her head," one of her closest friends said. "There were some things that were just not appropriate for a boy his age—or for a mother to be discussing with her son at all."

Perhaps. But Diana did not consider William to be like other little boys. She told Greene that he was "a very sensitive soul" with "deep feelings and an understanding far beyond his years." She referred to William as "my little old wise man."

Indeed, William had spent his entire life dealing with the myriad sordid dramas that seemed to be constantly swirling around the House of Windsor. Long before he would have to deal with the shock of his mother's violent death, William coped with his parents' stormy marriage. "It was a situation waiting for him when he arrived," observed Lady Elsa Bowker, another of Diana's closest friends. Diana, distraught over her husband's ongoing affair with Camilla, threw herself down the stairs at Sandringham, the Windsors' 20,000-acre country estate. She was three months pregnant with William at the time.

In the wake of his parents' quarrels, William tried to cheer up his mother by making reservations at her favorite restaurant, San Lorenzo, or bringing her candy. After one particular nasty spat at Highgrove, Mummy locked herself in the bathroom. "I hate to see you sad," eight-year-old William told her and began shoving Kleenex under the door.

William was not rattled at all when his mother sat the boys down and explained the facts of life to them (Harry, two years younger at age eight, ran away). Nor did William refuse to listen when his mother asked him about some of the men in her life—

and how to cope with the headline-making scandals both she and the Prince of Wales were making.

When it was published in the spring of 1992, Andrew Morton's book *Diana: Her True Story*—essentially dictated to Morton in secret by the Princess herself—unleashed a series of royal scandals. It was followed in quick succession that August by the release of highly personal cell phone conversations between Diana and her car-dealer friend James Gilbey. He called her "Darling," she called him "Squidgy," and the "Squidgygate" tapes caused a sensation. These private phone conversations had, in fact, been recorded by government intelligence and then leaked to the press by factions loyal to Charles. According to Diana's longtime personal protection officer Ken Wharfe, "The tapes were transmitted regularly at different times to ensure the conversation was heard, knowing that it would eventually reach the media."

For his part, Charles was far from blameless when it came to embarrassing the young Princes. Just five months after Squidgygate, Britain's tabloids published transcripts of an intimate phone conversation between the Prince of Wales and his mistress. Once again, the conversation was recorded by British intelligence and then broadcast—this time by agents who were sympathetic to Diana—at frequent intervals so that it would be picked up by ham radio operators and passed on to the tabloid press. The raunchy highlights:

CAMILLA: *Mmmmm, you're awfully good at feeling your way along.*

CHARLES: *Oh stop! I want to feel my way along you, all over and up and down you and in and out.*

CAMILLA: *Oh!*

CHARLES: *Particularly in and out . . .*

CAMILLA: *Oh, that's just what I need at the moment.*

CHARLES: *Is it?*

CAMILLA: *I know it would revive me. I can't bear a Sunday night without you.*

CHARLES: *Oh, God.*

CAMILLA: *I can't start the week without you.*

CHARLES: *I fill your tank!*

CAMILLA: *Yes you do.*

CHARLES: *What about me? The trouble is I need you several times a week.*

CAMILLA: *Mmmm. So do I. I need you all the week, all the time.*

CHARLES: *Oh God, I'd just live inside your trousers or something. It would be much easier!*

CAMILLA *(laughing): What are you going to turn into? A pair of knickers? Oh, you're going to come back as a pair of knickers?*

CHARLES: *Or God forbid, a Tampax. Just my luck!*

CAMILLA: *You are a complete idiot! Oh, what a wonderful idea.*

CHARLES: *My luck to be chucked down the lavatory and go on and on forever, swirling round the top, never going down!*

CAMILLA: *Oh darling!*

CHARLES: *Until the next one comes through . . .*

CAMILLA: *Or perhaps you could come back as a box.*

CHARLES: *What sort of box?*

CAMILLA: *A box of Tampax, so you could just keep going. Oh darling, I just want you now.*

CHARLES: *Do you?*

CAMILLA: *Mmmm.*

CHARLES: *So do I.*

CAMILLA: *Desperately, desperately, desperately!*

The conversation would continue for another three minutes, with Camilla referring contemptuously to her husband, Andrew Parker Bowles, as "*it*": "While you're rushing around doing things," she complains to Charles, "I'll be, you know, alone until *it* reappears."

While Charles's expressed desire to be reincarnated as Camilla's tampon—or box of tampons—understandably resonated with the public, another exchange was more revealing:

CHARLES: *Your great achievement is to love me.*

CAMILLA: *Oh darling, easier than falling off a chair.*

CHARLES: *You suffer all these indignities and tortures and calumnies.*

CAMILLA: *Oh darling, don't be so silly. I'd suffer anything for you. That's love. It's the strength of love. Night night.*

With that, Charles reverts to his randy self when he tells Camilla he will hang off by "pressing the tit"—a Briticism for the button on his mobile phone.

"I wish," Camilla purred, "you were pressing mine."

Camillagate more than made up for Squidgygate, but few went behind the lurid headlines to determine the original source of the tapes—who in fact had been listening in on the royals, and for what purpose. Investigators eventually concluded that rogue elements within the British security services—either MI5 or MI6—had been bugging the Royal Family.

That finding sent shock waves through Buckingham Palace. It would also confirm what the Queen, who spent much of her day sifting through highly classified communiqués in her role as head of state, had long known—that there were clandestine elements inside the intelligence services who were actively pursuing an agenda of their own.

For the press and the public, however, it was hard to focus on anything beyond the Prince of Wales's expressed desire to be magically transformed into his mistress's tampon. Harry was too young to fully comprehend what the steamy transcripts meant, but not William. Yet as long as his parents remained above the fray, refusing to dignify the stories with any sort of comment, Wills could at least try to convince himself that none of the stories were true.

"Children don't want to know that their parents are doing it," Diana's friend Vivienne Parry said. "It's out of the question. So when it's obvious that your parents *are* doing it—and with different people—it's a bit disturbing."

Still, one of William's former teachers recalled, "Even at the height of 'Camillagate,' Prince William outwardly seemed to be happy and full of fun. Of course he had to have known what was going on. It must have been hell for a child to keep up this cheerful facade when the whole world was watching both of his parents behave so horrendously."

It was a facade William could no longer maintain after his father was quoted in 1994's *The Prince of Wales: A Biography* that he had never loved Diana and had only married her after he was ordered to do so by his father, the Duke of Edinburgh. "Why, Papa?" demanded William, devastated by Charles's public declaration that he had never loved his sons' mother. "Why did you do it?"

Diana was left to reassure her sons that their parents were in love at the time of their fairy-tale wedding on July 29, 1981—a spectacle witnessed by a live television audience of 750 million worldwide. While Diana claimed to be "madly, desperately" in love with Charles, it was obvious at the outset that the feeling was not mutual.

From the beginning "there were three of us in this marriage," Diana later said, "so it was a bit crowded." Less than forty-eight hours before the wedding, Diana had stumbled upon a bracelet with the intertwined initials *G* and *F*—for "Gladys" and "Fred," the pet names Charles and Camilla had given each other after characters from the satirical British TV series *The Goon Show*. Even as she walked down the aisle at St. Paul's Cathedral, Diana could not keep her eyes off Camilla—"pale gray, veiled pillbox hat, saw it all, her son Tom standing on a chair. . . ." Diana was unaware that, according to one of the Prince's closest aides, Charles had slept with Camilla just two nights before the wedding.

Diana's insistence to William that she had loved his father would soon ring hollow as well. Two months after Charles's hurtful comments in *The Prince of Wales*, Diana's infidelities again took center stage when it was revealed that the Princess had made harassing phone calls to another of her boyfriends, millionaire art dealer Oliver Hoare. Not long after, Captain James Hewitt recounted his torrid six-year-long affair with Diana in his lurid tell-all *Princess in Love*. Diana's former riding instructor, whom the boys had considered a friend, wasn't exaggerating about the intensity of their affair. "He treated me," Diana admitted to Simone Simmons, "like a sex slave."

There would be others during this period, including rugby star Will Carling, whose wife publicly accused Diana of ruining her marriage; British businessman Christopher Whalley; Canadian rocker Bryan Adams; silver-maned American billionaire Theodore Forstmann; and—most important—a thirty-nine-year-old Pakistani heart surgeon named Hasnat Khan.

A paunchy, chain-smoking Muslim who shunned the spotlight, Khan was the unlikeliest of Diana's lovers. Yet he would eventually emerge from the pack to become the focus of her romantic life.

Even as she embarked on her secret romance with "Natty" Khan, the media-savvy Diana decided it was time to level an attack against her enemies inside Buckingham Palace. Just as she had with Andrew Morton, Diana secretly taped an interview inside Kensington Palace with BBC television correspondent Martin Bashir. In the interview, which caused an international sensation when it aired on the BBC program *Panorama*, Diana accused the Royal Family of trying to portray her as "unstable" and talked candidly not only about Camilla but also about her own love affair with James Hewitt.

Diana soon realized that the *Panorama* interview had been a grave miscalculation. Three weeks later, after consulting with the prime minister and the Archbishop of Canterbury, the Queen wrote letters to both Diana and her son essentially instructing them to proceed with a quick divorce. It arrived one week before Diana and the boys were to join the rest of the Royal Family at Sandringham for the Christmas holidays. "Diana was crushed," said her friend Elsa Bowker. "She did not want a divorce. She viewed the Queen as a friend, but the Queen had had enough of scandal, enough of the constant fighting between Diana and Charles."

Later, in a lengthy private meeting with "Mama," as she called the Queen, Diana aired a number of concerns. She was reluctant to give up her royal "HRH" status, though in the end she acquiesced to the Queen's wishes. She worried about William and his father flying together on the same plane; if something happened, the crushing weight of succession would all fall on Harry. The Queen replied that that was unlikely. Her Majesty also stressed to Diana—without ever mentioning the name of Charles's mistress—that she believed the Prince of Wales would never remarry.

After four months, a divorce settlement was finally hammered out. Diana would be paid a cash settlement of $22.5 million plus $600,000 to run her offices. She would also be allowed to remain at Kensington Palace and would share custody of her sons with Charles. When he heard that she would be losing her royal status, William threw his arms around her. "Don't worry, Mummy," William told her, "I will give it back to you one day, when I am King."

In the meantime, the Princess took solace in having found the only lover she would ever refer to as her "soul mate." She now became obsessed with the idea of marching down the aisle with Hasnat Khan. The Princess would don a leather jacket, glasses, jeans, and a dark wig, then drive a borrowed Range Rover or her own BMW to pick up Khan at Royal Brompton Hospital in Chelsea. With Khan crouching in the backseat beneath a tartan blanket, she would smuggle him into Kensington Palace. More often, Diana's butler did the smuggling.

For the last two years of her life, Diana pursued Kahn and often shared her deepening feeling for the doctor with William. After she donned a surgical mask to view the surgeon at work in the operating theater, the Princess breathlessly described the experience to her thirteen-year-old son. Realizing that she might have to convert to Islam if she was to marry Khan, she asked for William's approval. "Mummy," he replied, "you have to do what makes you happy." What she did not tell her son was that she also wanted more children. "Elsa," Diana told Lady Bowker, "I want two girls."

Although she was now spending up to two hours a day secretly studying the Koran, Diana worried about the impact converting to Islam would have on William and Harry—and on the monarchy. Acting on impulse, she traveled to Pakistan in May 1997—without telling Khan—to see if his parents would accept a non-Muslim as their daughter-in-law.

As it turned out, they would. Diana told her hairdressers Tess Rock and Natalie Symonds that there was "absolutely no problem" about her not being a Muslim, and that now the path was open for her to marry Khan. Unfortunately, the intensely private Khan had no intention of marrying the Princess or anyone else. Finally, after a particularly bitter quarrel, he abruptly ended the relationship. Once again, William was left to console his mother in the wake of another catastrophic love affair—and to listen patiently as she hatched a scheme to make Hasnat Khan jealous by dating another Muslim, Dodi Fayed.

The Dodi-Diana affair began on July 14, 1997, with a food fight aboard Mohamed Al Fayed's sleek 195-foot yacht, the *Jonikal*. "They were chasing each other and laughing and giggling like a couple of kids," recalled the *Jonikal*'s chief stewardess, Debbie Gribble. Thrilled to see his mother happier than she had been in months, William encouraged her to pursue the relationship. "Dr. Khan made you very unhappy, Mummy," William reasoned. "Dodi makes you laugh."

Over the next six weeks, Diana would heed her son's advice, spending time with Dodi at his lavish Mayfair apartment and cruising the Mediterranean aboard the *Jonikal*. By the time they arrived in Paris on the last, fateful leg of their journey, Diana was eager to return home. She had accepted a $3,000 Bulgari band from Dodi but wore it on the fourth finger of her right hand. She had no intention, she told several friends, including Rosa Monckton, Lana Marks, and Annabel Goldsmith, of marrying Dodi. "The last thing I need is a new marriage," she told Goldsmith. "I need it like a bad rash on my face."

If the Princess had been considering marriage, she would have run the idea by William for his approval. Instead, their last phone conversation, just hours before her death, revolved around William's concerns for his brother. Harry was no intellectual match for his brother and had been held back a year at Ludgrove. Now that Wills was about to start his third year at Eton, he was afraid that a staged photo opportunity to mark the event would leave Harry feeling shunted aside. Diana promised that she would figure out a way to keep Harry from feeling overshadowed by his older brother—once she returned from Paris. . . .

Now that Diana was gone forever, her onetime rival for the boys' affections, Tiggy Legge-Bourke, did what she could to keep the boys from becoming "shut down" and "emotionless"—two words

Diana often used to describe the Windsors. William appeared to have bounced back quickly—too quickly, family and friends would later speculate. But as he faced the prospect of his first Christmas without Mummy, Harry veered from euphoria to depression—"up one minute, without a care in the world," said a former maid at Highgrove, "and the next he is crying."

Two weeks before Christmas, the boys took one last look at the apartments they had shared with Mummy at Kensington Palace. They were driven up to the front door of the "KP," as the boys called it, by William's improbably named Royal Protection Officer, Graham Craker. Walking from room to room, they selected mementos to take with them to Highgrove and their new rooms at York House, the wing of St. James's Palace that served as the official residence of the Prince of Wales. Among other things, Harry picked out the sapphire-and-diamond engagement ring given by Charles to the bashful "shy Di" when she was just nineteen. William selected the Cartier Tank watch the Princess always wore—a gift from her late father, the eighth Earl Spencer—and the giant stuffed hippo mother and sons leaned against while watching television.

When he was told that Earl Spencer wanted the Princess's wedding dress to be displayed at Althorp, the Spencer family's magnificent five-hundred-year-old country estate in Northamptonshire, William objected. "No!" he insisted. "I definitely do not want them to have that!"

"Why not?" Harry asked. After all, Diana was buried on an island in a small lake at Althorp, and there were plans to build a Princess Diana museum on the site.

"I just don't, that's all," William replied, unable to conceal his growing distaste for the Spencers. As his mother's chief confidant, William knew full well that Diana had not spoken to her mother,

Frances Shand Kydd, for months. He was also aware that relations with her only brother had long been strained. Now firmly in the Windsor Camp, William had not appreciated his uncle's sneak attack on the Queen, his father, and the Royal Family in general.

Yet Diana's distrust of the Windsors ran deeper than any feelings of antipathy she may have felt toward her own family. The contents of Diana's last will and testament, which would remain sealed until five years after her death, revealed that she feared her sons would be, in the words of one observer, "inhaled" by the Royal Family. She stipulated that, should she predecease Charles, he would consult with her mother "with regard to the upbringing, education, and welfare of our children." In the event the Prince was also dead, Diana did make it clear that she wanted them to grow up Spencer, not Windsor: "I appoint my mother and my brother Earl Spencer to be the guardians. . . ."

The bulk of Diana's $35 million estate, to be divided equally between the boys, would be placed in trust until the Princes turned twenty-five.

One week after the boys returned to KP for one last time, Paul Burrell paid a call on the Queen. While ten plump corgis lumbered around the monarch's private sitting room, the Queen and the butler stood talking by her paper-strewn desk facing a bay window for nearly three hours.

When the butler announced his intention to "protect the Princess's world" by keeping the documents and objects she had given him in a safe place, the Queen did not object. But she did offer words of warning. "Be careful, Paul," she said. "No one has been as close to a member of my family as you have. There *are* powers at work in this country about which we have no knowledge." Then she paused and glared at him intently over her half-rimmed reading spectacles. "Do you," she asked, "*understand?*"

The Queen's cryptic reference to malevolent "powers at work in this country" spoke volumes about the suspicions she harbored regarding the circumstances regarding Diana's death. She had wondered aloud about the length of time it took to get Diana to the hospital, and about the mysterious white Fiat Uno that had brushed Diana's car in the Alma Tunnel, presumably precipitating the accident. Over time, her suspicions would grow as she read reports about mechanical problems that had plagued the Mercedes in which Diana was driving, about driver Henri Paul's possible connections to various intelligence agencies, and about the partial embalming that rendered a thorough autopsy impossible.

"The 'powers' the Queen was referring to are MI5 or MI6," said Harold Brooks-Baker. "She had been on the throne for nearly a half century, and of course she knew the kinds of dirty tricks that were played on enemies of the Establishment—right up to and including assassination." British intelligence was "particularly famous for staging accidents of all kinds, but especially automobile accidents, and the Queen was well aware of this."

At the time, Her Majesty was completely unaware of the October 1996 letter in which Diana had predicted that she would be the victim of just such a staged car crash. Had the Queen known, a former palace aide later speculated, "the Queen might have come to the conclusion that Diana had been murdered. I doubt, however, that she would have done anything about it. She is not one to rock the boat."

Although she was not close enough to Charles to broach the subject with him, the Queen did bring herself to ask Prime Minister Tony Blair, "Is it at all possible that Diana met with foul play?" Blair's less-than-comforting reply: "I believe it was an accident, Your Majesty. But am I certain? I do not know, Your Majesty. I'm not sure we'll ever know beyond any shadow of a doubt."

While she remained outwardly the cynosure of self-control, the Queen confided to her advisors and to family that her world had been turned upside down by Diana's death—or, more accurately, Her Majesty's own botched reaction to it. For the first time the palace went outside its own public affairs office and hired a public relations firm to "sell" the monarchy to the British people. Guided by this expert advice, Her Majesty became the first English monarch to ride in a London cab and step into a pub. More significantly, she also gave the public its first look at the financial records of the Royal Family—revealing for the first time that the Windsors cost British taxpayers somewhere in the vicinity of $90 million a year and that her personal worth hovered somewhere around $2 billion.

Then there was the problem of the Prince of Wales's mistress. In the months following the funeral, pressure mounted on Charles to either turn his back on Camilla once and for all or, as his great-uncle the Duke of Windsor had done sixty years earlier, give up the throne for the woman he loved. Leading the charge was the Queen's private secretary, Sir Robert Fellowes. Despite the fact that he was married to Diana's sister, Lady Jane, the Princess had viewed Fellowes as one of her chief enemies inside Buckingham Palace. "He's absolutely dreadful," Diana told Burrell. "He's so pompous, he's a bully, and he's insecure."

Now Fellowes wanted Camilla out of the picture. He believed Camilla was "endangering the future of the monarchy," said one friend of the Queen, "and that it was therefore his duty to give her up. His view, I believe, had a considerable influence on the Queen."

Not surprisingly, Charles refused. Given his upbringing, it was not difficult to understand why the Prince of Wales felt no particular need to please his mother. As a child, he seldom saw her, and on those rare occasions when he did, she insisted he bow to her—even in private. Once they grew to adulthood, the Queen's children found that it was almost impossible to simply pick up the phone and get through to their mother; she required them to make an appointment to see her in person.

Now that he was nearly fifty, Charles chafed at the notion of his mother interfering in his private life. According to one member of the household staff at Buckingham Palace, Prince Charles "would raise his voice to his mother in the most demeaning, hurtful way. She behaved as any mother whose son was yelling at her would. You could see that she was often quite upset."

"Prince Charles has respect for the Queen as the Queen," said Brooks-Baker. "But when he was growing up and needed her as a mother, well, she wasn't there for him. If anything, Camilla was more of a mother to him than the Queen ever was."

For the time being, Camilla would remain in seclusion while Operation PB regrouped. In the meantime, Buckingham Palace would deploy the monarchy's latest secret weapon: William and Harry. Accompanying their father on a tour of western Canada in March 1998, the Princes caused pandemonium among the hordes of teenage girls who waited for them at every stop.

When he was an awkward thirteen-year-old still painfully self-conscious about his braces, Wills had met Cindy Crawford,

Christie Turlington, Claudia Schiffer, and Naomi Campbell—meetings at Kensington Palace that had been arranged by Diana as surprises for the supermodel-smitten Prince. For his part, Harry had met the Spice Girls and would later invite them to Highgrove for tea. But the Canadian trip marked the first time blond, blue-eyed, six-foot-one-inch Wills realized the power he had over girls his age—thousands of whom showed up to scream, sob, toss flowers and teddy bears at him, and generally behave as if he were a Beatle.

Tiggy Legge-Bourke, who had been invited to tag along, chided William when he claimed to be embarrassed by all the fuss. "Oh, come on," the nanny laughed. "You *know* you love it. You just love it!"

Still holed up at her home in Wiltshire, Camilla followed the tour intently on television. She was not pleased when she spotted Tiggy in the background. Like Diana, Camilla resented the large role Tiggy played in the lives of the Princes, not to mention the fact that her new living quarters just down the hall from the boys in York House put her in uncomfortably close proximity to Prince Charles. Camilla routinely referred to Tiggy as the "Hired Help" and, when she was feeling particularly vindictive, "Big Ass."

At Camilla's urging, Tiggy was slowly nudged out of the Windsor family picture. By the spring of 1998 she was no longer invited to accompany the Princes on all their trips to Balmoral, Sandringham, or even to Highgrove. On those increasingly rare occasions when she did chaperone the boys, Tiggy was faulted for not supervising them closely enough. On a trip to Wales in the summer of 1998, for example, the adventurous Miss Legge-Bourke was photographed looking on as both William and Harry rappelled down the face of a dam without helmets or safety harnesses. The apparent lapse on Tiggy's part hastened her departure from the boys' everyday lives.

With the two women who had been closest to the Princes— Diana and Tiggy—out of the way, Camilla wasted no time stepping in to fill the void. The boys had actually seen her years earlier, riding with their father at the Beaufort Hunt near Highgrove, and the newspapers were filled with photos of the couple when Charles had hosted Camilla's fiftieth birthday party in July of 1997. But they had never actually met their mother's arch-nemesis.

Now was the time, Camilla, Charles, and media spin doctor Mark Bolland agreed, for the boys to meet the real love of Papa's life. It would best be handled in stages—first Camilla would meet William, the more conciliatory and less emotionally fragile of the two. If that went well, then a separate introduction to Harry would be arranged.

On June 12, 1998, Camilla sat in the living room at York House, waiting for William to arrive from Eton. As she often did when she was nervous, Charles's mistress was literally vibrating. When William finally strode into the room, Camilla leapt to her feet and curtsied. Trying to make her feel at ease, William chatted on happily about their shared interest in country pursuits—particularly foxhunting—then left to go to the movies with friends.

Continuing in his self-appointed role as peacemaker and fixer, William was willing to forgive and forget—a daunting task, given the pivotal role Camilla had played in destroying his parents' marriage. They had witnessed firsthand enough domestic strife to last several lifetimes, and what both William and Harry wanted now was "just a little peace and harmony in their household," said a family friend. "The only way to get that is to go along with Papa."

And with Camilla. After that first meeting, the most hated woman in England realized she had just gotten over a formidable hurdle in her marathon effort to become Princess of Wales and ultimately Queen. Charles could scarcely contain himself. "Isn't he wonderful?" he asked, sounding very much like Diana. "Just really splendid, don't you think?"

Camilla took a deep breath and held out her hand to show that it was still trembling. "Darling," she said, "I *really* need a vodka and tonic."

It's the perfect country house
for a future king. The only thing
missing is a future queen.

> —*Camilla to Charles, after he purchased*
> *Highgrove in 1980*

Charles: Your great achievement is to love me.
Camilla: Oh darling, easier than falling off a chair.

It's ironic that he was cheating on his
mistress with me.

—Janet Jenkins, whose on-again,
off-again affair with Charles
lasted twenty years

3

She stood slightly apart from the rest of the spectators at Smith's Lawn near Windsor, hoping to catch the attention of the Prince of Wales as he climbed off his sweat-drenched mount. "That's a fine animal, Sir!" said the young blonde in tight jeans and a green Barbour jacket. "I thought," she added with a smile, "you played wonderfully well."

On this drizzly August afternoon in 1971, Charles recognized most of the beautiful faces in the crowd. He had never seen Camilla Rosemary Shand before, and while she was certainly not in the same league with the model-perfect young women who usually swarmed around the royal enclosure, there was something about her that intrigued him. Before leaving, he stopped to chat with her for a few moments about horses and polo. "They looked," an onlooker recalled, "completely relaxed in each other's company."

Several weeks later at a dinner party, Lucia Santa Cruz cornered

Charles at a dinner party and breathlessly declared, "I have found the perfect girl for you!" Santa Cruz, the voluptuous daughter of Chile's ambassador to the Court of St. James's, was more qualified than most to make such judgments; it was with Santa Cruz that Charles allegedly lost his virginity while a student at Cambridge.

Santa Cruz disappeared into another room and returned with Camilla. "Your Highness," Santa Cruz said as Camilla curtsied, "I would like to present Miss Camilla Shand."

"Yes," Charles said, looking directly into Camilla's unblinking blue eyes, "I believe we've already met."

For the rest of the evening, Charles and Camilla, who at twenty-four was sixteen months older than the Prince, seldom left each other's side. She wasted no time cutting right to the chase. "My great-grandmother and your great-great-grandfather were lovers," she said. "So how about it?"

Bluntness was obviously a quality Camilla inherited from her great-grandmother Alice Keppel, celebrated mistress of King Edward VII. "My job is to curtsy first," she once proclaimed of her position as the official "other woman" in the monarch's life, "and then jump into bed." While other relatives built up the family's sizable fortune in real estate, namely by developing London's posh Belgravia and Mayfair districts, it was Alice Keppel who captured Camilla's imagination at an early age.

Keppel's position was so widely acknowledged that, as Edward VII lay dying, his wife Queen Alexandra summoned Alice to join her at his bedside. (Camilla's great-aunt Violet Trefusis added to the family lore by having a lesbian affair with the Bloomsbury writer Vita Sackville-West, one of Virginia Woolf's lovers.)

Rather than shy away from mentioning her notoriously naughty forebears, ten-year-old Camilla boasted about them to her schoolmates at the presciently named Queen's Gate, a boarding school in London's South Kensington district not far from Kensington Palace. "My great-grandmother was the lover of the king," classmates remember little "Milla" saying as she jokingly commanded them to bow before her. "We're practically royalty."

According to another Queen's Gate alumna, the school was perfectly suited to Camilla—and vice versa. "Landing a rich husband was the top of the agenda," actress Lynn Redgrave recalled of her time at the school. "There would be endless classes teaching us to be good wives and mothers. . . . Camilla reveled in the whole concept. She wanted to have fun, but she also wanted to marry well because, in her mind, that would be the most fun of all."

Milla certainly wasted no time getting started. "Even when she was too young for them to have a sexual interest in her, Camilla always had lots of boyfriends," said her classmate Carolyn Benson, who recalled that Camilla really excelled at only one thing at the school: fencing. "She could talk to boys about things that interested them. She was never a girls' girl. She was always a boys' girl."

A ruddy-faced, jut-jawed tomboy with stringy blond hair and dirty, bitten-to-the-quick fingernails (a habit she shared with Diana), Camilla was no match in the looks department for the well-bred beauties who made up most of the Queen's Gate student body. But her lack of self-consciousness—and the fact that she was not viewed as a threat by the other girls—made Milla a favorite of both sexes. By the time she graduated from Queen's Gate at sixteen, Camilla "exuded a sexy confidence over men," Benson said. "She was quite a flirt, she liked men. She still does."

Camilla also loved the country life and spent every weekend at The Laines, the Shand family estate fifty miles south of London in rural East Sussex. There Camilla, her brother Mark, and younger sister Annabel indulged their shared passion for horses and, more specifically, the Shand family's love of foxhunting.

Following a year at finishing schools in Paris and Geneva, Camilla returned to London to become a debutante and—more important—collect the $1.5 million she inherited from a distant relative. Although she clearly did not need the money, Camilla took her first—and only—job as a receptionist at Colefax & Fowler, a decorating firm owned by her roommate's aunt. Her roommate, Jane Wyndham, would go on to marry Winston Churchill's grandnephew, Lord Charles Spencer-Churchill. Camilla's next roommate, Lord Carrington's daughter Virginia Carrington, went on to marry Camilla's wealthy uncle Lord Ashcombe.

"It was an unbelievably ambitious, highly incestuous lot," said a longtime friend of the Shands. "Daughters of lords were marrying lords, daughters of marquesses were marrying marquesses. Camilla knew she had her work cut out for her if she was going to marry well. She laughed it off and said she was holding out for a king, like her great-grandmother did."

Until then, her roommates would have to put up with Camilla's less-than-pristine personal habits. By all accounts, she was already an unrepentant slob. Her room looked, said Virginia Carrington, "as if a bomb had gone off in it." Nor did Camilla bother making the bed, cleaning up after herself in the bathroom, cleaning her clothes or, for that matter, even hanging up her clothes. "As soon as she walked in the door, her coat and shoes and everything else hit the floor—and that's where they stayed until someone else came to pick them up." But, added Carrington, "She was so sweet it was impossible to be angry with her. She was like a big, boisterous puppy."

Camilla was eighteen when she began dating nineteen-year-old Etonian Kevin Burke, son of aviation pioneer Sir Aubrey Burke, deputy chairman of Hawker Siddeley Aircraft. Burke's principal recollection of Camilla, aside from the fact that she was "always great fun," were her constant references to Alice Keppel. "It was constantly on her mind," Burke said. "It was almost like a talisman, something she wanted to equal, if not better."

Yet Camilla would soon leave Burke not for a titled aristocrat, but for a man in uniform. In 1966, she met twenty-seven-year-old Sandhurst graduate Andrew Parker Bowles, a lieutenant in the Blues and Royals regiment of the Royal Horse Guards. The movie star–handsome Lieutenant Parker Bowles was already a formidable ladies' man with a reputation for bedding some of London society's most beautiful and highborn women. But he was intrigued by the plain-spoken, earthy, overtly sexual Camilla Shand.

If Andrew wasn't quite of royal blood, at least his family, which called Donnington Castle in Berkshire home, was well connected. Andrew's father was a distant cousin and longtime confidant of the Queen Mother, and at the age of fourteen Andrew had been a page at Queen Elizabeth II's coronation.

The courtship of Camilla and Andrew would last seven years, during which Parker Bowles aggressively pursued other women. "Andrew," allowed their friend Lady Caroline Percy, "behaved abominably to Camilla, but she was desperate to marry him."

They had a particularly rough patch in 1970 when Andrew began dating the Queen's only daughter, Princess Anne. The following year, Camilla sought her revenge by accepting Lucia Santa Cruz's invitation to meet the world's most eligible bachelor, Princess Anne's brother, the Prince of Wales.

Charles and Camilla hit it off instantly—in large part because, unlike the other "suitable" young ladies who had been brought to meet him—Camilla was down-to-earth, casual in manner and appearance, and completely at ease. Years later, Camilla mentioned to an American friend that she sometimes wondered if she wasn't the reincarnation of Alice Keppel. "Strange, but I never felt intimidated in his presence, never," she explained. "I felt from the beginning that we were two peas in a pod. We talked as if we'd always known each other."

At the time, Charles needed someone to talk to. After a miserably solitary childhood followed by what he called a "prison sentence" at the spartan Scottish boarding school Gordonstoun, Charles had made few friends at Cambridge. Now that he was about to embark on a seven-year tour of duty as an officer in the Royal Navy, the Prince of Wales felt more lost at sea than ever.

Before Camilla, there was only one person Charles felt he could confide in completely: his beloved great-uncle Lord Louis Mountbatten. The legendary Mountbatten, a World War II hero who later served as Viceroy of India and First Sea Lord, invited Charles to spend weekends at Broadlands, his baronial estate in Hampshire. It was there that Mountbatten introduced the future king to several marriageable young women, most notably his teenage granddaughter (and Charles's distant cousin), Lady Amanda Knatchbull. Unfortunately, Lady Knatchbull was only fourteen at the time.

Mountbatten's intention of having another Mountbatten marry into the family notwithstanding, Camilla soon joined Charles on his weekend trips to Broadlands. "Dickie," as Mountbatten was known by the royals, approved. "He knew," said Mountbatten's longtime private secretary John Barratt, "that Camilla would make a perfect mistress for Charles until his granddaughter was of marriageable age." As if to underscore what he viewed as the historic significance of Camilla's role as royal mistress, she was always given the Portico Room at Broadlands, the room where Prince Philip and the Queen consummated their marriage on their wedding night in 1950.

Charles and Camilla were now calling each other "Fred" and "Gladys" after *The Goon Show* characters, and even appearing in public at restaurants and nightclubs around London. By the time Charles departed on an eight-month tour of duty in the Caribbean at the beginning of 1973, it appeared to royal watchers—not to mention the Prince himself—that Camilla was the one.

Over the coming weeks and months, Charles poured his heart out to Camilla in dozens of letters, and she reciprocated. Marriage, however, was never mentioned, in large part because Mountbatten had urged Charles to wait until he was thirty to marry.

Not surprisingly, that spring Charles, who was still at sea, was devastated to learn that Camilla had accepted Andrew Parker Bowles's marriage proposal. When the couple was wed at the Guards Chapel on July 4, 1973, Charles read in the papers that Princess Anne and the Queen Mum were given a place of honor in the front row. The reason: the Parker Bowleses are also Bowes-Lyons. The Queen Mother's maiden name: Bowes-Lyon.

When Camilla gave birth to her first child, Thomas Henry *Charles*, in December of 1974, Prince Charles agreed to be a godfather. By this time, he had already undertaken to forget Camilla by sleeping with dozens of women, including the Duke of Wellington's daughter, Lady Jane Wellesley; Georgina Russell, daughter of England's ambassador to Spain; Lady "Kanga" Tryon; and brewery heiress Sabrina Guinness.

It was just one month after attending the christening of his godson Tom Parker Bowles that Charles, on a visit to Canada, met a comely blond receptionist at the British consulate in Montreal. Her name was Janet Jenkins, and she was four years older than the twenty-six-year-old prince. They made love for the first time in her apartment while Charles's security detail waited outside in the hall.

Over the next several years, Jenkins would become one of Charles's favorite—if little known—companions. "There was one girl who managed to remain very nearly anonymous," recalled Charles's longtime valet Stephen Barry. "The Prince saw more of her than anyone realized. Her name was Janet Jenkins, and she was a Welsh girl living in Canada."

In a series of passionate love notes, Charles left no doubt about his feelings for Jenkins, who was also married. In 1976, he wrote a four-page letter telling Janet he had found the perfect excuse for seeing her—flying to Montreal to watch his sister, Princess Anne, compete as an equestrienne in the 1976 Olympic Games. "If you could bear to see me, I would have thought your apartment is the quietest place," he wrote. "If we went anywhere out the press would be on to it in a flash and that would be misery. It will be something marvelous to look forward to as far as I'm concerned and I can't wait to see you again."

On another occasion when he was in Montreal but could not find time in his schedule, Charles lamented, "It was marvelous to hear your voice again the other day from the Ritz. I am desperate being unable to see you."

When Jenkins divorced her first husband, Charles, feeling the pressure to wed, wrote of his own fears about matrimony. "Thank goodness you discovered the mistake early enough and didn't start a family," he wrote. "Making a mistake like that is, frankly, something which concerns me enormously."

Nevertheless, out of loyalty to his great-uncle, Charles proposed to Lord Mountbatten's granddaughter Amanda Knatchbull as soon as she came of age. She declined, claiming she was not prepared to give up her private life to become Princess of Wales. Now that he had done what he could to please his great-uncle, Charles moved on to Lady Sarah Spencer. It was while visiting Lady Sarah at Althorp in 1977 that he met Sarah's younger sister Diana, sixteen and home from a year away at a Swiss finishing school. The encounter was far from romantic, since both Diana and Charles were standing ankle deep in the mud of a freshly plowed field.

Charles stopped seeing Diana's sister not long after and moved on to Venezuelan socialite Cristabel Barria-Borgia, then Scottish heiress Anna Wallace. There was talk of an imminent engagement when the fiery-tempered Wallace—known as "Whiplash" to her friends—stormed out of a birthday party for the Queen Mother because Charles had spent the entire evening dancing with his old flame Camilla. "Nobody treats me like that," she reportedly shouted at him. "Not even you!"

Even as he cut a wide swath through British aristocracy—and not a few well-heeled foreigners—Charles maintained his special friendship with Camilla. They spoke frequently on the phone and exchanged letters—all part of her continuing role as, in Charles's words, "my sounding board and touchstone. The only person I can truly rely on."

Among other things, Camilla played a significant role in helping Charles decide what he wanted to do with his life. "My great problem is that I do not know what my role in life is," he admitted after six years in the navy. "At the moment I do not have one. But somehow I must find one." It would not be easy. After toying with the idea of accepting an appointment as governor-general of Australia, he settled on bettering society through nonprofit work.

Toward that end, he set up the Prince's Trust, an umbrella organization that over the next thirty years would raise hundreds of millions of dollars for British charities.

Not all of his time would be spent on ceremonial duties or
steeped in philanthropic pursuits. Most of Charles's income would
be derived from the Duchy of Cornwall, a vast real estate empire
set up by Edward III in 1337 to provide an income for future kings.
Comprising 135,000 acres spread out over Cornwall, Devon, and
twenty other counties, the duchy includes forests, farmland, water-
front property, London real estate, and even a cricket stadium. Eventually, it would provide Charles with an annual income approaching
$30 million.

While Camilla urged Charles to create a job for himself where
none had existed, she was also someone the Prince could turn to
in times of crisis. Camilla was the first person Charles turned to
in 1979 when IRA terrorists blew up Lord Mountbatten's fishing
boat off the coast of Ireland, killing Mountbatten and two others,
including Mountbatten's fourteen-year-old grandson. Shattered by
the loss, Charles wept to Camilla over the phone. Now, he told
her, there was only one family member left he could talk to—the
Queen Mother.

Charles was still grieving when he ran into Lady Diana Spencer
a second time—at a barbecue in the summer of 1980. The tall,
captivatingly sweet nineteen-year-old was now sharing a flat with
three friends and teaching part-time at a kindergarten in central
London. When she told Charles that she could not forget how
"desperately sad" he had looked at Mountbatten's funeral, Charles
was genuinely touched. He was also impressed, he later said, at
how "she sensed my loneliness."

However impressed he was with Diana's innate sensitivity,

Charles might never have taken a second look at Diana if it weren't for three people who felt she would make an excellent wife for the Prince of Wales. Ironically, all three would become Diana's arch enemies: the Queen Mother, whose lady-in-waiting was Diana's grandmother, Lady Fermoy; the Queen's private secretary, Robert Fellowes, who happened to be Diana's brother-in-law; and Camilla Parker Bowles.

Diana met all the criteria: she was from one of England's oldest families—far older than the Teutonic Windsors, whom Diana would later refer to derisively as "The Germans." She was a virgin with virtually no romantic history to speak of, and—perhaps most important—she could be molded by the powers that be into the perfect royal wife and mother.

"They thought of me as a blank slate," Diana told Lady Elsa Bowker, "and they didn't expect someone like me could possibly have a mind of her own. They were wrong." What they had not taken into account was the lonely childhood that had forged a steely strength of will in Diana. When Diana was six, her mother walked out on the family. She was then left to be raised by a series of nannies, each apparently more coldhearted than the last. "I cried myself to sleep every night," Diana said, "but in the end I think it helped me become a better person. I can appreciate other people's pain because I've experienced it." But, she went on, "It also made me a stronger person. I had to be strong to survive my childhood."

Camilla was delighted with the choice. "Diana is a very sweet girl," she told Harold Brooks-Baker, "and she will give Charles beautiful children." More important, Brooks-Baker said, "Camilla felt Diana was too naive to suspect anything and too weak to do anything about it if she ever found out. She gave every indication of being someone who would simply do what was expected of her and bend to the will of the Royal Family."

Camilla understood the pressure Charles, now thirty-two, was under to marry and produce an heir—particularly from Prince Philip. According to Elsa Bowker, Camilla—a passionate horse-woman—reached for a familiar metaphor to describe the role Diana Spencer was now chosen to play. "Diana," Camilla said, "will make a beautiful brood mare." According to Bowker and others, it was not the sort of remark Camilla would have meant as an insult.

Even with the Queen Mother, the Queen, and Camilla urging him to propose to Diana, Charles dawdled. He knew that the ha-bitually unfaithful Andrew Parker Bowles, who was stationed in Rhodesia to help in that nation's transition to full independence as the state of Zimbabwe, had already been involved in two high-profile romances there. Charles held out hope that, if the Parker Bowleses divorced, he could still end up married to the woman he really loved.

Hotly pursued by the press, "Shy Di" became increasingly con-cerned that the Prince might never pop the question. "He won't ask me," she sobbed to her roommates. "I don't understand. Why won't he ask me?"

Once Charles did knuckle under to pressure from his father and propose in the gardens at Bolehyde Manor, the home of none other than Andrew and Camilla Parker Bowles, Diana was re-lieved—but only for a moment. Asked by a television reporter if they were in love, Diana blurted "of course" without hesitation. Charles, on the other hand, had to think about what Camilla's re-action would be. He paused for a moment before replying, "Whatever 'in love' is."

To the world, the wedding of Charles and Diana at St. Paul's Cathedral surpassed all expectations. Charles's on-again, off-again lover, Janet Jenkins, was certainly impressed. Charles's longtime valet, Stephen Barry, was frequently called upon to smuggle Jenkins into the Prince's hotel room whenever he was traveling. Now she was attending the wedding of Charles and Diana as a guest of the groom. Jenkins, enthralled by the spectacle, paid particular attention to Camilla. "Charles often talked to me about how wonderful Camilla was—he never spoke of Diana," Jenkins recalled, "so of course I was fascinated to get a look at this woman he preferred to his gorgeous young bride. Camilla had this cool, Cheshire cat grin as she watched them march down the aisle. She just seemed so delighted with the whole arrangement."

Charles and Diana's picture-perfect family seemed complete with the arrival of Prince William in 1982 and Prince Harry two years later. "The Heir and the Spare," as the boys were promptly dubbed, injected new life into the monarchy, assuring its continuation far into the next century. All appeared well and good in the House of Windsor.

Nothing could have been further from the truth. Scarcely a week after the engagement, Charles had told the five-foot-eleven-inch Diana that she was "getting a little chubby"—an offhand remark that resulted in her becoming a full-blown bulimic. By the time she threw herself down the stairs at Sandringham House to the horror of the Queen, Diana was making herself throw up five and six times a day.

Diana, now being treated by a battery of psychiatrists and taking large quantities of Valium, became increasingly self-destructive. On one occasion she stabbed herself in the chest with a pocketknife, on another she threw herself against a glass display case, shattering it and cutting herself badly. Another time, she slashed her wrists with a razor.

Diana was so focused on Camilla—and vice versa—that both women failed to notice that another old flame had reentered Charles's life. When Janet Jenkins was visiting friends in England in the fall of 1983, Prince Charles invited her to Highgrove. According to Jenkins, they "slipped back into the familiar intimacy that predated the marriage."

Neither his wife nor his mistress knew that Jenkins was again sleeping with Charles—and not using contraceptives because they had never used birth control before, and "neither of us thought of using protection."

Nine months later, on June 13, 1984, Jenkins gave birth to a son she named Jason. She had married a Canadian businessman six months earlier, and he was listed as the child's father on the birth certificate. Despite repeated suggestions that the Prince of Wales was her son's father, Jenkins eventually insisted that was not the case.

Charles, whom Diana periodically referred to as "The Boy Wonder" and "The Great White Hope," had essentially moved out of Kensington Palace and permanently into Highgrove by 1987. Highgrove was scarcely a twenty-minute drive from the Parker Bowles estate. The following year, Diana worked up the courage to confront the person she blamed most for the destruction of her marriage. At a fortieth birthday party in honor of Camilla's younger sister Annabel—a party that Charles originally planned on attending solo—Diana showed up unexpectedly with her bodyguard and went through the house looking for Charles.

She found him and another male guest chatting with Camilla in the nursery. "OK, boys," Diana told the startled men, "I'm just going to have a quick word with Camilla and I'll be up in a minute." At that point, Diana later recalled, Charles and the other man "shot upstairs like chickens with no heads and I could feel, upstairs, all hell breaking loose."

With Charles upstairs pleading "What is she going to do?" to his aides, Diana cornered his quivering mistress.

"Camilla, I would just like you to know that I know exactly what is going on between you and Charles," Diana said. "I wasn't born yesterday."

To the Princess's surprise, Camilla was anything but contrite. "You've got everything you ever wanted," she told Diana. "You've got all the men in the world to fall in love with you and you've got two beautiful children. What more do you want?"

"I want my husband," Diana replied without hesitation. "I'm sorry I'm in the way, I obviously am in the way and it must be hell for both of you but I do know what is going on. Don't treat me like an idiot."

Camilla, shaking, turned on her heels and fled. Charles chased after her. On the ride home that night, he angrily chastised Diana. Then he called Camilla and apologized for his wife's "outrageous" behavior. Humiliated and distraught, Diana sobbed herself to sleep.

Diana's decision to confront the Other Woman would alter Camilla's view of the Princess. "Camilla is not a very complicated person, and she underestimated Diana completely," said a longtime acquaintance of both women. "Camilla felt that somehow Diana hadn't caught on to their little game, or that if she had, she would play by the rules as all royal wives have done and say nothing." Once Diana squared off with her in public, Camilla "saw the Princess through new eyes. Now Diana was the enemy."

What she had not known was that Diana had already been working behind the scenes to destroy Camilla's relationship with

Charles. At one point, she had friends make a series of anonymous calls to Charles's private numbers at Highgrove, St. James's, and Balmoral. The callers all tipped Charles off to another man with whom Camilla was supposedly having an affair.

The ruse worked. Charles confronted Camilla about her secret paramour. "Camilla was absolutely perplexed when he started babbling about another man in her life," Diana's friend and confidante Simone Simmons said. "It took her days to allay his suspicions. He couldn't believe he'd been hoaxed. . . . For weeks after he hardly let Camilla out of his sight." Apparently neither Charles nor Camilla ever traced the anonymous calls to Diana.

The mischievous Princess often thought about ways to get even with her rival. One of her favorite fantasies involved surprising Camilla at her own birthday party. "Charles will be there, and they'll be having this massive cake," Diana told Simmons. "When they come to light the candles I want to be hidden inside and suddenly jump out. Picture their faces!"

For the most part, however, Diana regarded Charles's affair with Camilla as anything but a laughing matter. When she felt overwhelmed, the Princess sometimes felt compelled to take her case to the top. On several occasions over the years Diana appeared unannounced at Buckingham Palace and would typically be kept waiting in the page's vestibule outside Her Majesty's study before she was finally allowed in. With its overstuffed furniture, large windows, and calming blue-green wallpaper, this was both a working office and a refuge for the monarch. The antique desk was covered with the Queen's famous red boxes and blue boxes brimming with matters of ceremony and matters of state, but there were also framed photographs and knickknacks—personal items that her staff was under strict orders never to touch.

In this setting, Diana would pour out her heart to the Queen—about her marriage, about the pressures of her royal schedule, about her sense of isolation and the forces within the palace power structure she felt were aligned against her. Did she know that her son placed many of his calls to his mistress from his bathtub? Once, Diana told the Queen, she listened at the bathroom door and heard Charles whisper to Camilla over the phone, "Whatever happens, I will always love you."

If she was shocked, Mama, as the Queen encouraged Diana to call her, never allowed it to show. She listened calmly and patiently but in the end offered no solutions. Clearly, her own stiff-upper-lip sensibility precluded her from ever fully empathizing with Diana. After one particularly emotional session, the Princess fled in tears. When the Queen's private secretary was summoned into the study a few moments later, he found his boss sitting at her desk, her doughy face etched with exhaustion. "She cried," said the Queen, "nonstop."

Another time the Queen—"Top Lady," as Diana would sometimes refer to her behind the monarch's back—seemed equally exasperated with Charles's behavior. When Charles told Diana that he refused to be the only Prince of Wales who never had a mistress, the Princess went to her mother-in-law and tearfully asked, "What do I do?"

The Queen threw up her hands. "I don't know what you should do," she replied, shaking her head. "Charles is hopeless."

"And that was it," Diana later recalled of the Queen's offer of advice. "That was 'help'!"

The Queen would later concede that she sometimes felt as if she had failed her daughter-in-law. "I tried to reach out to Diana many times," she would try to explain to Paul Burrell.

"The trouble was, Your Majesty," he replied, "that you spoke in black and white. The Princess spoke in color."

Beneath the Queen's fabled facade, insisted her cousin Margaret Rhodes, there was a woman who keenly felt what Diana was going through. "She is not what is now called a 'touchy-feely' person," Rhodes said of the monarch. "She is a self-contained person, but an incredibly generous person."

Charles's reputation and the fate of the monarchy were at stake, but no matter. The Prince of Wales and his married mistress were determined to be together. So that they could spend more time together a favorite ploy of Camilla's, according to two of her former employees, was faking illness. "She had a smoker's cough already, so it wasn't very difficult for her to pretend she had a bad case of the flu," one said. On one occasion when she was supposed to attend a dinner at Whitehall in honor of her husband's commanding general, Camilla went to bed with a bad virus. As soon as Andrew—who by now had attained the rank of brigadier with the title Silver Stick in Waiting to the Queen—departed, "Camilla jumped out of bed and ran downstairs. Within minutes, Prince Charles was outside in his car waiting for her."

At other times, Camilla would start coughing and sneezing one or two days before the Parker Bowleses were supposed to leave town for a weekend with friends. Again, no sooner would Parker Bowles leave on his own than the royal car from Highgrove would pull up the drive to pick up Camilla.

Even in the face of a family emergency, Camilla would not disappoint her prince. After her mother, Rosalind Shand, fell ill and was rushed by ambulance to the hospital, Camilla held off visiting her until the next day. No explanation for the delay was necessary when Charles's car pulled up to the house later that evening.

"She loved her mother," said a member of the household staff, "but Camilla wasn't going to let *anything* get in the way of seeing the Prince. He came first, always."

At Highgrove, their affair had all the hallmarks of a Feydeau farce. During the week when Diana was in London, Camilla would be given a guest bedroom. Late at night, she would sneak into Charles's room—but not before the Prince had disarmed the elaborate security system that protected him from intruders. "It was a big risk," said Charles's valet, Ken Stronach. "A stupid thing to do." To make it look to the servants as if Camilla had spent the night in the guest room, it was Stronach's job to mess up the bed and the pillows—"but only on one side of the bed, so that it looked as if only one person had been sleeping there."

For all intents and purposes, Stronach said, "We were told to treat Camilla as if she was mistress of the house. It was as if Princess Diana had never existed." When Diana did show up at Highgrove on weekends, Charles would rendezvous with Camilla at a prede-termined spot just inside the garden walls. On those nights, Charles would sneak back into his room and change into a new pair of pa-jamas. It was then Stronach's job to scrub the grass stains out of the old pair so Diana would be none the wiser. "There was mud and muck everywhere," the valet said. Charles and Camilla had, he added, "obviously been doing it in the open air."

For years, Charles actually kept a framed picture of Camilla next to his bed at Highgrove. In the photo, Camilla is sitting on a bench outside Birkhall, the Queen Mother's house at Balmoral, with William in the background playing with Prince Charles's Jack Rus-sell terrier, Tigger. Whenever Diana came to stay at Highgrove, Ken Stronach was instructed to hide the photo—along with any other telltale signs of his boss's affection for Camilla.

When Charles and Camilla weren't trysting at Highgrove, the Prince drove to Middlewick House, the Parker Bowles family residence just twelve miles from Highgrove. In a ploy reminiscent of the biblical King David, who sent Bathsheba's soldier-husband into battle so that they could carry on their notorious affair, Charles allegedly used his influence to make certain Andrew Parker Bowles's assignments kept him away from home—better yet, out of the country—for weeks and months at a time.

Even when Camilla's husband was working in London during the week, Charles would show up at Middlewick House just minutes after Parker Bowles left on Sunday night. At that time, Camilla would have turned off the lights so that her lover could drive up and enter the house under cover of night. Camilla's servants called this precaution—which took place up to four times a week—"The Blackout." Charles would stay the night with Camilla in her room, then drive home just before dawn. Accordingly, the staff at Middlewick House referred to Charles as "The Prince of Darkness."

Meanwhile, back at Highgrove, Stronach circled TV programs in the newspaper and left them by the Prince's bedside with a half-empty glass of sherry and a partially eaten snack to make it look as if Charles had spent a quiet night at home. "It didn't," the valet said, "fool anybody."

Especially not Diana. Not surprisingly, most of the confrontations between the Prince and Princess took place at Highgrove, where Diana was fully aware of Camilla's near-constant presence. Despite the fact that Stronach had strict instructions to make sure all glasses were washed to remove any lipstick traces and to empty all the ashtrays, the acrid smell of Camilla's cigarettes lingered.

The rows between Charles and Diana grew more and more

heated. The housekeeper at Highgrove, Wendy Berry, recalled that screaming and slammed doors soon became the norm. Every day the two were under the same roof, there would be shouting matches that invariably led to Diana dashing down a hallway, sobbing hysterically. One day Stronach watched as the Princess went on the offensive, chasing her husband from room to room and taunting him about his obsession with another man's wife.

"How dare you talk to me like that!" he shot back. "Do you know who I am?"

"You," Diana replied, "are a fucking animal."

Enraged, Charles swung around and hurled a heavy boot at the wall as Diana made her exit.

As tensions mounted, there was real concern that something truly violent would happen at Highgrove. There was the distinct possibility that one of the many hunting rifles kept on the premises might, in the heat of anger, become a murder weapon. Just as likely was the chance that one or the other might use one of the guns to commit suicide. Diana had already made several half-hearted attempts to kill or injure herself, and royal lawyer Lord Arnold Goodman determined after talking to Charles that the Prince of Wales was clinically depressed and "suicidal." Royal Protection officers assigned to Highgrove moved quickly to gather up all the firearms at the estate and lock them away.

Incredibly, the public remained blissfully unaware of the turmoil inside the royal marriage until May 1991. It was then that Fleet Street noticed that Camilla and Charles were each vacationing in Italy without their respective spouses—and that the villas they rented in Florence were just a stone's throw from each other.

A month later, Charles and Camilla were together at Highgrove when they got the call that William had been rushed to Royal

Berkshire Hospital with a head injury. While horsing around with some other boys at Ludgrove, William had been struck full force in the forehead with a golf club and knocked unconscious. Diana, who had been lunching with a friend in London, rushed to join her husband at William's bedside.

Doctors were concerned enough to have the young Prince taken by ambulance to the prestigious Great Ormond Street Hospital in London, where it was promptly determined that William's injury was serious. Surgery would be required to check for bone fragments and to determine whether there had been any brain damage. Barring that, there was always the possibility of infection triggering meningitis or seizures.

Understandably shocked and upset, Diana remained at the hospital during the delicate seventy-five-minute operation on her son's skull and for hours afterward. Charles, however, saw no reason to hang around. Since his own parents had never interrupted their schedules to dote on him when he was sick, Charles had no reason to believe he should behave differently. To make sure his instincts were right, he called Camilla with news of William's condition, and to ask her opinion. Camilla insisted that Charles should go ahead with whatever he had planned. "It's in the doctors' hands now, Darling," Camilla assured him. "There's really nothing you can do. It would be silly to stop everything you're doing to just sit there in a waiting room."

As he always did, Charles took Camilla's advice and went as planned to a performance of *Tosca* at Covent Garden. Once the curtain came down, he went straight to an environmental conference in North Yorkshire. The Prince of Wales popped back into the hospital the next day for a brief visit with William, then headed off again—this time to see his mistress at Highgrove.

The headlines were scathing if predictable: WHAT KIND OF DAD ARE YOU? demanded the *Sun* on its front page. Similarly, the *Daily Express* began its attack on Charles's insensitive behavior with "What kind of father . . ."

It was a major public relations victory for Diana, who once again proved just how insensitive and self-centered the royals could be. Dismayed, Charles again turned for solace to Camilla, who laid it all at the feet of a scheming Diana. "She knows how to use the press to her advantage, Charles," Camilla said. "Diana is very cold and calculating that way. You're just not that kind of person. You're entirely too good for that sort of thing."

Yet there was no denying that Charles had not fully appreciated how grave William's situation could easily have become. Nor could it be overlooked that Camilla shared her lover's apparent lack of compassion for others—even his own child—as well as his chronic cluelessness when it came to shaping public perceptions.

The marriage of Charles and Diana would continue to unravel through 1991, but it was the following year that Queen Elizabeth would dub her true *annus horribilis*. It would begin with Andrew Morton's Diana-sanctioned blockbuster. As it happened, Camilla and Andrew Parker Bowles were guests of the Queen at the Windsor Great Park polo match the day *Diana: Her True Story* hit bookstores. That same year, the marriage of Prince Andrew and Sarah Ferguson came to a sordid end, Princess Anne divorced, and the Queen stood by helplessly and watched as Windsor Castle nearly burned to the ground.

It was not a particularly good year for Camilla's husband either. In the wake of all the revelations regarding Charles and Camilla, Andrew Parker Bowles was now publicly ridiculed as Britain's No. 1 cuckold. At Ascot in June 1992, Lord Charles Spencer-Churchill loudly compared Parker Bowles to Ernest Simpson, the man Wallis Simpson left so she could marry the Duke of Windsor. Andrew replied by grabbing Lord Spencer-Churchill by the arm and shaking him. "He was very, very angry indeed," Spencer-Churchill said. "The next day I was black and blue with bruises." On another occasion, Camilla's husband was publicly chided by another friend as "the most patriotic man in Britain. He is prepared to lay down his wife for his country."

By the time of "Camillagate"—the release of those intimate taped conversations in which Charles voiced his desire to become one of Camilla's tampons—Andrew Parker Bowles could no longer keep up the charade. Their marriage would limp along for another eighteen months before officially ending in divorce in 1994.

As his own marriage came tumbling down around his famously protruding ears, Charles turned to an old flame for consolation. He invited Janet Jenkins to Highgrove in July of 1992, and over a four-hour period poured out his heart about the impending divorce and what impact it would likely have on his sons. Then they slept together—"the last time," Jenkins said, "we were sexually intimate." At the time, she claimed to have no idea that Charles was still involved with Camilla.

Camilla was certainly unaware of Charles's infidelity to her— in large part because of her growing fear of what Diana might do next. Camilla came face-to-face with Diana again that October, at a service in Westminster Abbey to mark the fiftieth anniversary of the Battle of El Alamein. Camilla attended the ceremony with her father, Major Bruce Shand, a decorated World War II veteran. When the Prince and Princess of Wales entered the abbey and made their way to the front pew, Diana turned her head and glared at Camilla. "It was like going into the lion's den," Camilla later said of the mob of reporters who descended on her as she tried to leave. "But I guess all they're going to care about was that my hair was in a mess."

The press would, in fact, have a field day comparing the sleek, glamorous Princess of Wales to her frumpy, comparatively ill-kempt competition. "They were like the twin faces of war—the dullness of defeat and the radiance of victory," sniped the *Daily Mail*. "As a piece of theater it was compelling. The Princess of Wales, her eyes wide, bright, and open, wearing a jacket of shimmering silvery gray and tight-fitting white skirt. Camilla Parker Bowles, a funereal figure, pale, thin, and hair flecked with gray, in shapeless, somber blue." Camilla, the piece went on, looked "so much more like her forty-three years as she shuffled out of the abbey." Yet the press did not seem to fully comprehend that it was Camilla who was the victor here; she could always return home to Highgrove knowing that she, not Diana, was the true mistress of the house.

That was particularly evident to Janet Jenkins when she was invited to Highgrove again in 1996 and was seated next to Camilla at dinner. Jenkins found Camilla "absolutely charming—either she didn't know that Charles and I had been lovers or she didn't care, because she treated me wonderfully."

Jenkins was being, in the words of one longtime friend of Charles, "a tad naive if she thought it was all an accident. The divorce was under way, and the last thing Charles needed was another batch of stories in the papers about what a randy cad he had been. They also worried about the child [Jenkins's son Jason was then twelve years old] who may or may not have been Charles's, for all they knew." But was Camilla aware that Janet Jenkins had still been sleeping with Charles just a few years earlier, and at Highgrove? "No, *that* is something Camilla did not know."

If she had only a fleeting familiarity with Janet Jenkins, Camilla was well aware of the important role another of Charles's married mistresses played in his life. Off-again and on-again for a quarter century, Lady Dale Tryon not only shared Charles's bed with Camilla but also served as his second-most-trusted female confidante—"the only woman," the Prince of Wales once said, "who really understands me."

On his way home to Highgrove, Charles frequently bypassed Camilla to make a "comfort stop," as Lady Tryon wryly referred to their assignations, at the Tryon estate. "He would ring out of the blue," Lady Tryon remembered years later, "and say he would be passing by and would I mind if he popped in. I'd make sure a whiskey was ready for him, then we'd chat before making ourselves more 'comfortable.'"

Nicknamed "Kanga" by Charles because of her bouncy personality, the flamboyant Australian-born beauty got together with Camilla at Charles's request to come up with a suitable young bride. Kanga Tryon claimed she and Camilla were "most civilized toward each other" when they met to consult on a list of potential princesses. "We came up with three names each," Kanga recalled. "The only name Camilla and I both came up with was Diana Spencer, so she went to the top of the list. I thought she'd look great in a tiara—and Camilla liked the fact she was shy and unlikely to cause trouble. How wrong can you be!"

In contrast to the grudge she harbored against Camilla, Diana liked Kanga; after her marriage to Charles, the Princess of Wales and the *other* other woman became friends—so close that Lady Tryon reportedly shared her prescription for the powerful sleep medication Rohypnol with Diana. "She'd get up at night and even go for drives," Kanga recalled. "She told me once that she'd been out in the car after taking Rohypnol and had no recollection of it until she came to getting out of the car. She had no idea where she'd been."

Born with spina bifida, Kanga managed to overcome uterine cancer but was less successful battling the symptoms of clinical depression—a condition that worsened when she realized in the mid-1990s that she had been completely supplanted by Camilla as Charles's closest confidante. In 1996, while the divorce of Charles and Diana dominated the news, Kanga Tryon checked herself into Farm Place, a drug and alcohol rehabilitation center in Surrey. While being treated there, she suffered a mysterious fall from a third-floor window, breaking her back and fracturing her skull.

The following June Kanga, now confined to a wheelchair, suffered a nervous breakdown and was detained under Britain's Mental Health Act after she repeatedly claimed that someone was trying to kill her. The following day her husband, Lord Tryon, filed for divorce. "She has flipped before," he said. "She has said in the past I am going to murder her." Several months later, after undergoing a minor skin graft procedure at a London clinic, Kanga developed septicemia and died. She was forty-nine.

Coming just nine weeks after Diana's death, the unexpected loss of Kanga Tryon—and under circumstances that could only be described as bizarre—hit Charles hard. Camilla, still in hiding, could only offer words of comfort over the phone for the loss of the one woman who was truly a rival for Charles's affections.

Camilla would have to wait until May 1998 before being permitted to venture out in public, and then only to dash in and out of her godson Henry Dent Brocklehurst's wedding. Three months later, following her historic first meeting with Prince William at Clarence House, Camilla joined with the boys to plan a fiftieth birthday bash for Charles at Highgrove. No longer willing to languish in the shadows, she made a dramatic entrance. Camilla slowly stepped out of her Bentley wearing a clingy green velvet dress and an eye-popping necklace of sapphires and diamonds and smiled for the cameras.

Inside, Camilla had re-created the Prince's walled garden using tree stumps, leaves, flowers, vines, and grass. After 340 guests lifted their glasses in a toast to the birthday boy, everyone was riveted by the sight of Charles and Camilla boogying to the music of Abba and the Village People. Yet the Queen, still objecting to the presence of Camilla in her son's life, refused to attend. And Camilla was explicitly excluded from attending Charles's more formal, official birthday party at Buckingham Palace.

Still, a newly emboldened Camilla continued to play up her connections to Princes of Wales past and present. Now a portrait of Alice Keppel hung in a prominent spot over the mantel in her house, and Camilla made a point of wearing Keppel's jewels to high-profile affairs. "Oh, this necklace belonged to my great-grandmother Mrs. Alice Keppel," she would tell anyone who inquired before loudly adding, "she was the mistress of Edward VII, you know."

That first summer following Diana's death, Charles stuck to the plan carefully devised by Mark Bolland to win back the affection of the British people. For the first time, the Prince of Wales was photographed on the tarmac at Heathrow, kissing William goodbye as both prepared to take separate flights to Greece. Once there, they boarded billionaire John Latsis's lavish, four-hundred-foot yacht *Alexander* (named after Alexander the Great) for a week-long cruise of the Aegean with several of Charles's closest friends. It was too soon, however, to be seen vacationing in the company of his mistress.

It had only been a few years since Charles and Diana had taken a "second honeymoon" cruise aboard the *Alexander*—an attempt at reconciliation that fell apart when Diana discovered her husband making furtive ship-to-shore calls to his mistress. Now the Prince of Wales spent much of his time staring silently out to sea. One day he turned to one of the other passengers and sighed. "I just so wish," he said, "she could be here with me."

"Diana?"

"Oh, heavens no," Charles snapped back. "Camilla, of course."

I think both me and William
are different from the rest of
the family. The world is changing
. . . and we've changed with it.

—Harry

4

"Shit!" William yelled, grabbing his ear. The spray of buckshot had passed uncomfortably close. A few yards behind the Prince stood the Eton classmate who had fired the shot, frozen in terror as four Royal Protection Guards came running. "Sorry," the teenager managed to sputter, his twelve-gauge shotgun rifle now pointed safely at the ground. "I guess I'm a bit . . . off."

"It's OK," the future King said, trying to calm himself and everyone else. "But could you *please* be bloody more careful next time?"

It would not be the first time a member of the Royal Family came perilously close to being killed in a hunting accident, nor would it be the last. On this particular occasion William and Harry, who joined his brother at Eton in September of 1998, had invited fourteen of their school chums to dine with Granny at Windsor just five days before Christmas.

First, all the students—ranging in ages from fourteen to sixteen—met the Queen in the Green Drawing Room for a drink. At dinner, they were served wine—white with the Dover sole, red with the pheasant, tawny port with the cheese. After the Queen retired for the evening, the boys then helped themselves to Her Majesty's abundant liquor supply.

Shortly after sunrise, the Princes and their friends—now mightily hung over—grabbed shotguns and headed off on a rabbit hunting expedition in Windsor Great Park. As was the practice at such royal venues as Balmoral, Sandringham, and even Highgrove, the teenage hunters—accompanied by a battery of guards and gamekeepers—stopped for a picnic lunch that also included wine. Unlike the hunting parties at Balmoral, Sandringham, and Highgrove, they would not have the time to stop several more times during the day to nibble on chicken served up by the Queen in Tupperware and chase it down with a beer.

Blinded by centuries of tradition, the Royal Family and their handlers were oblivious to the dangers inherent in mixing youth, alcohol, and firearms. While several of their fellow Etonians had virtually no experience handling weapons of any kind, William and Harry had grown up enjoying what their mother called the "glorious Windsor pastime of killing things."

Both Princes were "blooded" at the age of fourteen: after killing their first buck, each was daubed on the face with the dead animal's blood. Diana was only thirteen when she shot her first stag, but for her the experience was far from exhilarating. "I can't understand how anyone can take pleasure in killing a beautiful creature," she said. "But it is part of the boys' heritage, and I won't stand in the way of it."

A determinedly hands-on mum, Diana worried about the royals' casual approach to drinking and shooting—and to drinking and driving, for that matter. There were no speed limits on the royal estates, and it was not uncommon for family members, friends, and employees to hoist a few before getting behind the wheel of a Land Rover or Jeep and tearing off across the countryside.

However, if it was a drink they wanted, William and Harry didn't have to go farther than the students-only pub at their own school. Etonians sixteen and older were allowed to belly up to the bar at The Tap and order up to two pints of hard cider or beer per day. Will and Harry quickly discovered that these restrictions were easily circumvented.

Alcohol and drug abuse were just two of the problems Eton shared with any high school—public or private. During the time William and Harry were enrolled there, students were disciplined for taking speed, painkillers, and cocaine, for smoking pot, and for smuggling a variety of weapons, from stun guns to knives and pistols, into the school.

Yet the most shocking tragedy to occur at the school during William's tenure there apparently had nothing to do with substance abuse or student-on-student violence. When one of the Prince's classmates, sixteen-year-old Nicholas Taylor, was found hanged in his own room in early 1999, his death was at first thought to be a suicide.

Soon, however, investigators were exploring another theory: one that involved a bizarre nocturnal diversion at Eton called the Fainting Game. This particular practice involved two students looping a bathrobe belt around the neck of a third student and pulling it until he passes out. As a precaution of sorts, the boy with the noose around his neck taps on his thigh while the belt is tightening to indicate that he is still conscious. Once the tapping stops—the sign that the boy has either had enough or has lost consciousness—the noose is quickly loosened. At this point in the alarmingly widespread practice of voluntary strangulation known as autoerotic asphyxia, the boy who has passed out has supposedly experienced an orgasmic high.

Not surprisingly, the Fainting Game can lead to severe injury, brain damage, or death. (One of the better known victims was Katharine Hepburn's brother Tom, who hanged himself in this fashion at the age of fourteen.) Like young Hepburn, Taylor had apparently been attempting to play the Fainting Game alone.

Though William and Harry were shocked when classmates approached them to play the Fainting Game, they did nothing to warn school officials about what was going on. "The Princes both knew how to have fun, and they were very well liked," classmates recalled. "They would never inform on their friends. But they also never forgot who they were, or how what they did would end up in the newspapers. That's where they drew the line—doing anything that would embarrass the Royal Family."

Not that the Princes didn't overimbibe, and with some frequency. Royal Protection officers, lurking just out of sight even when the boys were on school grounds, were under strict orders not to interfere with William and Harry experiencing something akin to a normal adolescence. That meant trying to give the boys a sixty- to one-hundred-foot zone of privacy. At least once a week, that meant standing at a respectful distance while the Princes partied with their friends. "They got lashed like everyone else," said one Eton student who was a year younger than William and a year older than Harry. "Their bodyguards just looked the other way while they threw up."

Scotland Yard also ordered the Princes' security detail to look the other way whenever they witnessed any drug use in the boys' presence. A Scotland Yard official told the Sunday *Times* of London that, while it was the natural inclination of any law enforcement officer to arrest someone smoking marijuana or snorting cocaine, such an action would only compound the "potential for embarrassment."

At a time when Camilla could not afford to be portrayed in anything but the most favorable light, the greatest "potential for embarrassment" would come from her own unruly clan. Four years after his 1995 arrest for possessing marijuana and the drug Ecstasy, Tom Parker Bowles—now regarded by William as the big brother he never had—admitted to cocaine use. The resulting scandal unleashed a torrent of revelations about Camilla's son—including the night he attended a "Fetish Party" brandishing a whip and dressed as a dominatrix in fishnet stockings, a black plastic dress, and stiletto heels. (By all accounts, Tom's younger sister, Laura, was far more level-headed. Also a regular on the nightclub circuit, Laura nevertheless managed to avoid the pitfalls of substance abuse.)

Charles gave his godson Tom a stern talking to—"Your mother is very upset. For God's sake, think of what all this is doing to her"—and warned him to stay away from William and Harry until he conquered his cocaine dependency.

But Tom Parker Bowles's drug scandal was only the first in a series involving several members of William's inner circle. Tara Palmer-Tomkinson, the daughter of Charles's longtime skiing buddy Charles Palmer-Tomkinson, went into rehab in 1999. Another attractive young female pal of William's, Izzy Winkler, confessed to using cocaine. So too did Lord Mountbatten's great-grandson Nicholas Knatchbull. The young Princes' cousin and William's closest chum at Eton, Nicholas went into rehab twice in two years.

Yet another cousin, Lord Frederick ("Freddie") Windsor, grappled with a dependence on cocaine. A particular favorite of the Queen ("Freddy's manners are *impeccable*"), the son of Prince and Princess Michael of Kent cautioned his royal cousins about being sucked into the world of drugs. "It is very difficult to avoid getting into this sort of thing," Freddy said, "when you move in these circles."

Unfortunately, the Parker Bowles name would again be dragged into the spotlight when Emma Parker Bowles, Camilla's niece and William's first serious crush, was also treated for cocaine and alcohol dependency. "It's all," Emma said when tabloid photographers discovered that she was spending a month drying out in an Arizona clinic, "very upsetting."

By all accounts, at this stage both William and Harry scrupulously avoided illegal substances of any kind. But the fact that they seemed to be running with a drug-taking crowd—and that two of its members bore the Parker Bowles name—raised serious concerns. Clearly Charles was in no position to bar Tom Parker Bowles from contact with his sons, or vice versa. "The Queen never liked Camilla, never trusted her," one courtier observed. "But once it looked as if Prince William and Prince Harry were being dragged down by the Parker Bowleses as well, she became very cross."

Buckingham Palace and Charles's advisors agreed that, for the time being at least, Tom should not be seen in public with either William or Harry. Camilla was asked to stay out of the public eye until the drug scandals had blown over.

It was a devastating setback for Charles and Camilla, who seemed to have been making great strides toward public acceptance as a couple. In January 1999, they had made their first public appearance together since Diana's death. They were seen standing on the steps of the Ritz Hotel in London, where they'd come to celebrate the fiftieth birthday of Camilla's sister Annabel Elliott. Of all the galas, parties, and events where Camilla could have chosen to make this statement, she chose this particular date and occasion for a reason: it had been ten years to the day since Diana confronted Camilla and humiliated her at Annabel's fortieth birthday party.

"People often say that Camilla is such a sweet and uncomplicated woman," Lady Elsa Bowker observed, "but all you have to do is look at how she plots, schemes—the deception. She despised Diana in life, and I think even more so in death, because Diana was even more beloved for her kindness in death."

With Mark Bolland pulling the strings, Operation PB had continued in May of that year, when Camilla returned to the London Ritz—this time to host a dinner for the National Osteoporosis Society. To underscore her status as the future King's official mistress, she wore a diamond brooch bearing the distinctive plumed emblem of the Prince of Wales. Later, Camilla accompanied Charles to a Buckingham Palace dinner for wealthy Americans who gave sizable donations to his charitable Prince of Wales Foundation.

Now, in the wake of more summer headlines linking the drug-abusing Parker Bowleses to her grandsons, Her Majesty had more reasons to resent Camilla. Over her son's angry objections, the Queen had banned Camilla from attending the June 19, 1999, wedding of Charles's brother Prince Edward and Diana look-alike Sophie Rhys-Jones. Asked to explain if this meant that Camilla had taken a major detour on the road to acceptance by the Crown, a palace spokesman sniffed that the Queen had "made it clear that any rapprochement is out of the question."

She did take some solace, however, in the fact that Camilla would be withdrawing from public view. This time, however, neither Charles nor his mistress were willing to comply with Her Majesty's wishes. In direct defiance of the Queen, Charles invited Camilla to join him and the boys aboard the *Alexander* when they embarked in July on their annual ten-day cruise of the Aegean. What's more, in spite of the damaging news about his drug use, Tom Parker Bowles was also on the guest list, along with his sister, Laura.

Once again, Diana's friends believed Camilla and Charles both showed a callous disregard for the Princess's memory. Just seven years earlier on the occasion of their tenth anniversary, Charles and Diana had set sail aboard the *Alexander* on their ill-fated "second honeymoon." Another of Diana's friends believed that "each of these places represented something in the rivalry between Diana and Camilla, and Camilla was simply going back to each spot to make it clear that she had won. It made a lot of people angry."

By way of damage control, St. James's sought to deflect attention away from Camilla and toward William, whose popularity now exceeded that of the revered Queen Mum. Charles's spin doctors came up with the specious story that William had insisted on inviting Camilla and her children, and then leaked information concerning three beautiful last-minute additions to the passenger list—all invited by Wills. With the press frantically speculating about which of the three young ladies—Emilia ("Mili") d'Erlanger, Mary Forestier-Walker, or Davina Duckworth-Chad—had the inside track with the seventeen-year-old heir, interest in Camilla's presence on the cruise quickly faded.

It was no accident that Mark Bolland went along as Camilla's handler when the woman who would be Queen made her first trip to New York that October. The highlight of the visit was a lunch hosted by the doyenne of New York society, Brooke Astor. Among the guests were media mogul Mortimer Zuckerman, future Mayor Michael Bloomberg, U.N. Secretary-General Kofi Annan, *Vogue* magazine editor Anna Wintour, designer Oscar de la Renta, and Henry Kissinger. More exciting, however, was another glitterati-sprinkled cocktail party that ended when police arrived to announce that they had received a credible bomb threat. Just as the bomb squad arrived, Camilla stepped out a side exit and discreetly into a waiting Rolls-Royce.

On the trip, Camilla had been eager to hear the then ninety-seven-year-old Brooke Astor regale her with stories about Alice Keppel, whom Astor had actually met. Out of concern for her guest's feelings, Astor neglected to mention that by the time she met Alice Keppel in the 1930s—more than twenty years after Edward VII's death—Camilla's great-grandmother was a social pariah, cast out by the upper classes, who viewed her as immoral and predatory.

Astor also spared Camilla the truth concerning Keppel's appearance—she was never considered a beauty, even at the height of her affair with King Edward. "Her charm," said the novelist Dame Rebecca West, "was not in her looks. George [Alice's husband George Keppel] was the only beauty of the two."

Astor also refrained from telling Camilla that the great-grandmother she so idolized was shunned for bearing two children out of wedlock with two different lovers—one by Lord Grimthorpe, the designer of Big Ben. Keppel moved into the Ritz Hotel during World War II, and it was there that she died in 1947 of cirrhosis of the liver. "A very sad end, as I understand it," Astor later recalled. "But not entirely unexpected."

Nevertheless, Camilla charmed her American hosts, and her progress was anxiously monitored by Charles back in London. He had paid $33,000 out of his own pocket to defray Camilla's expenses—a small fraction of the $250,000 he was already spending on his mistress annually. He could well afford it—and the $80,000 a year he spent on clothes alone. By the year 2000, according to official financial records made public by St. James's Palace that year, Prince Charles was worth well in excess of a half-billion dollars.

For the moment, he was determined to bolster Camilla's image as a worthy successor to Diana when it came to pressing the flesh abroad. The Prince instructed Bolland to make sure the Queen's new private secretary, Robin Janvrin, passed the positive U.S. press clippings on to his boss. "Prince Charles was keen to prove Camilla could do the job—the boring ceremonial duties that went with being his wife and a member of the Royal Family," said a longtime friend of the Parker Bowleses. "He wanted the Queen to know that in her own way Camilla could be a valuable addition to The Firm. She was no Diana, of course . . ."

That, to a large extent, was Camilla's saving grace—especially when it came to winning over Diana's sons. And once they were fully in Camilla's corner, the Queen would surely follow.

It was precisely because she was so little like their mother that Camilla seemed nonthreatening to William and Harry. She was like the furniture she favored, classic English shabby. Her wardrobe of boxy sweaters, torn riding pants, manure-caked Wellingtons, and frayed head scarves reeked of cigarette smoke. So did her uncombed hair, a tangle of split ends from which, at any given time, one could pluck the stray twig, or perhaps a brittle leaf or the odd bit of grass. Her crooked teeth had been stained corn kernel yellow from decades of heavy smoking, and black dirt formed a crescent beneath her jagged nails.

Camilla was equally fastidious about her surroundings. At her house in Wiltshire, the carpets were threadbare, the upholstery soiled. Tabletops, armrests, chenille throws, and even curtains were spotted with cigarette burns. Muddy boots were heaped in the hallway. Beds looked as if they had been hit by a tornado. Bathroom counters were strewn with wads of crumpled Kleenex, toothpaste oozed out of capless tubes, underwear hung from curtain rods, and damp towels were piled on the wet tile floor. Despite the fact that there was always a full contingent of servants—at a bare minimum a cook, a housekeeper, two maids, a gardener, and a driver—it was impossible to stay ahead of their employer's messy habits.

As earthy as Diana was urbane, Camilla was happiest riding to the hounds, tromping through open fields, or digging in the dirt alongside her man at Highgrove. Her attitude toward child rearing was as relaxed as Diana's was hands-on. When William took up smoking—something that the health-conscious Diana would never have countenanced—Camilla remained mum. No surprise there, given the fact that she had not yet resolved to quit her own two-pack-a-day habit.

With the exception of his fondness for Marlboro Lights, there actually seemed little about William that needed improvement. An outstanding athlete, William Wales—the name under which he was enrolled at Eton—was captain of the swim team (his mother had been an avid swimmer) and a hard-driving member of the rugby, rowing, and water polo teams. ("I think William chose to play it," Diana once said of his foray into water polo, "because it was a way of pleasing both Charles and myself.")

William's grades placed him in the top 10 percent of his class, and as a member of the student leadership society called "Pop," he was essentially in a position to tell the rest of the student body what to do—"good training for a King," one of his teachers quipped. William also showed a keen interest in all things military, and as a member of Eton's cadet force was awarded the force's highest accolade, the Sword of Honor.

Camilla could take credit for none of William's achievements, and she sought none. On the rare occasions when she did encourage him—to go public with his passion for the controversial blood sport of foxhunting, for example—the result was often a public relations disaster.

Wills had been riding to the hounds at Sandringham, Balmoral, near Highgrove, and on other family estates ever since he turned sixteen. The Spare, an even more avid athlete and outdoorsman than the Heir, would soon follow in his brother's footsteps. But when the press photographed a red-capped William on horseback, sailing over fences in hot pursuit with other members of the Beaufort Hunt Club near Highgrove, animal rights activists were appalled. Polls showed that most Britons regarded foxhunting as unspeakably cruel, while its defenders viewed it as just one more cherished British tradition under attack.

William brushed aside his critics and vowed to continue foxhunting. "The departure of their mother pushed the Princes into the traditional 'maleness' of the Royal Family—the foxhunts and the polo," Richard Greene said, "and away from the emotional, raw, open, honest side of their psyches that Diana was reinforcing."

Even after William was denounced on the floor of the House of Commons for his "insensitivity" and "upper-class arrogance," Camilla and Charles failed to see what all the fuss was about.

"These bloody people have never done it, I mean they can't even *afford* to do it, and therefore have no idea what they are talking about," Charles told another member of the Beaufort Hunt Club. "They are the ones who are arrogant—imagine trying to tell us what we can or cannot do?"

Imagine, indeed. William ignored the criticism in much the same way he ignored his father's attempts to steer him away from some of the London clubs he now frequented—places like China White, Mimo, Crazy Larry, Foxtrot Oscar, and K-Bar. William was, in some ways, proving to be a typically defiant teen. Without warning, he would arrive home at York House with a half-dozen Eton chums, order up food from the royal kitchens, and then have his friends crash on the floor of his room in sleeping bags.

"Prince Charles really had no concept of how teenagers behave," said a former St. James's Palace footman. "He wanted to know who was being invited, who their parents were—and why, in a palace with seventy-five rooms, they weren't each given one of their own."

While William scrupulously avoided drugs, alcohol was quite another matter. A favorite hangout was the Rattlebone Inn, a four-hundred-year-old pub just four miles from Highgrove. According to one eyewitness, William hid in an alleyway behind the pub when local constables raided the place, looking for illegal after-hours drinkers. Harry, who sometimes tagged along, occasionally had to be reined in by his big brother. Pierre Ortet, the Rattlebone's French-born owner, remembered the night when Harry called him "Froggie." According to Ortet, "Prince William told his brother to apologize." William reportedly told his brother "to remember what happened to royalty in France" as he grimaced and ran his finger across his throat.

For the most part, tavern owners and shopkeepers viewed the Princes as well mannered and polite. The bartender at Nam Long Le Shaker, a Vietnamese bar in Kensington frequented by the brothers, tentatively admitted to preferring one over the other. "I like Harry better," he said. "Harry comes and talks with me; William is more reserved."

Conscious of the constant scrutiny they were under, both Princes always made certain they had settled their tab before leaving—a courtesy not generally observed by other royals who never carried cash and expected somebody else to pick up the check. As small children Diana had taught them to refer to money in a way that only they could. Since the Queen's face appeared on British currency, they referred to each bill as a "granny": a five-pound note was a "blue granny," a ten-pound note was a "brown granny," and a fifty-pound note a "pink granny." Whenever Diana had asked them how much spending money they needed, William would always reply, "Oh, a pink granny, please!" It was not uncommon for William to lean over to his brother after a night of drinking, reach into his pocket, and ask conspiratorially, "How many grannys do you need? I've got a brown and three blues. . . ."

As the twenty-first century approached, Charles offered Highgrove as the site of his son's much-hyped "Willennium" celebration. He was nonplused when William turned him down, and even more mystified when his son declined to tell him the party's secret location. Ultimately, as William would later put it, he got "very seriously, seriously drunk" partying with a group of friends at a tin-roofed village hall near Sandringham House. The hangover, again by his own account, would last two full days.

1.

2.

3.

A Royal Lovers' Gallery: Diana presented
James Hewitt with a polo trophy in 1991.
Hewitt's confession that his affair began in
1981 instead of 1986 fueled even more gossip
regarding Harry's paternity. Meanwhile,
Charles carried on simultaneous affairs with
glamorous Lady "Kanga" Tryon and Camilla,
"the most hated woman in England," hiding
out at her Wiltshire home shortly after
Diana's death in 1997.

4.

5.

6.

7.

8.

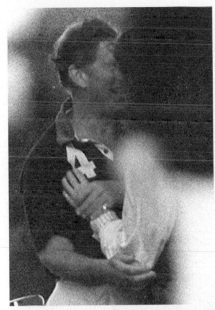

Prince Charles plays cat-and-mouse with Tiggy Legge-Bourke after a polo match in June 1999. Diana was convinced that the two were having an affair, and reportedly even suggested that both she and Camilla would be put out of the way so that Charles would be free to marry Tiggy.

9.

11.
William taught English to children like six-year-old Alejandro Heredia during his pre-university "gap year" doing volunteer work in the remote Chilean village of Tortel.

12.

At St Andrews University, William and two classmates surfed in chilly North Sea waters. The atmosphere was decidedly warmer at the student fashion show, where Wills cheered his new girlfriend, Kate Middleton, as she modeled lingerie.

13.

14.

The Royal Family gathered outside Clarence House to greet well-wishers on the occasion of the Queen Mother's 101st birthday on April 8, 2001. The following March, William, Harry, and an obviously grief-stricken Charles attended the Queen Mum's funeral services at Westminster Abbey.

15.

16.

Three months after the Queen Mother's death, Camilla sat in the royal
box at the pop concert in the Buckingham Palace Gardens celebrating the
Queen's fiftiethth year on the throne. It marked the first time she was
permitted to appear in public with the Royal Family—albeit two rows
behind Charles, William, and the Queen.

17.

18.

19.

Charles and his sons compete
in the *real* sport of kings.
In 2005 injuries forced Papa, who
got a congratulatory kiss from
Camilla, to give up polo. After a
fierce skirmish with his brother,
William took a nasty spill.
Amazingly, he suffered no serious
injuries from the fall.

20.

21.

Outside Windsor Castle, a bobby chatted amiably with self-styled
"comedy terrorist" Aaron Barschak. Later Barschak, dressed up like
Osama bin Laden in drag, exposed serious flaws in royal security when
he leapt onstage at William's twenty-first birthday party and grabbed
the microphone from the hand of the startled Prince.

22.

Both Harry and William fought back tears at dedication ceremonies
for the Diana Memorial Fountain in Hyde Park on July 6, 2004.

23.

Ignoring protests from animal-rights groups, Charles and Camilla refused to quit fox hunting—a sport William also enjoyed. The royals were forced to give it up, however, when Parliament outlawed fox hunting with hounds in 2005.

24.

From "Harry Pothead" to "Harry the Nazi" to "Dirty Harry," Harry has
supplied England's tabloids with one racy headline after another.

25.

Charles's relations with the press suffered a setback when, during a photo
op in Switzerland just days before his wedding, he insulted reporters
under his breath. Unknown to the Prince, his remarks were picked up by
microphones and were clearly audible.

Before the Archbishop of Canterbury, Charles and Camilla confessed their "manifold sins and wickedness." After the Windsor Castle ceremony, the Queen warily eyed the newlyweds. During their honeymoon at Balmoral, Charles risked overexposure, wearing a kilt on a windy day.

26.

27.

29.

William and Kate
Middleton had lived
together for three years
by the time they both
graduated from St
Andrews University in
June 23, 2005.

30.

Now that she was
Duchess of Cornwall,
Camilla often wore her
predecessor's jewelry—
including Diana's
favorite $5 million
Prince of Wales emerald
brooch. While Diana
wore it on a necklace
with matching drop ear-
rings Charles gave her as
a wedding present,
Camilla preferred to pin
it to her shoulder.

31.

32.

33.

"My crown is bigger than yours": The Queen lent Camilla Queen Mary's magnificent Delhi Durbar tiara for the Duchess of Cornwall's first royal banquet, held at Buckingham Palace in honor of Norway's King Harald V in October of 2005.

During their first official visit to the United States together in November 2005, Charles and Camilla sniffed organically grown garlic at an open-air market in Point Reyes, California. A few months later, while touring India with her husband, Camilla nearly collapsed twice from the intense heat.

34.

35.

As Harry grew older, his resemblance to Diana's lover James Hewitt (below) grew stronger—and so did the controversy surrounding Harry's paternity. "It's not just the hair and the eyes and the nose and the chin," said a friend of Diana's. "They have the same expressions and mannerisms. It's uncanny."

36.

37.

38.

During a break after graduating from Sandhurst, Harry worked as a "Jackaroo"—one of Australia's famous cowboys—on a 40,000-acre ranch in Queensland. Later, he co-founded a charity in South Africa for children orphaned by AIDS.

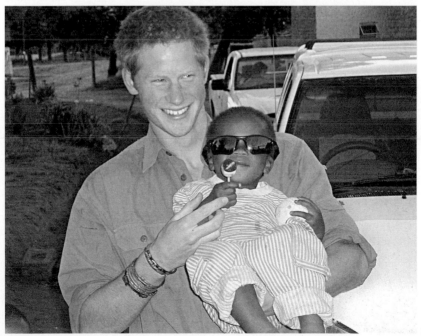

39.

40.

Surrounded by his stone-faced fellow soldiers,
Harry grins as Granny reviews the troops
during graduation ceremonies at Sandhurst.
Later, junior cadet William leans over to kiss
Camilla before everyone—including Charles
(far left), Philip (third from right), William
and Harry in uniform—posed for a family
portrait. Camilla is partially obscured
behind the Queen.

41.

42.

Harry relaxes with his serious girlfriend Chelsy Davy at the Windsor Great Park polo grounds. At the Beaufort Polo Club near Highgrove, both Windsor women-in-waiting—Chelsy and Kate Middleton—showed up to cheer on their respective Princes.

43.

44.

45.

Like his brother before him, William could not keep a straight face when the Queen reviewed the troops at his Sandhurst "passing out" (graduation). Wills also followed Harry into the Blues and Royals of the Queen's Household Cavalry.

46.

"I do enjoy running through a ditch full of mud, firing bullets," said Harry, who resumed combat training in late 2006. "It's the way I am." He was headed for front-line duty in Iraq in the spring of 2007.

47.

48.

49.

Kate Middleton moved closer to becoming Mrs. William Wales when the Queen invited her for several private chats at Buckingham Palace. More important, the Queen allowed one meeting to be photographed. In early 2007, Woolworths in England was already selling souvenir plates "commemorating" the couple's nuptials.

Afraid that the woman he loved would be hounded to death by paparazzi the way his mother was, William ordered his lawyers to bring action against anyone who threatened Middleton's safety.

50.

51.

Kate and the Queen shared a growing concern for William's obsession with speed. He has since traded in this Triumph 600 Daytona for two "superbikes" capable of reaching speeds in excess of l60 miles per hour.

The future King and
his love soak up the
sun off Ibiza. After
more than five years
together, William and
Kate Middleton had
cemented the bond his
parents never had.

52.

53.

54.

Conversely, Charles and Camilla celebrated the arrival of the new millennium with only a few close friends at Highgrove. They wound up, Camilla later said, holding hands in the garden. "After all we had been through," she explained, "we wanted to be alone together. There was no one else who could possibly have understood the feelings we had that night."

"William has a mind of his own, and he wants to live his life without people knowing what his every move is going to be," said Diana's friend, the journalist Richard Kay. "It's understandable, but so is the concern for his safety."

Occasionally William gave his bodyguards the slip, but for the most part he tolerated their near-constant presence with no small degree of grace and even humor. "I don't know what their game is," he cracked whenever someone mentioned the hulking figures trying so hard to be unobtrusive, "but they are constantly following me around."

At times they came in handy for unexpected reasons. When William was caught on a security camera entwined with a half-dressed young woman in the stairwell of a London nightclub, one Royal Protection officer frantically warned him to stop. Then he confiscated the tape.

The one place William was relatively free to pursue his romantic life was at York House. Several times a week, and at virtually any time of the day or night, young ladies were invited up to the Prince's rooms for "tea." In early 2000, perhaps no one joined William upstairs for tea more frequently than the winsome Alexandra Knatchbull—Nicholas Knatchbull's sister and the niece of the woman who had turned down Charles's first marriage proposal, Amanda Knatchbull.

Of more interest to William's growing legion of female fans was his odd cyber-friendship with pop diva Britney Spears. Then just eighteen and single, Spears began corresponding with the Prince when she learned he had tacked up a poster of her on his wall at Eton. William, not above inviting the reigning teen sex symbol for tea at York House, suggested a Valentine's Day meeting. The plan was scrubbed by St. James's Palace, however, once news of the budding romance was leaked to the press.

William would somewhat disingenuously dismiss his e-mail correspondence with Spears as "a lot of nonsense." But he never denied that he had also exchanged a series of torrid e-mails with another beautiful young American woman, model Lauren Bush. A niece of U.S. President George W. Bush and granddaughter of former U.S. President George Herbert Walker Bush, Lauren had been a guest aboard the *Alexander* immediately before Prince Charles's party boarded it the previous summer. She left a signed glossy of herself for William in a stateroom, and from that point on they conducted an e-mail friendship that one Bush family friend described as "flirty," "sexy," and "quite intimate." The romance would never get beyond the virtual stage, however, as William found love in the arms of another runway star—this one home-grown.

"His Royal Sighness," as the tabloids were now calling William, coped as best he could with the hoopla surrounding his impending eighteenth birthday—the age of majority in Britain—on June 21, 2000. From now on, he was warned, dealing with the press was going to be even trickier than usual: Fleet Street's self-imposed ban on covering the boys in the wake of their mother's death was about to expire.

By way of tossing the press a bone, Buckingham Palace released a series of photographs showing Wills studying and competing in sports at Eton. The Prince would also agree to his first-ever interview, sort of. The British Press Association's veteran royal correspondent Peter Archer was invited to submit written questions to William, and the answers were far from revealing. On the subject of the girls he was seeing, William was especially closemouthed. "I like," he said, "to keep my private life private." As for how he determined whether a young woman might be worth getting to know, William was equally evasive. "Trying to explain how," he cannily replied, "might be counterproductive."

Unbeknownst to William, his milestone birthday would be further used by the Royal Family to heighten the image of Charles as a father and erase the memory of Diana from Britain's collective consciousness. To mark the occasion, for example, the Queen personally approved thirty-five commemorative stamp designs to be issued in Britain as well as in more than a dozen other Commonwealth countries. When Earl Spencer pointed out that Charles was included in the designs but not Diana, a spokesman for the Crown Agents Stamp Bureau issued a flat denial that there was any "hidden agenda" to ignore the Princess of Wales.

Yet, despite the fact that the vast majority of Londoners favored building a statue honoring Diana in their city, the Queen and Charles were adamantly opposed to such an idea. Instead, Her Majesty focused her attention on throwing a get-together for seven hundred guests at Windsor Castle. The party actually celebrated the juxtaposition of five benchmark birthdays occurring in the year 2000: William's eighteenth, Prince Andrew's fortieth, Princess Anne's fiftieth, Princess Margaret's seventieth, and the Queen Mother's one hundredth. Harry dropped in, as did Papa.

Andrew Parker Bowles attended, but given the Queen Mother's lingering resentment, Camilla did not. By this time, Windsor

Castle was the only royal residence where Camilla had not been an overnight guest; she had already slept over at Sandringham, at Balmoral and Holyrood in Scotland, and even at Buckingham Palace when the Queen was not in residence.

Despite the fact that he could have walked from his rooms at Eton to Windsor Castle in less than ten minutes, William was a no-show at his own official birthday party. His excuse: he was cramming for final exams.

Ten days later, William again ignored an invitation. Only this time, both he and Harry stunned their countrymen by joining the rest of the Royal Family in boycotting the dedication of the first official London memorial in Diana's honor: the $3 million Princess Diana Playground near Kensington Palace. "We were all so saddened when no one from the Royal Family showed up," one of the organizers of the event said. "You can only imagine that the Princess would have been shattered that her own boys didn't think it was important to be there."

William did feel it was important to leap to his mother's defense two months later, however, when one of her most trusted aides published a tell-all book. In his damning memoir *Shadows of a Princess*, Diana's longtime private secretary Patrick Jephson depicted his former boss as conniving, insecure, unbalanced, devious, and at times malicious—someone who combined "a radiant smile with a knife between the shoulder blades."

On September 29, 2000, William took the extraordinary action of stepping before television cameras with his father at his side to denounce the book. He told reporters that he and Harry were "both quite upset" that his mother's "trust had been betrayed and that even now she is still being exploited."

For Camilla and Charles, *Shadows of a Princess* was nothing short of a godsend. For the first time, someone who had been close to Diana was painting a portrait of Diana the way Charles, Camilla, and the Queen saw her—as spoiled, neurotic, and highly manipulative. "At last," Charles told one of his advisors. "I wondered how long it was going to take for *someone* to tell the truth about her." According to a friend of the Parker Bowles family, "Camilla read the excerpts from the book in the *Sunday Times* with absolute glee. She called me up and said, 'Have you read this, Darling? Do you think people will finally understand what she put poor Charles through?' "

Notwithstanding being banned from the royal birthday extravaganza at Windsor, Camilla had seen a softening in the Queen's attitude toward her. A major breakthrough came during a sixtieth birthday party Charles threw at Highgrove that June for his friend King Constantine of Greece. As soon as Camilla entered the room, the Queen walked over to her, and a startled Camilla did a deep, formal curtsy. Then the two women chatted for ten minutes before the Queen moved on to other guests.

Camilla and the Queen had met several times in passing during the 1970s, but this was the first known encounter between the two since Charles and Diana had wed. Three weeks later Camilla, wearing a pink Versace gown with a plunging neckline, was allowed for the first time to attend the glittering Prince of Wales Foundation dinner at Buckingham Palace. No mere guest, she served as hostess of the event, sitting directly across from Charles at dinner in the Queen's Drawing Room. To underscore Camilla's newfound status, those in charge of Operation PB invited *Vanity Fair* to cover the affair. The next week, Charles and Camilla kissed publicly for the first time—a fleeting peck on both cheeks—in a receiving line at yet another charity event, this one hosted by their friend Lord Jacob Rothschild.

"At this point, Camilla was pretty shameless about staking her claim on Prince Charles at every available opportunity," said a leading American fashion designer who had known both Charles and Camilla for years. "She suddenly seemed to be everywhere, making up for all those years she had to sneak around."

While Camilla ricocheted from one glittering gala to the next, William started off his post-Eton, precollege "gap year" by training with a unit of the Welsh Guards in the steaming jungles of Belize. From there, he joined the Royal Geographical Society's marine observation program on Rodrigues Island in the Indian Ocean.

William had hoped to spend the last few months of 2000 playing polo in Argentina. But when his handlers nixed the idea as frivolous, he opted for something far less glamorous. Starting in October, he spent ten weeks with 110 other young volunteers—including a number of juvenile offenders and recovering drug addicts—chopping wood, scouring toilets, and tutoring children in the remote Chilean province of Patagonia.

Even in this desolate outpost, William was not without ample female companionship. According to another volunteer, recovering heroin addict Kevin Mullen, at the volunteers' farewell party the future King was "dirty dancing with a lot of girls and making a spectacle of himself." Nevertheless, Mullen had to concede, "The girls didn't seem to mind."

William wasn't the only one in the royal circle making a spectacle of himself. While the Prince of Wales nonchalantly read briefing papers poolside in the south of France, his mistress dropped the top of her bathing suit and then had him slather her with suntan oil before returning the favor. The British papers, jockeying to gain more access to William and Harry, refrained from publishing paparazzi photos of the bare-breasted Camilla. But when the Queen was informed that topless pictures of Camilla were popping up in various European tabloids, she was, in the words of one courtier, "once again disappointed in the woman her son and heir had chosen to love."

The Queen's frustration was shared by the Earl of Powys, owner of historic Powys Castle in Wales. For years, Charles had stayed at the thirteenth-century castle whenever he made his annual official visit to the region as Prince of Wales. But when the earl, John George Herbert, discovered that Charles had also been using his castle for secret assignations with Camilla, he made it clear that the Prince was no longer welcome. "You don't sleep in the same bed if you are not married," Herbert said flatly. "That applies to everyone."

At around the same time, Camilla's name was tied to yet another scandal when her cousin and fellow descendant of Alice Keppel, Judith Keppel, became the first person to win a million pounds in the history of the British version of the TV game show *Who Wants to Be a Millionaire?* No sooner had the twice-divorced Keppel pocketed the prize—roughly the equivalent of $1.44 million at the time—than there were charges that the show had been rigged.

BBC officials charged that producers at the rival ITV network had needed a big winner to boost ratings, and that they "dumbed down" the questions so that Camilla's cousin could become the first contestant in 122 episodes to win the top prize. The million-pound question: Which king was married to Eleanor of Aquitaine of *The Lion in Winter* fame. The answer—Henry II—was known to virtually every British grade-schooler.

It hardly seemed coincidental, the BBC officials added, that Keppel's big win was scheduled against the series finale of the BBC'S top-rated sitcom, *One Foot in the Grave*. "It's very suspicious," claimed *One Foot in the Grave* star Richard Wilson. "There's no doubt it was planned."

There was no way of proving the allegations were true, but the last thing Charles wanted to read about was yet another controversy involving a member of Camilla's family. Yet the Prince and his lover could point the finger at no one else when Camilla, appearing in public with Charles for only the third time, wore a dazzling $100,000 necklace that had belonged to Diana. "It's simply heartbreaking," said Vivienne Parry, "to see someone else wearing Diana's things."

Diana wasn't the only person that "someone else" had supplanted. No longer around to comfort a still-uncertain Harry was Tiggy Legge-Bourke. At her wedding to former army officer Charles Pettifer in late 1999—a wedding that, in light of Camilla's hostility toward the bride, Charles did not attend—Harry allegedly entertained the assembled guests by scooping a goldfish out of a tank and swallowing it.

Thanks to Camilla, Tiggy was no longer the "surrogate mother" Diana once accused her of being. But Tiggy did what she could to remain an influence in the boys' lives. "We speak all the time—constantly, the way people who care deeply for each other do," she said.

Within two years, Harry would pay a call on Tiggy and her newborn son Freddie—his godson—at the Pettifer home in South London. "There is no doubt he's missed a mother figure in his life," said author Penny Junor, one of the Waleses' Gloucestershire neighbors.

"And finding that he was no longer Tiggy's number-one little boy may have affected him deeply."

Tiggy was not the only palace staffer who had, in Camilla's opinion, grown too close to the Prince of Wales. Sarah Goodhall was twenty-four when she was hired to answer Charles's mail in 1988, and she quickly rose to become the secretary handling all of the Prince's correspondence. In that capacity, she spent late hours with him in his offices at St. James's Palace and at Highgrove, and traveled with the Prince on official state visits to such far-flung locales as South Korea, Japan, South Africa, Spain, and Swaziland. She also accompanied him when he toured abroad with Diana. "After her death," Goodhall recalled, "I just tried to be as supportive as possible."

Eight months after Diana's death, Goodhall was among only five people invited to join the Prince for a week's vacation at Birkhall, the Queen Mother's house on the grounds of Balmoral. Since Camilla had been careful to remain out of sight during that sensitive period, Goodhall was surprised to see her there.

Camilla watched from the sidelines as Charles flirted harmlessly with his secretary. "I hope you like caviar," he joked, "because there are mounds to get through." He also continued with the sort of banter that had always characterized their working relationship. "You're still not married yet?" he chided Goodhall. "How many boyfriends have you got?"

As she had with Janet Jenkins, Camilla positioned herself next to Goodhall at dinner and charmed her with talk of friends, charity work, horses, even their mothers' battles with cancer.

Once Goodhall and the other guests had left Balmoral, Camilla let Charles know that she disapproved of his secretary's easygoing manner. She also told Mark Bolland that she was not happy with the "forward" way in which Goodhall behaved toward the Prince.

A few days later, Bolland called Goodhall into his office and told her there been "complaints" about her behavior at Balmoral—that she had been "rather familiar" with the Prince. It was the beginning of the end for the secretary. From that point on, she said, "The atmosphere in the office changed. I started to feel that I was being ganged up on. Camilla had made it clear she did not want me working there." At the end of 2000 Goodhall was abruptly dismissed, told to clean out her desk, and after surrendering her security pass, escorted from St. James's by palace security guards. "Charles is not strong enough to say no to Camilla," Goodhall observed. "Or to have said, 'I like her. I'm keeping her.'"

It was Tiggy's departure, however, that was most keenly felt. For the moment, however, Harry could take some comfort in the fact that he would no longer have to settle for trudging along in his brother's shadow at Eton. The Spare would soon show that, while no match for the Heir academically, when it came to sports he could equal or even outperform William. By the time Harry turned sixteen, he was outskiing, outshooting, and even outswimming his older brother—much to William's chagrin. "William is very physical," said a former royal bodyguard. "But he is more hesitant where Harry is absolutely fearless."

There were also noticeable differences in temperament. As he prepared to enter college, William was described by those closest to him as thoughtful, deliberate, bullheaded, and at times, moody. "William carefully weighs everything," Peter Archer observed. "He has very definite ideas about things—something he got from both his mother and his father. No one is going to make William do something he doesn't want to do." Harry, on the other hand, seemed by far to be the more easygoing of the two—"someone who is always looking for a bit of fun," Archer said, "but also the kind of person who does what is asked of him without question or complaint. He's less inquisitive than his brother, and more eager to please."

Yet Harry's cheerful exterior belied no small degree of inner turmoil. "The pressures on Prince Harry are just enormous," a former teacher claimed. "He tries to act like he hasn't a care in the world, but he is still clearly feeling the effects of his mother's death."

It certainly did not help Harry's state of mind when, just prior to Christmas 2000, he and Wills were both asked by Buckingham Palace to help plan their own funerals. Hoping to avoid the sort of confusion that surrounded their mother's funeral, the government wanted Diana's sons to design their own services—right down to the music and the type of guest list they would like followed in the event of their deaths.

It had long been customary for older members of the Royal Family to be consulted on their funerals. In the case of the most senior royals, such as the Queen and the Queen Mother, there were practice funeral processions conducted in the streets of London at least once a year under cover of darkness. But the decision to consult William and Harry signaled a new desire on the part of the monarchy to avoid the kind of squabbling that occurred following Diana's death. "It seems entirely sensible to me," said Charles, who long before had written down highly specific instructions concerning his own funeral service.

Harry dealt with the macabre request by suggesting that the traditional dirge be replaced with a live performance by his favorite group at the time, the Spice Girls. There were certain things, however, that Harry could not shrug off with a laugh.

Most disturbing of all for Harry was the incessant drumbeat of gossip concerning his paternity. As the Prince grew older, his resemblance to Diana's lover James Hewitt—rusty hair, ruddy complexion, distinctly upturned nose—became more pronounced, as did the rumors that Hewitt was his biological father. Diana and Hewitt had always insisted that they had not even met before 1986, when Harry was already two years old. But that, and the fact that redheads run in the Spencer clan, did little to stop the speculation.

At one point, a young lady who had met Harry at a party was purportedly enlisted to clip a strand of the Prince's hair for DNA analysis. The tale of the purloined lock turned out to be apocryphal, but no matter: before it could be disproved it spawned more seamy tabloid stories.

Of all the stories that circulated about his family, Harry found most hurtful the suggestion that he might not be a Windsor at all. "It is appalling for anyone to have to put up with," said Harry's godfather, Gerald Ward. But, he continued, the brothers "are both very balanced people, and they and their father are very close and support each other."

Camilla, who by now had taken up official residence both at St. James's Palace and Highgrove, tried to be part of that equation, while at the same time not giving the impression that she intended to replace the boys' mother. "That is probably why," said a friend of Camilla's, "the Princes do not feel they are betraying Diana's memory by accepting Camilla."

On February 7, 2001, Camilla would take yet another step toward respectability when, in a manner of speaking, she, Charles, and William appeared together for the first time in public. The occasion was William's first official public engagement—an appearance at the tenth anniversary of the Press Complaints Commission. Harry had remained at Eton, studying for exams.

Billed as the young Princes' way of thanking the press for keeping a respectful distance since their mother's death, the royal visit also gave William an opportunity to persuade more than five hundred journalists face-to-face that the policy should continue at least until Harry turned eighteen the following year.

From the beginning, Charles also saw this event, at Somerset House in Central London, as the perfect opportunity for Camilla to court the press. The Queen, however, was not so enthusiastic about the idea. Her Majesty and her Men in Gray made it clear that William and Harry were never to appear publicly in the company of their father's mistress.

Harry was left back at Eton while his father and brother arrived at Somerset House together. They then went off in separate directions, working the room like seasoned politicos. Drink in hand, six-foot-two-inch-tall William towered over the other guests as he moved from one cluster to the next, making cocktail party chitchat with hundreds of reporters and editors. "He was," observed *Tatler* magazine editor Geordie Greig, "surprisingly at ease." Wills even managed to get the phone numbers and e-mail addresses of several attractive single women. "Prince William was not at all shy about asking," said one female staffer at the *Daily Telegraph*. "He was very confident. I must say he possessed a great deal of poise for a nineteen-year-old."

Not long after the Princes began their campaign to win over the press, Camilla arrived to flashing cameras at the opposite end of the building. To ensure that she never inadvertently crossed paths with William and Charles, Camilla stayed where she was at the far side of the room. Nearly two hours after they arrived, the

Princes left in triumph. Once she got the word, Camilla waited another thirty minutes before making her exit. While she was never actually seen with William, guests were well aware that Camilla had actually attended the same high-profile event at the same time. "It was definitely a victory for Camilla," Richard Kay said. "Whatever the reality of her relationship with Prince William and Prince Harry, it left one with the general impression that she was being accepted into the family."

The strategy now being implemented at St. James's Palace was simple: the larger the role Camilla played in their lives, the more William and Harry would have to let go of their mother's memory. As a result of that policy, no one bothered to inform the Princes in March 2001 that they had been invited to the dedication of France's official memorial to the late Princess of Wales— the Diana Garden and Nature Center in Paris.

"We were very surprised and hurt when no one from the Royal Family accepted our invitation," said Claude Lefevre, one of the volunteers who worked on the Diana memorial gardens for more than fourteen months. "We all admired and respected Princess Diana for the care she showed the less fortunate. People all over the world loved her, she was a shining star in the Royal Family, and now it looks as if they want to disown her. I suppose I can understand the Queen not coming, or even Prince Charles. But when her own children did not even respond to the invitation, it was very sad, very disappointing."

Once they read about the dedication in the papers, both of Diana's sons were annoyed that they hadn't been informed of the invitation that had been extended to them by the French government. William and Harry had already been roundly criticized in the press for missing the opening of the Diana Playground in

Kensington Gardens, and their failure to appear for the ceremony in Paris only added to the growing perception that they no longer cared.

"There was no particular desire on the part of anyone in the Royal Family to wallow in the cult of Diana," one of Charles's senior aides said. "Prince William and Prince Harry were very close to their mother and they will always miss her very much. They do not need to prove that fact to anyone."

The brothers did, however, end months of debate about what would be a fitting tribute when they gave their official blessing to the Diana Memorial Walkway. Winding from Kensington Palace to Westminster Abbey, the seven-mile-long path would be marked by seventy plaques, each engraved with an English rose.

Camilla maintained an understandable public silence when it came to anything regarding the late Princess of Wales. But privately, she shared Charles's oft-expressed exasperation over what he snidely referred to as "those Diana people." According to a former member of the household staff at Highgrove, "Mrs. Parker Bowles was very good at never sounding bitter about the Princess, but she left the distinct impression that she felt they ought to just hurry up and build a statue to Diana in Hyde Park or Kensington or somewhere and just move along. She was eager to be the next Princess of Wales, and she couldn't do that with everybody still trying to decide how they were going to honor the last one."

On June 17, 2001, Charles paid a call on his mother at Buckingham Palace and asked if she might soften her attitude toward Camilla. The Queen refused, making it clear that she—like the Queen Mother—saw no reason to change her mind about the problematic Mrs. Parker Bowles. Charles stormed out, and for the next two months the two did not speak to each other.

The tension would continue at Balmoral, where the Queen hiked and picnicked on the shores of the River Muick while Camilla stayed with Charles at Birkhall, the Queen Mother's residence on the grounds of the Scottish castle. Yet even though the Queen drove herself past Birkhall on several occasions on the way to and from the castle itself, she did not drop in on her son and his mistress. Nor were they invited to visit her. To compound the irony, the one person whose opposition still made it impossible for the Queen to give Charles and Camilla her blessing—the Queen Mother—was apparently perfectly happy to have the couple stay at Birkhall in her absence.

For the time being, William, who had done all he could to make Camilla feel like part of the family, was determined to make the most of what remained of his gap year. Just a few days after missing the ceremony honoring his mother in Paris, the future King headed off for yet another exotic locale. This time, he was going to spend four months working on a 55,000-acre game preserve in Kenya (arguably the world's largest rhino sanctuary). Between digging ditches and tracking endangered species in the wild, he would also manage to squeeze in a brief romance with Jessica "Jecca" Craig, the nineteen-year-old daughter of the game preserve's owner. At one point during William's African idyll, this relationship became so intense that the couple staged a mock engagement ceremony at the foot of Mount Kenya.

William was still in Africa coping with vipers, hyenas, and a lack of any modern plumbing facilities when his mother's memory was assailed by yet another member of the Royal Family. Taped by an undercover reporter she thought was a potential client for her public relations firm, Prince Edward's wife, Sophie—the Countess of Wessex—ridiculed Diana for her visits to the sick and dying.

Sophie, who bore a distinct physical resemblance to the late Princess, also thought it was "ridiculous" that the press expected her to take up where Diana—whom she described as "scheming" and "publicity mad"—left off.

"When we got engaged, they were very keen to put me on the empty pedestal left by Diana," Sophie said. "But I don't have armies of hairdressers and makeup artists at the drop of a hat." The press was disappointed, the countess added, when they realized she was "not going to be turning up every day in different outfits, opening children's homes like Diana."

As for Diana's role in the divorce: "A lot of things came out after Diana's death about the way she behaved," Sophie said. "I think everybody realized it takes two. You'll get the fanatical Diana diehards who'll always blame the Prince of Wales for everything." Sophie also made the mistake of talking about Charles and Camilla, and referred to the Queen as "an old dear."

Outraged at the attack on their mother coming from within the Royal Family, William and Harry demanded that their father do something. Under pressure from Charles, the Countess of Wessex dashed off a series of written apologies to everyone mentioned in the tapes, then resigned from her PR firm.

To the Princes, Harry told an Eton confidant, it often seemed that life was just "one betrayal after another." Yet no one could have anticipated what, for a time, looked like the most shocking sellout of all.

People who try to take advantage of me
and get a piece of me, I spot it quickly
and soon go off them.

—William

William and I try to be normal.
It's very difficult but, you know,
we are who we are.

—Harry

The Princes are accustomed to seeing
the people they once trusted sell them out.
They grew up in an atmosphere
thick with betrayal.

—a longtime friend of Diana's

I always go into my own little world. . . .

—William

5

"Paul? Stealing Mummy's things?" Harry asked his brother as he held up the headline in the *Daily Mirror*. "*Paul?* What a joke!"

When Paul Burrell was first arrested for stealing 342 items worth an estimated $7.7 million from the Princess's Kensington Palace apartments, William and Harry were, in the words of one of the boys' godfathers, "in a complete state of disbelief." This was, after all, the man Diana had often called "My Rock," the man who dressed her body for burial, who kept a solitary vigil by her coffin the night before her funeral, who took the Princes by the hand and led them from room to room in Kensington Palace as they picked out mementos of their mother.

Burrell had tried in vain to convince authorities that the items were either gifts to him and his family from the Princess, or had been entrusted to him for safekeeping. But Diana's Spencer relatives, who were unaware of the close bond between the Princess and Burrell, were unconvinced. As the investigation progressed, it had become increasingly apparent that the Spencers—specifically Diana's estranged mother Frances Shand Kydd (no relation to Camilla Shand Parker Bowles) and her sisters Lady Jane Fellowes and Lady Sarah McCorquodale—were in the prosecution's corner and would even testify against him.

William and Harry promptly demanded that their father come to Burrell's defense. But Charles, who had always viewed the close relationship between Diana and her butler warily, was reluctant to become involved. Once again, the Prince of Wales turned to his mistress, who reminded him that Burrell had been the keeper of Diana's secrets. Should it become necessary to prove in court just how much she trusted him, the butler might well offer up testimony that was embarrassing, to say the very least.

There was another reason for the Royal Family to try and get the case against Burrell dropped: Diana's boys would almost certainly be called to testify on the defendant's behalf. "I will not," Charles told a senior aide at the time, "have William and Harry questioned in open court about their mother and Paul. It is completely inappropriate, and it would be too painful for the boys."

Yet, even after Burrell wrote directly to Charles in January and to William three months later, no one from the Royal Family spoke up. "Why was the Royal Family not defending me?" Burrell wondered. "The silence," Burrell later recalled, "was deafening. . . . I thought I was being fed to the lions."

Finally, Mark Bolland, the public relations wizard who was masterminding Operation PB, called Burrell and arranged for a secret meeting with his boss. The Prince of Wales and both his sons were eager to hear Burrell's side of the story and find a way to put the whole, ugly matter behind them. The meeting was set for the afternoon of August 3, 2001, near Highgrove. "All I knew," Burrell later said, "was that it was going to be held after Prince Charles finished a game of polo."

But Charles didn't finish. Instead, in the middle of the match he was pitched off his horse and knocked out cold. Even as he was lifted into an ambulance and taken to a nearby hospital for observation, William and Harry—fierce competitors on the field even when they are on the same team—resumed playing. The accident would be used as an excuse for calling off the meeting, but that's all it was—an excuse. Even before the polo match began, Scotland Yard investigators visited Charles and William and told them that there was substantial evidence Burrell was selling Diana's belongings in the United States. They also told the Princes that there were photographs of several staff members wearing Diana's clothing to a party. Eventually, the police would have to admit in court that they never had any such evidence.

Police investigators also pointed to Burrell's "drastically improved financial condition," specifically large amounts of cash that were moving in and out of his accounts. They did not inform the Princes that the money had come from Burrell's book *Entertaining with Style* and his income on the lecture circuit. Swayed by Scotland Yard's campaign of disinformation, all the royals were left to believe the worst about Diana's "Rock."

On August 16, 2001, Burrell was formally charged with theft. The Spencers continued to press the case against him while the Windsors remained silent. Along with Diana's old friends, the Spencers were no longer a part of the boys' lives. One of Charles's friends now pointed out that William and Harry "didn't understand why the Spencers seemed so eager to see Paul put in jail."

As the case headed for trial, William pressed again for his father to intercede with Granny on Burrell's behalf. But he said nothing publicly. "William knows Paul Burrell better than anyone," said Richard Kay. "Everyone wondered why he wasn't coming forward early on to say, 'This is crazy. Paul Burrell would never steal anything from Mother.' "

There were certainly times when William might have questioned Burrell's claims of complete innocence. William, according to Scotland Yard investigators, reacted with surprise when informed that their raid on Paul's Cheshire home yielded thirteen letters Diana had written to him at Ludgrove and Eton. Each handwritten letter was addressed using her favorite nickname for her elder son: "Dear Wombat."

In the coming months, Burrell would be driven to the brink of financial ruin, physical collapse—and suicide. Apparently unmoved, the Royal Family continued to do nothing. Then, during the second week of the trial, in October 2002, prosecutors were forced to reveal what they were looking for when they raided Burrell's house: the mahogany box marked with a *D* in which the Princess had kept her secrets.

Inside the box, investigators were told by an informant, they would find the signet ring James Hewitt had given Diana, scathing correspondence to Diana from Prince Philip, and a taped interview the Princess conducted with former Kensington Palace footman and valet George Smith in 1996. On the tape Smith, who was suffering from clinical depression and drinking heavily, claimed that his problems stemmed from an incident in 1989. It was then, Smith told Diana, that he was raped by one of Prince Charles's most trusted manservants—and that he had also witnessed the alleged rapist in a compromising position with a member of the Royal Family.

When Diana called her ex-husband and angrily demanded that the alleged rapist be fired, Charles refused. Instead, he cautioned her not to pay attention to "staff tittle-tattle." Over the next year, Charles would reportedly spend 100,000 pounds covering the legal bills of the alleged rapist. Smith, who left his job with a $59,000 lump sum payment from the palace, would eventually drop the matter.

For the moment, however, the "rape tape" was nothing less than a ticking time bomb tossed in the Royal Family's collective lap. Not only would the tape expose the Windsors to even more ridicule, but it would also raise serious questions of a royal cover-up. "You wait," a veteran palace watcher told American journalist Dominick Dunne, "the rape tape is going to become the story."

Before it could, Charles would have to act. Once more it was Camilla, the woman he called his "touchstone," who urged Charles to tell the Queen what was on the tape. Yet again Robin Janvrin, who replaced Sir Robert Fellowes as the Queen's private secretary, stressed that his boss was reluctant to interfere in any matter before the courts. Now frantic that William and Harry would be drawn into the seamy affair once they were called to the stand, Charles looked for one more chance to plead with the Queen to intervene.

He would get the chance in the backseat of the Queen's Rolls-Royce, as he rode with his grim-faced parents to an October 25 memorial at St. Paul's Cathedral for the 202 victims of a terrorist bombing on Bali. Burrell was only days away from testifying, Charles told his mother, and time was running out for her to act. Finally, Prince Philip spoke up. "It's a bit tricky for Mummy," he said, "because she saw Paul, you know."

Stunned that his mother had kept the details of her private 1997 meeting with Burrell to herself, Charles went to his private secretary, Sir Michael Peat, with the new information. The next day, St. James's Palace informed Scotland Yard. On November 1, the day Burrell was scheduled to take the stand in his own defense, prosecutors told the court that they had just been told of Burrell's meeting with the Queen—that he had, in fact, told the monarch of his intention to keep Diana's things for safekeeping. The case was summarily dropped.

"It's the Queen," Burrell sobbed as he left the Old Bailey. "It's all thanks to the Queen." She had rescued Burrell at the eleventh hour, but for the Royal Family it was too late. I WAS RAPED BY CHARLES' SERVANT screamed the *Daily Mail's* full-page headline, followed the next day by PANIC GRIPS THE PALACE. As it turned out, there was ample reason for panic: George Smith was now charging that he had witnessed a separate "incident" between another male servant and an unidentified member of the Royal Family.

Amid the larger issues of rape and cover-up were the kinds of minor details about Windsor life that seemed every bit as illuminating. For example, it was the job of Charles's valet, Michael Fawcett, to squeeze toothpaste onto the royal toothbrush. The valet was also reportedly responsible for selling off some $150,000 worth of unwanted royal gifts each year, with the proceeds going to the Prince. And when, during a hospital visit, Charles was asked to supply a urine sample, Fawcett held the bottle while the prince complied.

William and Harry cheered the news of Paul's acquittal, and Granny's role in securing it. That she could have spoken up anytime while the trial dragged on for months appeared to be of no consequence to them. "My brother and I are very glad for Paul," William said. "We always knew he was completely innocent, of course."

Nevertheless, it's doubtful they would have pressed Papa to come to Burrell's defense if they'd had any idea what the butler was going to do as soon as he was sprung. After his deposition was leaked to the press, Burrell sold his story to the *Daily Mirror* for $468,000. He revealed, among other things, that once when her lover Hasnat Khan came to visit, she greeted him at the door of Kensington Palace wearing nothing but diamond earrings and a mink coat. At one point, Burrell said, Diana begged Khan to marry her and even considered tricking him into marriage by becoming pregnant.

"I will never betray your mother or you for as long as I live," Burrell tried to explain in a public plea to William and Harry. "Some things will go to my grave with me. You have nothing to fear from me. Remember," he went on, alluding to an incident known only to them, "what we said and how we felt standing in that special place in Kensington Palace? Our hearts were breaking. You will know I will always protect you. If I betray you, I will be betraying everything I ever felt or thought, everything I stand for, and I will never do that."

The ploy seemed to work well enough. In response to tabloid stories that said he had branded Burrell "Paul the Betrayer," William had St. James's Palace issue a denial. Even Granny seemed willing to let Burrell off the hook. "There is no suggestion that the Queen is furious or unhappy," a palace spokesman said. On the subject of Burrell's revelations, he added, "The Queen has not said anything."

What she had said to Paul—specifically her warning that he be aware of sinister "powers at work" in the land—must have come as news to William. Not that the Heir was entirely unaware of the plotting that went on; his mother had often complained to him about the entrenched bureaucrats and court advisors surrounding the monarchy. "William knew all too well what the Men in Gray had done to his mother," one ex-member of the staff at St. James's said. "But it must have been sobering to hear that the Queen was also intimidated by them. William," he continued, "would have to be wondering what intrigue lies in store for him."

For all the headlines it generated, the Burrell affair was scarcely the Windsors' sole concern. During the summer of 2001 when Prince Charles and William were away from Highgrove, Harry was left to his own devices. The Spare, still two years under Britain's legal drinking age of eighteen and without the steadying influence of his big brother, was spending more and more time downing pints of Stella Artois beer with vodka and gin chasers at the nearby Rattlebone Inn. At one point, Harry thought it would be amusing if he and his friends pretended to exchange blows over a game of pool. This time without Wills to rein him in, Harry used profanity and was ejected from the inn.

No matter. Harry could always repair to his father's estate down the road—often in the company of one of the well-born young ladies who attended nearby Westonbirt School. As he approached his seventeenth birthday, the Spare was unashamedly employing a line available to only the rare few: "Do you want to come back to my palace for a drink?"

At Camilla's urging, Charles had done his best to make Highgrove an appealing refuge for his teenage sons. "Club H," the young Princes' basement retreat, featured a fully stocked bar, a dance floor, video games, a jukebox, and a state-of-the-art sound system.

It was at Highgrove where staff members first noticed the scent of marijuana following one of Harry's parties and reported it to Prince Charles. It turned out that Harry had also been smoking pot in a toolshed behind the Rattlebone Inn.

Concerned that his youngest son was going the way of Tom Parker Bowles and so many of William's friends, Prince Charles sent Harry to spend a day talking to recovering cocaine and heroin addicts at the Featherstone Lodge Rehabilitation Centre in south London. "I think he was quite shocked," said Featherstone staffer Wilma Graham, "that you can be using 'soft' drugs and that suddenly you're moving toward hard drugs. I think it was quite an eye-opener for Harry." Incredibly, St. James's was able to keep the pot-smoking incident and the visit to Featherstone out of the papers—at least for a time.

As "eye-opening" as Harry's visit to Featherstone may or may not have been, two weeks later he was hitting the bars on Spain's Costa del Sol. In Marbella, the Prince was spotted knocking back drinks at a club called Olivia Valere's until he passed out on a couch. Over the next few months, Harry—now nicknamed "The Sponge" by his fellow pub crawlers—was photographed making bleary-eyed, predawn exits from discos in London and bars around Highgrove.

Nick Hooper, a bartender at the Vine Tree pub near Highgrove, watched as Harry switched from red wine to whiskey to Smirnoff ice in a single evening. "Harry would never come in and have one drink," Hooper said. "With him it was binge, binge, binge. . . . His speech was always slurred, and he would stumble about." One evening when Harry and his friends were "very rowdy," said Hooper, the Prince and several of his friends went into the street and became sick. After wrestling with his buddies, Harry walked back into the pub, Hooper recalled, "smeared with vomit."

"Maybe Harry stopped smoking pot," said an Eton classmate, "but there was no chance that he was going to give up going to the clubs, fooling with the girls, and maybe drinking too much. He's *seventeen*."

At the Beaufort Christmas Ball that year, Harry, fortified by two bottles of champagne, made a play for twenty-three-year-old model Suzannah Harvey. Once he had pulled her out the back door, he pulled Harvey toward him and surprised her with an openmouthed kiss. "I forgot he was seventeen," she said. "He handled me like a grown man."

Neither Charles nor the Queen was there at the time, but Camilla witnessed the entire incident. "She could have taken the role of the adult, but she wasn't the slightest bit interested," Harvey said.

William, on the other hand, scowled in disapproval from the sidelines and later took his brother aside. "You've got to be more careful," he warned Harry. "What you do reflects on all of us. Think of Papa and Granny. . . ."

The following January Fleet Street finally uncovered the story of Harry's visit to a rehab center, and Britons were shocked by the lurid accounts of binge drinking and marijuana use. HARRY'S DRUG SHAME blared the *News of the World* front-page headline, while the *Daily Mail* went with the more direct PRINCE HARRY: I TOOK DRUGS. Yet there was also considerable sympathy for Harry's plight, even among tabloid editors. "We should be wary of pouring too much vitriol on poor Harry's head," editorialized the *Sun*. "This is an all-too-common rite of passage being lived out in public."

On the floor of Commons, Prime Minister Tony Blair, whose own son Euan had been arrested for public drunkenness in London's

Leicester Square when he was sixteen, praised Prince Charles's handling of the situation. Earl Spencer disagreed; the boys' uncle told friends he did not approve of the way Charles's handlers had stage-managed the entire episode to cast the Prince of Wales in the most favorable light. "Diana," Spencer said, echoing the sentiments of many in both camps, "was by far the better and more attentive parent. She would never let things get out of hand the way Charles did."

Not that everyone liked the way Harry's drug use was handled. There were those who pointed out that Britain's harsh drug laws made possession of even a small amount of marijuana punishable by jail time. If he was anyone else's son, one member of Parliament pointed out, Harry might well have been prosecuted.

For all his usual bravado, Harry was distraught over having saddled his family with yet another front-page scandal. "I feel like a complete idiot," he confessed to an Eton pal. "Nobody understands how difficult things are for my father. I just feel that I've let him down." Said a friend: "Harry may look like a tough guy, but he is the most sensitive of any of them."

The owners of the Rattlebone Inn took it all in stride. Not long after the scandal hit, they placed a doctored Harry Potter poster over the bar. It showed Prince Harry smoking a joint under the title: THE RATTLEBONE INN PRESENTS HARRY POTHEAD AND THE PHILOSOPHER'S STONE.

With the rest of the Windsor men, Harry took his frustrations out on the polo field. At the Beaufort Polo Grounds—accessible directly from Highgrove via a three-mile stretch of unmarked country road—Charles and his sons competed against one another on horseback. Harry, more than William, seemed determined to challenge his father on the field. "Harry is certainly at an age when he wants to prove himself against the world," polo commentator Jim Hilston said of the then seventeen-year-old Prince. "So you see good rivalry between father and son."

Polo also offered ample opportunity for some old-fashioned sibling rivalry between Harry, who thanks to a recent growth spurt had shot up to a full six feet, and his six-foot-three-inch brother (William will be England's tallest monarch since Henry VIII). As usual, Harry proved himself to be the more dauntless competitor. "Prince Harry's a jolly good player," said Lady Apsley, whose family has owned the Cirencester Park Polo Club since 1697. "He's strong, and he doesn't hold back." In William's defense, he had to spend months training to become ambidextrous, since he was born left-handed and polo requires that all players "meet" right hand to right hand.

Not all the action was on the field. It was at the Beaufort Polo Grounds that Wills met his first serious girlfriend, Arabella Musgrave. The daughter of Major Nicholas Musgrave, who managed the rival Cirencester Park Polo Club, Arabella reportedly "worried" about his interest in other women and ended the relationship before he left for college. "Arabella was really William's first love," a friend of the Musgrave family said. "He was taken by complete surprise and, from what I understand, took the breakup quite hard."

Wills was still licking his wounds as the Royal Family decamped for its customary summer vacation in Scotland. The Windsors were all together at Balmoral on September 11, 2001, when Robin Janvrin called the Queen to tell her that planes had slammed into the World Trade Center and the Pentagon. Well into the evening hours, Her Majesty, the Queen Mother, Princes Philip, Charles, William, and Harry were glued to the astonishing images being carried live by the BBC.

"The Queen became very emotional," a member of the household staff said. "She does not let her feelings show very often, and when she does it is very moving." The following day, the Queen allowed that she was "watching developments in growing disbelief and total shock."

Ever since their first trip together to the United States in 1993, William and Harry had, like their mother, developed a keen interest in all things American. As might have been expected, the boys cheered her on when she fantasized about renting a seaside villa in Malibu where they might spend a month or two each winter.

Now William in particular wanted to show solidarity with the Americans. There would be the expected statements of sympathy and support, drawn up by the Foreign Office and bearing the Queen's signature. But William wanted something more palpable. By way of one small gesture, he suggested a musical tribute at Buckingham Palace. During the ceremonial Changing of the Guard two days later, the Coldstream Guards band opened with a stirring rendition of "The Stars and Stripes Forever" and then played a rousing "Star-Spangled Banner" before concluding with "When Johnny Comes Marching Home." Hundreds of tourists standing outside the palace, many of them Americans stranded in the wake of the attacks, burst into applause and cheered; many wept openly.

The next day, during a memorial service at St. Paul's for the thousands of Americans who perished in the terrorist attacks, the Queen stood to sing "The Star-Spangled Banner." It marked the first time that any British monarch had sung the American anthem. "For the Queen to sing like this is more than a gesture," Richard Kay observed. "The Queen does not 'sing' national anthems. Her mouth never opens when they are played. It was the ultimate sign of unity, friendship, and support for America."

The rest of the royals were moved to see tears well up in the sovereign's eyes when the choir sang "The Battle Hymn of the Republic," but no one was more devastated by the events of 9/11 than William. "Nothing since his mother's death four years ago has hit him harder than this," Harold Brooks-Baker said. "But the way he took charge to tell America 'We're with you' was . . . inspiring."

In the wake of the attacks, there was also a heightened concern that all members of the Royal Family—particularly the Queen, Charles, William, and Harry—were potential terrorist targets. (The royal who came closest to harm was actually Princess Anne, the target of an armed kidnap attempt in 1974. When the kidnappers cut off her car and then told her to get out, the Princess replied, "Not bloody likely!" A Royal Protection officer who was shot in the head and chest during the attempted abduction was later decorated for heroism.)

Security at Buckingham Palace had always been problematic. Since the Queen encountered an intruder sitting on the edge of her bed in 1982, there had been no fewer than eleven major security breaches at the palace—perhaps none more memorable than the nude American paraglider who landed on the roof in 1994. That same year, someone broke into the Prince of Wales's apartments at St. James's Palace. Even after a special panel determined that security precautions at St. James's were "abysmal," someone knocked on Princess Anne's bedroom door and asked for directions to Victoria Station.

The new "panic rooms" at Buckingham Palace and Windsor Castle in the wake of 9/11 were certainly not on any tour. Designed to cope with the possibility of an Al-Qaeda attack, the rooms were encased in an eighteen-inch-thick fire-retardant steel shell. According to the experts, this would presumably be strong enough to withstand the impact of a direct hit by a small aircraft or even sustained shelling. Gas masks and a state-of-the-art air-filtration system were also on hand for the Queen, her family, and even a few of the servants in the event of a chemical or biological attack on the palace.

Similar precautions were taken at the other royal residences; less elaborate panic rooms were installed at St. James's Palace, Balmoral, Sandringham, and Highgrove, while security details were beefed up dramatically. Yet one royal posed special problems. While Harry was safely ensconced at Eton, his older brother was bound for one of the most freewheeling university campuses in the British Isles.

While the Spencers pushed for Oxford, and Cambridge man Papa lobbied hard for his alma mater, William decided instead to listen to his house master at Eton, Andrew Gailey, and enroll in Scotland's University of St. Andrews. Granny could not have been happier. At a time when Scottish nationalists were demanding independence, there was an obvious political advantage to having a future King of England choose to attend college there.

St. Andrews, famous as the birthplace of golf (in the 1440s), had other advantages as well. Boasting a student body of just six thousand, Scotland's leading university had a more intimate, small college feel than either Oxford or Cambridge. In fact, it would be a stretch to describe St. Andrews and the tiny college town surrounding it as merely remote. Poking out into the North

Sea some seventy-five miles north of Edinburgh, St. Andrews was a fog-shrouded outpost dotted with tourist hotels, souvenir shops, and moss-covered medieval ruins.

Not surprisingly, then, more than twenty-two pubs lined St. Andrews's narrow lanes and alleyways—more per square mile than any other town in Scotland—earning it a place at the top of the list of U.K. party schools. According to student Beryl Finch, "Everyone thinks the number one sport at St. Randy's is golf, but it's really drinking. And not just drinking, but drinking *a lot*."

To be sure, William's fellow students had thought up some distinctive new approaches to binge drinking that they could call their own. At one end of the campus social spectrum was the James Bond Society, where martinis were downed shaken, stirred, and if need be through a straw. At the other end was the proudly decadent Dead Parrot Society.

For those who chose not to belong to any particular club, there were plenty of student activities. The Student Run, for example, required freshmen to consume as much alcohol as they could manage at five separate pubs. Weaving from one establishment to the next, they paused to urinate into the mail slots of local residences who hadn't the foresight to seal them shut. While that practice was largely (though apparently not exclusively) reserved for men, female students often scrawled their addresses on their forearms so they could be helped home in the event they drank themselves into a stupor.

Understandably, once Wills arrived on the scene, mayhem ensued. No sooner had he announced his intention to enroll at St. Andrews than applications climbed 44 percent over the previous year. Predictably, the increase was almost entirely accounted for by women.

His first day on campus, Wills waded into the crowd of more than four thousand screaming, camera-clicking fans held back by police barricades. Papa, who was on hand to lend William moral support, was taken aback by the rock star reception. "I almost," Charles conceded, "turned around and fled." Allie Giddings, one of the undergraduates who showed up hoping to catch a glimpse of St. Andrews's most famous "fresher," sympathized with William's predicament. "I feel kind of sorry for the dude," she said.

Once again, St. James's Palace had agreed to one strictly controlled interview with William in exchange for a continuation of Fleet Street's hands-off policy when it came to covering Diana's sons. Determined to be "treated like an ordinary student," the Prince expressed alarm at all the attention he was getting. "I'm only going to university," he protested to journalist Sam Greenhill. "It's not like I'm getting married, though that's what it feels like sometimes."

Still, just how would William—son of the most famous woman of her generation and a future King of England—fit in socially? "It's not as if I choose my friends on the basis of where they are from or what they are," he insisted. "It's about their character and who they are and whether we get on. I just hope I meet people I get on with."

The sleepy Scottish town would, in fact, never be quite the same. From this point on, women and men alike would flock to the wine bars, pubs, taverns, and assorted student hangouts, hoping for a glimpse of the strapping student prince. Only one person seemed confident that eventually it would all die down. "It will get easier as time goes on," William predicted. "Everyone will get bored of me, which they do."

Boredom was precisely what William's Royal Protection officers were praying for. Unfortunately, there was ample reason to believe that the Prince was in danger. Even before moving into his rooms at St. Andrews, William was the target of credible threats from an antifoxhunting group that had a record of firebombing stores that sell fur, as well as violent elements in the Scottish separatist movement (one pointed out on its Web site that security was lax at St. Andrews, "anyone could shoot the fucker any time they wanted"), militant antimonarchists, and of course the IRA.

Actually, what had authorities most worried was the "Real IRA," a splinter group of the Irish Republican Army that in 1998 detonated a bomb in Ulster killing twenty-eight people. Before Scotland Yard shut it down, the group offered details on its Web site concerning where William and his security detail would be staying, and spots on campus where he could be seen "at extremely accurate range."

While Scotland Yard, the Royal Protection Service, and Britain's various intelligence agencies sorted it all out, William fended off an attack of a very different kind. As part of the deal St. James's had struck with the press, camera crews were given access to William the day of his arrival on the condition they left within twenty-four hours. Everyone abided by the agreement, with one exception: Prince Edward, who sent a camera crew from his TV production company to tag along on his nephew's first few days at university. William and Charles were both, according to one St. James's spokesman, "incandescent with rage" over this betrayal from within his own family. Within minutes, an angry Charles was screaming at his youngest brother over the phone. Needless to say, Edward immediately canceled the planned documentary.

"It beggars belief when I think of the efforts we have gone to to allow William a normal undergraduate life," said Andrew Neil, rector of St. Andrews and a former Fleet Street editor himself. That the delicate pact with the press was "broken by a company owned by his uncle," Neil added, "'well, you just couldn't make it up.'"

William's new home was a fifteen-foot-by-fifteen-foot room at St. Salvatore's Hall ("Sallies" to students), an imposing Gothic residence next to the town's tourist information center and overlooking the sea. Whenever he wanted to leave for classes or dinner out, William buzzed the Royal Protection officer who bunked in the next room.

William, who majored in art history and geography, quickly buckled down, spending hours poring over his lecture notes in the library ("He must be a bit of a swot [nerd]," observed one student) and never missing a class. "He has always been," said his former Eton classmate Hamish Barne, "a very serious fellow."

"My father," Wills joked, "thinks I'm the laziest person on earth, but, surprisingly, I do actually get up for the lectures." Up each day, in fact, at 5:30 A.M. so that he could run unrecognized and under cover of darkness—always trailed by his security detail—through St. Andrews's narrow streets and alleyways. Back at his residence hall an hour later, William would shower and dress, then climb onto the 125 cc Kawasaki motorcycle (a gift from Papa) and head for class. Zipping north on The Scores street, William would then cut across an alleyway called Butts Wynd heading toward Union Street. There he parked his motorbike outside the Buchanan Building, a 1960s-era concrete monstrosity in the center of town.

Once inside Buchanan's airless, linoleum-floored lecture hall, William would climb a steep back stairway to the small balcony and slide into one of the child-size seats with a pull-down wooden desk. All were covered with graffiti—some of it hilarious, some of it poignant, most of it banal. KURT COBAIN LIVES ON was carved into the desk at seat K-10, while two seats away someone had scrawled I AM THE WORLD'S FORGOTTEN BOY. At M-1: A WOMAN NEEDS A MAN LIKE A FISH NEEDS A BICYCLE. Once when he sat at seat Q-2, Wills looked down to see that someone had written PRINCE WILLIAM IS A SEX GOD in block letters. He pointed out to friends that the same compliment had been paid to one of their lecturers at a half-dozen other desks in the balcony. The fifth day of William's week was devoted to his tutorial group, a small gathering of five or six students who then review what they've learned with an instructor.

Still, life for William at St. Andrews was not all work. "I'm not a party animal, despite what some people might think," he said. "But I like to go out sometimes like anyone else." His favorite haunt: Ma Bells, a cozy, pine-paneled bar in the St. Andrews Golf Hotel, where he would play video games, watch sports on the telly, and even take to the stage to belt out a few Beatles tunes on the karaoke machine. More often, he stuck close to home, ordering dinner from Pizza Express or Chinese takeout from Ruby on Market Street.

Party animal or no, William soon admitted to "feeling trapped" within the stone confines of St. Sallies. "Weekends at St. Andrews," he said, sighing to the British Press Association's Peter Archer, "are not particularly vibrant." Soon Wills was jumping into his white VW Golf nearly every Friday afternoon and driving seventy-five miles south to Edinburgh. There he dined at restaurants like Olorosso, owned by the former chef aboard the royal yacht *Britannia*, and danced the nights away at clubs like Opal and the Bongo Club. There were also five-hour train rides to visit Granny and the Queen Mum at Balmoral, and sojourns to London, where William reunited with many of the same "Throne Rangers" whose drug abuse had caused Papa so much concern.

The student prince was also making trips to Highgrove, trying to rekindle his romance with Arabella Musgrave. By then, she had moved on. "I hated being famous for going out with William," she said bluntly. "I have a new boyfriend who is in property [real estate]."

Sadly, these weekend jaunts only served to underscore the Heir's palpable sense of isolation. "If you have to drive hours and hours or take the train every weekend just to see friends," said William's old Eton pal David Walston, "it gets to be a huge problem. It's easy to feel cut off if you're not around the few people you can really count on."

William pleaded with Papa to let him transfer to Edinburgh University, but Charles's senior advisors, Sir Stephen Lamport and Mark Bolland, strongly opposed the idea. "It would have been a personal disaster for William," a royal aide told journalist Robert Jobson. "He would have been seen as a quitter, and it would have been an even bigger disaster for the monarchy, particularly in Scotland."

Citing the political ramifications, Charles managed to convince his son to at least give St. Andrews one more year. Then, to seal the deal, he rewarded his son for his impressive first-year marks with a gold-inlaid hunting rifle. The price: $32,000.

William's sophomore year would make all the difference—in no small part because of an important change in his living arrangements. Moving out of Sallie's, he now was shelling out the princely sum of 100 pounds (then about $165) a week to share a Victorian town house with three fellow students. His relationship with one of his new roommates, Kate Middleton, had already raised eyebrows after she modeled a bandeau bra and black bikini bottoms beneath a transparent lace sheath at a university fashion show sponsored by Yves Saint Laurent. William, who had paid two hundred pounds for a front-row seat, led the applause.

WILLIAM AND HIS UNDIE-GRADUATE FRIEND KATE TO SHARE A STUDENT FLAT, screamed the headline in *The Mail on Sunday* while the *Sun* proclaimed, WILLIAM SHACKS UP WITH STUNNING UNDIES MODEL. Trouble was, Kate had a boyfriend at the time: Rupert Finch, a star player on St. Andrews's cricket team. "William is sensitive to that," said a family friend of the Middletons. "Besides, there are always those bodyguards skulking about."

The bodyguards knew by now how to hide in plain sight, keeping a watchful eye over the Prince while giving him the privacy he required. "We don't get in the way," a former Royal Protection officer said. "We are just on the other side of the door, in the next room, outside the building—front and back. What he wants to do with a young lady in the privacy of his room is his business. I mean, he's entitled to a life, isn't he?" Soon, Middleton cut off her relationship with Finch and, despite constant statements to the contrary, began a serious affair with William.

The woman in William's life was—unlike his own mother—an untitled commoner, but a wealthy one. By the time Kate was six, her parents were well on their way to making a sizable fortune in the mail-order business. In 1987, businessman Michael and former flight attendant Carole Middleton started Party Pieces, a company specializing in children's party supplies. As a little girl growing up in the tiny Berkshire village of Bucklebury, Kate would try on princess gowns and tiaras before the items were packaged and shipped off to customers. "At the time," said the mother of one of

Middleton's childhood playmates, "I remember Kate in her sparkly princess dress and little rhinestone crown, watching Princess Diana on the television and imitating her. Of course, all the little girls wanted to be Diana."

Soft-spoken Kate, the oldest of three children, claimed she was bullied in grade school. But at Marlborough College, the elite $35,000-a-year coed boarding school she later attended, Middleton was, said her friend Gemma Williamson, "extremely popular. Good at tennis, swimming, running, maths and science. . . . Everything looked good on her because she had such a perfect body."

That aside, she was somewhat . . . straitlaced. Catherine, as Middleton was known at boarding school, "wasn't one for the random snog [kiss]," Williamson said. "She didn't need a guy to be happy." Then again, like William, Kate wasn't above the occasional outrageous antic. When several boys gathered outside her dorm window at Marlborough and began yelling up at Kate and her roommates, Middleton allegedly mooned them. That may have explained the nickname Kate's chums bestowed on Middleton. They called her "Middlebum."

As for the way Middleton treated other girls: "She was the most kindhearted woman," observed Williamson. "There are always cliques at school, but she would have time for absolutely everyone. That's what made her special."

It was Middleton's compassionate streak—in addition to the beautiful face and "perfect body," of course—that drew William to her. At the time he was having second thoughts about his choice of St. Andrews, she too was harboring doubts. After consulting with their parents, William and Kate made a pact to stick it out together.

Determined to keep the true nature of their relationship under wraps, Wills and Kate refrained from public displays of affection. Their housemates went along with the charade, insisting to anyone who would listen that the Prince and the coed were nothing more than "mates." The gambit worked so well that, despite the fact that they were a couple by the spring of 2002, more than a year later Kate's own father was still unaware of the romance. "I can categorically confirm that they are no more than just good friends," Michael Middleton said. "There are two boys and two girls sharing the flat at university. They are together all the time because they're the best of pals. . . . But there is nothing more to it than that. We are very amused at the thought of being in-laws to Prince William, but I don't think it is going to happen."

To be sure, at times William scarcely behaved like someone in a committed relationship. All three of the girls who cruised the Aegean with William aboard the *Alexander* in 1999—Mili d'Erlanger, Mary Forestier-Walker, and his distant cousin Davina Duckworth-Chad—were still seen cozying up to William at clubs in London and Edinburgh. Another striking blonde from William's club-crawling Eton days, the moneyed aristocrat Lady Isabella Anstruther-Gough-Calthorpe, also seemed to be back in the picture. Then there were St. Andrews classmates Olivia Bleasdale, daughter of a Royal Artillery officer, and Virginia "Ginny" Fraser, whose dad is Lloyd's underwriter Lord Strathalmond.

At the Beaufort Polo Club, William also began flirting between matches with athletic, fun-loving Amanda "Tigger" Bush, who worked for club owner Claire Tomlinson. "William was growing fonder of Kate the longer he stayed at St. Andrews," said a friend from Eton, "but what they had at the time wasn't exclusive—at least not as far as he was concerned. Don't forget, girls—gorgeous girls, and not just girls but older women too—were constantly throwing themselves at him."

While William coped with his fortunate dilemma, Granny was dealt two emotional hammer blows in early 2002. First, the death at seventy-one of her sister, Princess Margaret, followed just seven weeks later by the loss of her mother.

Neither death came as a complete surprise. The once-glamorous, high-living Margaret Rose, the Queen's only sibling and a lifelong smoker, had suffered a series of strokes before succumbing to a heart attack. And while the Queen Mum had always seemed indestructible, the fact remained that she was 101.

When she was 99, William and Harry introduced their great-grandmother to Ali G, the over-the-top rapper created by British comedian Sacha Baron Cohen of *Borat* fame. At the end of a lunch at Windsor, the Queen Mum stood up at the head of the table, snapped her fingers like Ali G, and said, "Dahling, lunch was marvelous—*respec*." At her 100th birthday celebration at Buckingham Palace, the Queen Mother was handed a card from the Queen. She fumbled with the envelope for a moment before turning to the Irish Guardsman standing nearby. "Can you use your sword?" she asked. And he did.

Charles, William, and Harry were on yet another ski holiday at Klosters in Switzerland when they heard the news of the Queen Mother's death. The Prince of Wales was her favorite grandchild, and he was devastated. "Somehow, I never thought her death would come," said Charles, who immediately flew back to London with his sons. "She seemed gloriously unstoppable, and ever since I was a child I adored her. She was quite simply the most magical grandmother you could possibly have and I was utterly devoted to her."

Charles would don his full military uniform to stand ceremonial guard by her coffin not once but twice as an estimated 500,000 mourners filed past. After a funeral service at Westminster Abbey attended by more than sixty heads of state, the Queen Mother was then interred beside her husband, King George VI, at Windsor. "Lilibet," as the Queen was known to her mother, then watched as the urn containing her sister Margaret's ashes was placed inside the vault with their parents' remains.

Camilla had been pointedly excluded from the celebrations surrounding the Queen Mother's centennial, but she was among the mourners invited to Westminster Abbey—shoved to one side, kept away from the Royal Family, but there nonetheless. "She knew the Queen Mother for thirty years," a spokesman for St. James's sniffed when asked why Camilla was there at all. The spokesman neglected to mention that the Queen Mother had stood in the way of Camilla's marriage to her favorite grandson.

Charles had, in fact, demanded that the woman he loved be allowed to pay her respects to the grandmother he loved. "The Queen knew how strongly he felt about the Queen Mother," Harold Brooks-Baker said. "She may not have liked the idea of Camilla being there, but she was not going to deny Charles the right to invite anybody he wanted to the funeral." Yet Camilla's mere presence sent a subtle but significant message to palace watchers—that, said Brooks-Baker, "now that the Queen Mother was gone, Camilla might be allowed to play a somewhat larger public role."

It was at Camilla's insistence that Charles now pressed the issue. On a more or less regular basis, he had had to tell Camilla she was not welcome at high-profile affairs, and Camilla, said Brooks-Baker, found that "totally humiliating. Just imagine how many times she has heard, 'No, dear, I'm afraid you've got to stay home tonight.' "

No longer willing to just stay home, Camilla insisted that she be included in the upcoming Golden Jubilee celebrations marking the Queen's fiftieth year on the throne. She got her wish. In what would be her biggest step toward respectability to date, Camilla was invited to sit in the royal box at the classical concert that kicked off the festivities on June 1, 2002. Although Camilla and the Queen never spoke or even made eye contact with each other—Camilla was actually seated directly behind Charles—it marked the first time Britons had seen the two women together, more or less. Camilla clearly found the experience unsettling. When a camera projected her image on a giant television screen, the crowd saw an obviously nervous Camilla licking her lips and fiddling with her hair.

Camilla seemed much more at ease two days later, when she also sat with the royals at the Queen's Jubilee "Party at the Palace" pop concert held in the Buckingham Palace gardens. Diana's name was never once mentioned during the festivities, although her presence was felt among those in the crowd. "You would not have seen a pop concert in the grounds of Buckingham Palace," said the Queen's biographer Robert Lacey, "had it not been for Diana. . . . The Royal Family is immensely the better off for what they learned from Diana."

Camilla was also an avid pop-rock fan, and when Phil Collins launched into "You Can't Hurry Love," Charles's mistress—who knew something about the subject—sang along. Then, when Tom Jones took the stage, Camilla also proved she knew all the words to "Sex Bomb."

Afterward, surrounded by the likes of Paul McCartney, Elton John, and Tony Bennett, Camilla appeared unfazed when Ozzy

Osbourne's wife, Sharon, approached her with outstretched hands and squeezed her breasts. "You've got gorgeous old tits," Sharon declared brightly. Camilla merely nodded in agreement. Apparently encouraged by Camilla's favorable response, Sharon went on to pinching the bottoms of William, Harry, and the Prince of Wales—none of whom seemed to mind.

The illusion of family harmony would be shattered a few weeks later, when Diana's brother denounced the Windsors for keeping William and Harry away from their Spencer relatives. Specifically, Charles had banned the boys from attending Spencer's wedding at Althorp to former nursery school teacher Caroline Freud.

Spencer, who had encountered Charles only once—and then purely by happenstance at a charity event—also criticized Charles for having never visited Diana's grave. "Not a single time," the Princess's brother said, "in five years." Nor, incidentally, had the Queen been to Althorp since Diana's death. But each year on Diana's birthday, the boys did make the journey to the Spencer estate, rowing out to the tiny, 75-foot-by-180-foot island on which she is buried to place flowers on her grave.

It had been only nine months since the horrors of 9/11, but the Queen's Jubilee celebrations had gone off without incident. In August, however, William became the target of a surreal threat when a twenty-two-year-old Montana woman spiked a bottle of Coke with cyanide and prepared to mail it to the Prince. Accompanying the poisoned soft drink was a note: "Have a Coke and a smile!" Before she could make it to the post office, the would-be terrorist, who had already mailed two bottles of cyanide-laced Coke to Senator Edward Kennedy, was arrested. At her house, police found a 9 mm handgun and a tranquilizer dart gun. The woman, a schizophrenic, would eventually be found innocent by reason of insanity and remanded to a federal psychiatric hospital for treatment. William took such bizarre incidents in stride. He had a much harder time, however, coping with the unrelenting attacks on his mother's memory. In September 2002, Diana's longtime personal bodyguard dealt the Princess's image another blow with the publication of *Diana: Closely Guarded Secret*. Among other things, Ken Wharfe alleged that the Princess apparently had no compunction about parading around in front of him in the nude, that she once withdrew $30,000 from the bank to buy her lover James Hewitt a sports car (Wharfe delivered the cash to Hewitt in a briefcase), and that she kept a vibrator in her handbag. She called the sexual aid "le gaget," and, according to Wharfe, it became her "secret mascot" on royal trips.

Branding Wharfe's book "a disgusting betrayal," Charles placed an angry phone call to Scotland Yard chief Sir John Stevens demanding that action be taken against the retired Wharfe. The Queen weighed in as well, though her concern was more for the impact such sleazy revelations would have on the boys. "The Queen is very perturbed," said the Queen's private secretary, Robin Janvrin. "She is extremely worried about the effect all this will have on her grandsons."

A palace official described William as "incandescent with anger" over the bodyguard's tell-all, but it was Harry who appeared to be most deeply affected. "Harry is *really* upset," William told his friend Guy Pelly. "It's just total treachery, that's all."

Wharfe had, in fact, been far more to the Princess and her sons than just another bodyguard. During his six years as Diana's minder, the ruddy-faced baritone (Wharfe was an accomplished amateur opera singer) became something of a father figure to the boys. When William and Harry were at Weatherby preschool in West London, it was Wharfe who ran in the father's race in place of Charles, cheered on by the young Princes.

The most tawdry revelations over the years since Diana's death had come from James Hewitt, Patrick Jephson, Paul Burrell, and now Ken Wharfe—all trusted advisors and friends. Yet there were many other damaging remarks concerning Diana's character that went unnoticed—remarks that often came from inside the royal circle.

Charles did not complain when the Queen's friend Lady Kennard appeared on a TV documentary with the palace's blessing and described Diana as "very damaged." Nor did he or any other member of the Royal Family protest when another of Her Majesty's chums, Lady Penn, raised the possibility of "mental instability" on the Princess's part. Countess Mountbatten, who was closely allied with Charles's camp, stated that "there were sides to Diana that were different to what was seen on public occasions." These random comments and worse from friends of the Windsors, observed the *Guardian*'s Catherine Bennett, would lead most to the conclusion "that the late Princess was barking mad—far, far madder than the character recalled by Wharfe—yet the palace registered no displeasure."

Charles's outrage was, without exception, reserved for those who dared to profit from writing about their years spent in service to the Royal Family. "The Royal Family has always counted on the discretion of the people who work for them," said a former St. James's Palace official. "Once that trust is broken, it really sort of shakes the foundations of their entire belief system. They simply can't afford to have their butlers and bodyguards running around spilling Royal Family secrets."

As for the sordid stories concerning Diana, there seemed little doubt that they bolstered the Royal Family's portrayal of the Princess as unbalanced. "There was a great deal of breast-beating for public consumption," said the ex-aide, "but inside the palace there were a lot of people saying 'Maybe now they'll understand what a difficult woman the Princess was.'" There was also a belief that, with each book filled with sordid stories about Diana, "you peeled away the layers of the myth until nothing was left. That was the objective—to allow Diana's memory to be debased to such an extent that Camilla looked good by comparison."

By the fifth anniversary of Diana's death, in 2002, there was no doubt in the minds of many who knew Diana that there was an organized plan afoot to downplay the Princess's place in modern British history. "It feels," said her friend Vivienne Parry, "like there's a conspiracy to forget Diana." Royals authority Judy Wade agreed that "her memory is fading. It's very sad, and I find it very difficult to understand." Earl Spencer theorized that "there is a feeling among those who were never Diana supporters of 'Let's try to marginalize her, and tell people she never mattered and tell people that in that first week of September in 1997 they were all suffering from mass hysteria.'"

Polls showed that the public agreed with Spencer. Over 74 percent of Britons believed that the Royal Family had "deliberately avoided" mentioning Diana since her death, and almost as many believed not enough had been done to honor her memory.

By way of evidence, the Princess's defenders pointed to the palace-approved Diana memorial fountain in Hyde Park—a $4.7 million, oval pool designed by Seattle landscape architect Kathryn Gustafson. "It's not a fountain," Diana's friend Arthur Edwards said of the two channels of water flowing in different directions and winding up in a children's wading pool. "It's a drainage ditch!" Sculptor Michael Daley, director of ArtWatch UK, concurred. "Diana deserves a proper memorial," Daley said. "This is not it."

Once again, Vivienne Parry was livid. "Here was the most celebrated Briton in twenty-five years, and this is something you'd trip over before you realize it is even there," she said. "It's not a national monument. It's a national nothing. We've remembered her with a puddle."

A more impressive gesture—renaming London's Heathrow after Diana—was nixed by the Queen and the Duke of Edinburgh. "People who remember Diana with love and pride are appalled at the way the elders of the Royal Family have acted," said writer Nicholas Davies, one of the Princess's more ardent defenders. "The Queen and Prince Philip particularly appear to have made definite attempts to besmirch the name and memory of the People's Princess by leaking and spreading disturbing innuendoes that she was mentally ill."

For William and Harry, every week seemed to bring a new indignity. In the aftermath of the sensational Burrell trial and Ken Wharfe's sleazy memoir came the news that former servants were selling locks of Diana's hair, her used Kleenex, even her toenail clippings on the Internet. Alicia Carroll, a California-based dealer in celebrity memorabilia, claimed to have grossed more than $1.5 million selling Diana memorabilia.

"William internalizes everything," Diana once said. "Harry is a survivor." Returning to gloomy St. Andrews, William buried himself in his studies. Harry, meanwhile, set aside the days leading up to his eighteenth birthday for a little damage control.

Declining a birthday bash and steering clear of bars and clubs altogether, he took part instead in ceremonies commemorating 9/11, visited a primary school, dropped in on homeless children and drug addicts in one of London's tougher neighborhoods, took a few practice kicks at a youth soccer club, and spent time with cancer patients at one of his mother's favorite charities, Great Ormand Street Children's Hospital.

If there was any doubt, Harry wanted his countrymen to know that he was a serious young man who intended to follow in his mother's footsteps. He praised "the way she got close to people and went for the sort of charities and organizations that everybody else was scared to go near, such as land mines in the Third World. . . . She got involved in things that nobody had done before: AIDS, for example."

As for his drinking and drug use, Harry was abjectly apologetic. "That was a mistake, and I learned my lesson," he insisted. "It was never my intention to be that way."

For his official coming-of-age portrait, Harry chose one of Diana's favorite photographers, Mario Testino. Harry's only condition: that he be allowed to style his own hair, using gel to create a tousled, just-got-out-of-bed look.

For those who viewed Harry's seemingly overnight conversion from party boy to social crusader with skepticism, the Prince insisted that his whirlwind tour of classrooms and hospitals "wasn't just a one-off thing. I've wanted to do something like this for a long time—especially after my mother died. It was quite difficult," he said of his visit with children undergoing chemotherapy, "but I've seen my mother do it many times. She was so good at it."

Now Harry looked forward to his final year at Eton, where he was holding his own academically and excelling at virtually every sport pursued on the school's celebrated playing fields. The Spare most looked forward to taking part in the Combined Cadet Corps, where he would get the chance to shout orders at his forty-eight fellow cadets during the colorful Eton Tattoo.

Yet when he arrived back at Eton, Harry was not prepared for yet another act of betrayal from a man her mother had once professed to love. Nor was he prepared when he overheard the cruel nickname some of the underclassmen were sniggering behind his back. "You know what they're calling him now, don't you?" asked someone who was not aware that the young Prince was standing directly behind him, "Harry—Harry *Hewitt*."

6

In several of the letters, she refers to his penis as "my friend." In others, she refers to his trysts with other women, or to pornography she has sent along. ("Nothing like whetting your appetite . . .") In all of the sixty-four letters Diana wrote to James Hewitt while he commanded a tank squadron in the Persian Gulf War, the Princess is unashamedly passionate.

"I felt your lips on my body last night as I slept," she wrote in one. "They were everywhere. I willed myself not to wake up. . . ." In another: "To see your form in those tight riding britches is more than a woman can bear. I long to slide my fingers inside and bury them in your skin."

Some of the torrid love notes, signed with the pseudonym "Julia" or simply "D," were written after Hewitt had been home on leave. In one of these, Diana complained that he had twice refused the Princess's plea to make love to her in a field near his mother's home. "You can be a beast one lusts after," she wrote, "and a beastly beast who drives a girl to weep tears of anger."

Although financially strapped, Hewitt turned down a $7 million offer from a private U.S. collector for the entire collection of love letters. Instead, he tried to sell the letters to Britain's *News of the World* tabloid. "I want ten million pounds [roughly $16.5 million at the time] for the lot," Hewitt said during a secret meeting at Claridges Hotel in London. "These letters are unique. It's the first time a member of the Royal Family is writing to a serving soldier at war."

Soon accounts of the "secret" meeting were splashed across the front pages of several papers, and Hewitt was again branded a cad. Meanwhile, the negative publicity scared away prospective buyers—including the American collector. Hewitt's dreams of instant wealth quickly faded, but not before Fleet Street again took the opportunity to speculate on Harry's paternity.

Now that Harry was eighteen, it was clearer than ever that he bore scant resemblance to the rest of the Windsor clan. He did, however, look an awful lot like James Hewitt. In addition to the red hair, the freckles, and the lanky six-foot frame that could all easily be attributed to Spencer genes, the two men shared the same jawline, the same eye shape and color, the same forehead and hairline, the same mouth, and—most strikingly—the same upturned nose.

The likeness, said one of Diana's closest friends, "is uncanny. It's not only that they look so much alike, but the mannerisms, the walk—it's the whole package."

Nonsense, Diana had claimed. She insisted that it was impossible for Hewitt to have fathered Harry for one reason: the Princess insisted that she and the dashing army officer had never even met until 1986, when Harry was already two years old. Hewitt's version of events varied somewhat from Diana's—he said he first set eyes on the Princess after a polo match in the summer of 1981—but he stuck to the story that they did not actually meet for another five years.

Yet there were eyewitnesses to the fact that Hewitt and Diana had at the very least known each other prior to Harry's birth. "I saw Diana and Hewitt out riding together one morning in Windsor Great Park in the *early* 1980s, and they were kissing," said journalist Nicholas Davies. "It was plain that they were lovers—and that was years before Hewitt claimed to have met Diana for the first time." Another courtier insisted he saw Hewitt and Diana together at a party at St. James's Palace. Prince Charles's former baggage master, Ronald Lewis, also confirmed that Hewitt often called on the Princess at Kensington Palace in 1983 and 1984.

According to noted British publicist Max Clifford, Hewitt approached him in 1988, asking for advice on how to keep his affair with Diana a secret. At the time, Hewitt allegedly told Clifford that he met Diana at a polo match in 1981, and that by January 1984—nine months before Harry's birth—they had become lovers.

"He was absolutely certain at that time that he didn't want anything to come out and I agreed to help him," Clifford said. "I told him to keep quiet and not to say anything to anyone. I explained that in these situations the papers might speculate but that there were only two people whose word would be taken as cast-iron evidence; his and the woman he was involved with. If they didn't provide that evidence then their relationship could never be absolutely confirmed."

Hewitt took Clifford's advice until Diana unceremoniously dumped him in 1992 without explanation. "He was hurt and upset, particularly as she didn't explain what he had done wrong," Clifford recalled. "He said it was a small comfort to know he wasn't the first friend she had dropped like a stone. He admitted he drowned his sorrows in drink and that he never really got over it."

In a tantalizing choice of words, Diana herself had told writer Andrew Morton that at a time when she and Charles were at each other's throats, "Harry appeared by a miracle." A friend of Hewitt's has also claimed that there is a sixty-fifth love letter from Diana to Hewitt in which she essentially tells him that he is Harry's father.

By the time Diana died, Charles had already proven himself to be a loving and attentive father figure to both boys. Even Diana frequently pointed out that Harry and his father had a special bond that mirrored her bond with William.

Yet Charles had his own doubts from the very beginning. There was, for example, a pronounced and telling difference in the way he reacted to the birth of his sons. Charles, who was at his wife's side during William's delivery, was emotionally overcome when William made his appearance. "Fantastic, beautiful," he whispered to Diana at that moment. "You are a darling."

Conversely, Charles, who supposedly had wanted a girl, did not try to conceal his disappointment the moment Harry arrived. "Oh, God," he said, shaking his head with obvious disdain. "It's a boy. And he even has red hair."

Diana was crushed. "At that moment," she later said, "something inside me closed off."

At Harry's christening, Charles complained that Diana had not only produced another boy, but one with—strangely enough— "rusty" hair. "You should just be thankful," Diana's mother Frances Shand Kydd admonished him, "that you had a child who was normal." She then reminded Charles that many Spencers had "rusty" hair. Unconvinced, Charles would treat his mother-in-law with frosty indifference from that moment on.

At the time Charles, unaware of Diana's ongoing affair with Hewitt, appeared satisfied with the explanation that Harry had merely inherited more than his share of Spencer family traits. But after Hewitt and Diana confessed their affair and tongues began wagging, Charles turned to Camilla for reassurance that Harry was in fact his son.

"Camilla sees her job as one of offering comfort and support to the Prince of Wales," a longtime neighbor and friend observed. "Even if she had doubts of her own, she could never hurt Prince Charles in such a fashion, never. Camilla told him that of course Harry was his son, and that it was absurd to think otherwise."

Perhaps. But Charles was upset enough about the gossip to consult his advisors on how best to bring a halt to it. While it would signal to Harry that indeed there were those in the Royal Family who may have harbored some doubts as to his paternity, the whole matter could be put to rest once and for all with a simple DNA test.

Charles would not be put in the painful position of having to ask his son to take the test; after the latest round of Hewitt headlines, Harry took the initiative and volunteered. The Queen, however, forbade it. Ostensibly, Her Majesty felt that it was degrading for any member of the Royal Family to have to prove his birthright. She also did not wish to set a dangerous precedent by acknowledging any of the salacious gossip that always seemed to be swirling around the Windsors. After all, for years the Royal Family had simply ignored similar rumors concerning Prince Andrew and the possibility that Prince Philip might not be his biological dad.

There was a more practical reason for not testing a sample of Harry's DNA: what if it turned out Charles *wasn't* his father? The possibility had, in fact, occurred to the Queen. At a closed-door meeting with one of her most trusted advisors, Her Majesty had spread out on her desk yet another tabloid story comparing photographs of Hewitt and Harry. "Good heavens," the Queen said, shaking her head as she looked down at the pictures. "You don't think it's true, do you?" Then, catching herself, she quickly answered her own question. "No, no. Of course not. How ridiculous . . ."

Several Men in Gray believed that—given intelligence reports that indicated Hewitt had known Diana as early as 1981—there was indeed a possibility that Harry was not Charles's son. A DNA test proving as much would be, in the words of one senior courtier, "catastrophic. Harry would automatically lose his place in the line of succession, and the monarchy would be dealt a terrible blow, perhaps even a mortal blow."

Left in a kind of tabloid limbo, Harry turned increasingly to alcohol. "He was out to the pubs whenever he got the chance," said a fellow Beaufort polo player, "and getting lashed quite a lot." Harry was reportedly so drunk at a shooting party hosted by the phenomenally wealthy Duke of Winchester that he crawled under a table and, to the amazement of fellow guests, vomited.

"Sadly, he fears he might not be who the world thinks he is," Brooks-Baker observed. "Those terrible doubts about who his real dad is have Harry looking for solace at the end of a joint and the bottom of a shot glass."

Notwithstanding his brotherly concern for Harry, William returned to St. Andrews with the hope of carving out something akin to a normal life for himself. This was only possible, his father insisted, if the press continued to leave him alone.

Still managing to conceal the increasingly serious nature of their relationship, William and Kate Middleton moved from their rooms in St. Andrews to a farmhouse on the outskirts of town. There, Middleton and William claimed to be living much like any other students—even to the extent of pushing a shopping cart through the aisles at Tesco supermarket. "I do all my own shopping," he said. "I go out, get takeaway, rent videos, go to the cinema, just basically anything I want to really."

Middleton was now secure enough in her relationship with Wills to ignore the women who flocked around him. She even found it amusing when, on one occasion, a young woman approached William and—in total seriousness—proposed marriage to him. "I laughed at first," he later recalled, "until I realized this girl wasn't joking."

On weekends and holidays, the young couple often hied away to Balmoral, where William and Harry now had exclusive use of a newly refurbished, three-bedroom stone "cottage" with four fireplaces and a staff of six (not counting the bodyguards). And William still enjoyed partying with friends in Edinburgh and London—only these days with Middleton discreetly tagging along.

That summer of 2002, however, William was anything but discreet when he attended a party at a friend's castle in Suffolk sans Kate. As the boozy affair dragged on into the early morning hours, an obviously tipsy William stripped down to a pair of swim trunks and took a midnight swim in the castle moat. Then, still dripping wet, the karaoke-loving Prince made his way across the dance floor, climbed onto the stage, wrapped a bright blue boa around his neck, and began doing an ersatz striptease. When an attractive brunette walked up and tied a pink boa around his waist, William threw up his arms and began dancing wildly. It would be a year before photographs of William's bizarre performance would—much to his embarrassment—surface in the Australian press.

In the meantime, he could not escape the unending stream of scandalous revelations, and the gnawing fear that his world was spinning out of control. The seamy stories unleashed by the Burrell trial—all of which involved members of William's family—reverberated throughout the fall. In addition to the ongoing investigation into charges by royal valet George Smith that he had been raped by a senior aide, there was the butler's claim that Diana drove around London and handed out "pink grannys" (fifty-pound notes) to prostitutes, imploring them to "go home."

Burrell also recalled being dispatched by the Princess to buy soft-core porn for the then thirteen-year-old William because, unlike most adolescent boys, he was a tad too recognizable to do it himself. Perhaps none of these disclosures was as disturbing to William as the assertion by Simone Simmons that she saw letters written by Prince Philip to his former daughter-in-law describing her as a "harlot" and a "trollop."

Even the more banal stories about the crowd he was hanging out with and the girls he might or might not be dating supplied what one close friend from St. Andrews called a "daily dose of dread mixed with anxiety." Nor did it help that the papers were running shots of William's thinning pate alongside headlines like SEXY HEIR LOSING HIS HAIR—JUST LIKE DAD and ONE DAY WILL WILLS BE AN HEIR WITHOUT HAIR?

As William sank into a discernibly darker mood, the contrast between him and his ostensibly more outgoing brother grew more apparent. "Harry is quick to share his emotions with other people," Peter Archer said, "and while that may get him in trouble in the short run, it's healthy in the long run. William tends to block unpleasant things out, to push them to the back of his mind, rather than face them."

If William learned anything at those afternoon tea tutorials with Granny, it was how to conceal his true emotions beneath an impenetrable mask of stoicism. But was he concealing his feelings, or suppressing them? "He pretends he's not affected," Archer went on, "but of course he is—deeply so. There's a very big worry that if William keeps repressing these things in this way it will just keep building up. . . . Something has to give." Fellow palace-watcher Brooks-Baker agreed. "No one knows how much damage has been done psychologically," he said. "Prince William is seriously shaken. He is very moody these days, and that is of concern to everyone around him."

In a rare display of temper that occurred as he returned on horseback from a foxhunting expedition, William hurled obscenities at a photographer before forcing him into a ditch. The photographer, Clive Postlethwaite, was waiting for the hunting party when "Prince Charles went by first and then William saw me and just went mad. He rode towards me with his eyes wide and his teeth showing."

"Fucking piss off!" William screamed as Postlethwaite dropped his camera and jumped into a ditch to avoid being trampled by the Prince's horse.

"I was shaken," recalled Postlethwaite, "and just about managed to shout out, 'Steady on, Wills.'"

Charles, meanwhile, was having his own problems with the press. Just as William and Harry were returning to school, their father was embroiled in yet another embarrassing brouhaha—this time over his habit of writing scores of letters to government ministers sharing his opinions on everything from human rights and nursing care to foxhunting and political correctness.

The uproar began when someone leaked several of the letters to the press. In one to Tony Blair, Charles defended such "country pursuits" as foxhunting and extolled the virtues of farmers who, he reportedly said, would get better services from the government if they were black or gay. In another letter, this one to Lord Irvine, the Lord Chancellor, Charles bemoaned the proliferation of lawsuits. "I and countless others dread the very real and growing prospect of an American-style personal injury 'culture' becoming ever more prevalent in this country," the Prince wrote, citing a decision by the government to chop down chestnut trees in eastern England out of concern that pedestrians would be injured by falling chestnuts.

Lord Irvine complained privately of being "bombarded" by letters from the Prince, as did other politicians who insisted the Prince of Wales had no business trying to influence government ministers. "Let's not kid ourselves," said Labor Party Member of Parliament Ian Davidson. "This is someone who was born with a mouthful of silver spoons, a megawealthy farmer who's looking for things to do, so he fires off letters. If he wants to be involved in politics, then he should stand for election."

At St. James's Palace, Charles seethed over the leaked correspondence that left him open to public ridicule yet again. "Is there no way," he complained at a meeting of his senior staff, "that I can write someone or speak to someone on the phone without having it broadcast all around the world the very next day?"

As it happened, virtually every member of the Royal Family was being bugged by Britain's domestic and foreign intelligence agencies, and in some cases, by foreign powers. When William originally enrolled at St. Andrews, MI5 did an electronic sweep of his rooms and discovered numerous listening devices that they

assumed had been planted by the Real IRA. It turned out, however, that the Royal Protection Service had installed the bugs and
wiretaps as a means of keeping tabs on the student prince. Moreover, Prince Charles, who was persuaded that such precautions
were necessary to ensure his son's safety, had known about the
listening devices installed in William's dormitory room.

An angry William confronted his father, demanding to know
how he could have permitted such a flagrant violation of his own
son's privacy. It seemed unfathomable that, after "Squidgygate"
and "Camillagate," Charles had failed to see how leaked tapes of
private conversations offered the potential for yet another hugely
embarrassing royal scandal—this time involving William.

In this instance, Papa promptly apologized to his son and ordered
that William's rooms at St. Salvatore's be swept clean of all eaves-
dropping devices. MI5 did, in fact, remove the Royal Protection
Service bugs—and replaced them with bugs of their own.

Glynn Jones, one of the British military surveillance experts
who was in charge of keeping an eye on Diana, said that every
member of the Royal Family is watched around the clock. "Their
personal conversations, both on the phone and sometimes person
to person, are monitored and recorded," Jones said, "and many of
their movements are captured on videotape. It's impossible for
them to keep any secrets. The most personal things are recorded.
Charles, Camilla, and William are always under surveillance by
secret service personnel."

Ken Wharfe was well aware, as were the other Royal Protection
officers, that England's intelligence agencies eavesdropped on every
member of the Royal Family. One who came to appreciate the extent of the snooping was Wharfe's boss, Princess Diana, who once
caught someone red-handed thumbing through her address book.

For her oft-repeated conviction that she was being followed and spied on, the Princess was dismissed as paranoid.

"They routinely taped the Princess's telephone calls," Wharfe said. "We, her protection officers, were trained to keep our conversations short and speak in code. Not Diana, however, who used the telephone incessantly and often spoke on it, literally, for hours." Wharfe conceded that Diana "was not being paranoid at all. She was quite right in suspecting that her every move was being watched. Princess Diana was under constant surveillance."

British investigators looking into the circumstances surrounding Diana's death would stumble upon the fact that the CIA had also been keeping tabs on the Princess—without the consent of the British government. While the CIA denied spying on Diana, spokesmen for the agency conceded that over the years she had occasionally spoken over the phone to people who were targets of CIA surveillance, and that her voice was picked up on tapes of those conversations. This did explain why, according to ex-CIA officials, the agency's secret dossier on Diana totaled more than a thousand pages.

In the wake of the infamous tampon conversation, Camilla had taken pains not to say anything she wasn't prepared to see splashed across the front page of *News of the World* or the *Daily Mail*. These days it was a particularly daunting task, since Camilla was now consulting with cosmetologists, dentists, dermatologists, dietitians, fitness experts, and even plastic surgeons—all part and parcel of the ongoing efforts to make her a worthy successor to Diana.

To be sure, what Charles had always loved most about Camilla was her love of the countryside and what amounted to a general disinterest in fashion. Yet it was also true that the Prince of Wales was a man of classic tastes who now spent in excess of $100,000 annually on his own wardrobe. The Prince's exacting standards applied to every aspect of his daily life, starting with the first meal of the day. "His daily breakfast tray," a former servant revealed, "has to contain a cup and saucer to the right with a silver spoon pointing outward at an angle of five o'clock. Plates must be placed with the Prince of Wales crest pointing to twelve o'clock. Butter must come in three balls (no more) and be chilled. The royal toast is always in a silver rack, never on a plate."

Charles also preferred round pieces of ice in his drinks rather than cubes because the angles made cubes "too noisy." Still attached to the now-tattered teddy bear he had as a child, Charles took it with him everywhere—even on state trips abroad. Each night one of the servants was assigned the task of tucking the teddy bear into bed up to its paws so, Charles patiently explained, "Teddy doesn't get cold."

Given his persnickety streak, Charles had no trouble urging Camilla to follow the advice of public relations experts and streamline her look so that she would be acceptable as a representative of the Royal Family. Over the course of six months, Camilla underwent a pricey royal makeover. She had her teeth recapped and whitened at a cost of $10,000, underwent Botox injections to smooth the furrows in her forehead, a series of face and neck peels, and laser treatments to erase her crow's feet and the lines around her mouth. She was also down two dresses sizes, to a size ten. Gone were the muddy Wellingtons and frumpy tweeds, replaced with tailored suits and slinky gowns designed by homegrown fashion talents Antony Price, Paddy Campbell, and Robinson Valentine.

Camilla's desire to look younger and more vibrant may also have had something to do with the growing importance of a younger woman in Charles's life. When the staid, dignified, and thoroughly reputable Sir Michael Peat took over as Prince Charles's private secretary in 2002, he made an attractive thirty-nine-year-old brunette named Elizabeth Buchanan his deputy. At that point Buchanan, who had worked as a spokeswoman for former Prime Minister Margaret Thatcher, had already been working for the Prince as a publicity consultant, at an annual salary of $150,000.

The daughter of a Sussex landowner, Buchanan had previously been linked with Winston Churchill's grandson and Charles's long-time confidant Nicholas "Fatty" Soames. She was so devoted to the Prince of Wales that her coworkers nicknamed Buchanan "Miss Nannypenny" after the Miss Moneypenny character of James Bond fame. Comparing her to Camilla, a colleague observed that Buchanan "wears sensible shoes, sensible hats, sensible skirts and she doesn't smoke like the resident horse in the stable."

As Miss Nannypenny assumed a larger role in shaping the Prince's public image, Camilla was spending more and more time with her elderly father in the countryside. Buchanan, meanwhile, remained almost continually at the Prince's side. "It was no secret that Elizabeth wanted Camilla out of the picture," said a former colleague of Buchanan's. "She apparently felt that Camilla was just too visible and that that was a detriment to Charles's public image."

Buchanan certainly had her employer's ear. Over the next several months, Charles reportedly visited Buchanan's London apartment no fewer than seventy-three times—purportedly, St. James's Palace tried to explain, to discuss "business." To further complicate matters, Buchanan's purse had been stolen from her locked car. It contained a security pass, an address book, and—perhaps potentially most embarrassing—personal correspondence from Charles to Buchanan.

"Elizabeth has a reputation for falling in love, in a hero-worship sense, with her bosses," said a former colleague who insisted Buchanan's relationship with the Prince was purely professional. Charles, in turn, "is in the habit of sending warm personal notes to his staff whenever he wants to express his appreciation for a job well done—particularly his close female staff. It is the kind of gesture which Elizabeth in particular treasures. The fact that she carries these letters with her in her handbag is entirely in character."

Buchanan's mother was more to the point. The senior Elizabeth Buchanan dismissed the speculation concerning her daughter and Prince Charles as "barking mad, absolute rubbish, a total load of nonsense, laughable."

Camilla, accustomed to competing with other women for Charles's attention, took Buchanan in stride. What Camilla could not accept, however, was the possibility of once again being relegated to the shadows. According to writer Penny Junor, a long-time acquaintance of Charles's, Camilla felt she was "being frozen out. . . . Elizabeth is close to the Prince—possessive and passionate about him—and would like Camilla to take a backseat."

By the spring of 2003, Camilla's makeover was nearly complete. Having allowed herself to play Galatea to Charles's Pygmalion, Camilla now allegedly demanded that he fire Buchanan. But Buchanan stayed, and two years later Miss Nannypenny would be promoted to the key post of private secretary to the Prince.

It was not only Camilla's appearance that the palace sought to overhaul. She was also pressured to give up tobacco—a forty-year addiction that left her newly upset coiffure and stylish clothes reeking of stale cigarette smoke. Over the years, Charles, who routinely referred to smoking as "a filthy habit," had begged Camilla to quit—a promise that was her birthday present to him when he turned fifty in 1998. But Camilla had been unable to keep that promise—not even when she was reminded that the Queen, whose chain-smoking father King George VI had died of lung cancer at fifty-six, was a rabid antismoker.

It would take a major health scare for Charles's mistress to finally quit. In May of 2003, Camilla was suffering from back pain so excruciating that she was rushed to the hospital for five hours of tests. Osteoporosis—the bone disease that had killed her mother—was quickly ruled out, but so was everything else. Even without a firm diagnosis, doctors convinced her that smoking was undermining her health. In addition to the damage it was doing to her lungs and her heart, smoking was now wreaking havoc with her sinuses. It was then that Camilla made the decision to quit cold turkey—and she did.

Now that Camilla had kicked the habit, Charles tried to enlist her in his ongoing campaign to get the boys to quit. In the wake of the "Harry Pothead" headlines, the Spare hardly concerned himself with concealing his smoking habit; Harry was often photographed with a beer in one hand and a cigarette in the other. William was more circumspect, allowing the palace to issue denials while at the same time carrying a pack of Marlboro Lights in his back pocket along with a silver lighter. According to friends, Wills also kept a small can of air freshener in the glove compartment of his VW Golf to mask the odor whenever he decided to light up while driving.

Despite the fact that she was their stepmum in all but name, Camilla refused to speak to the boys about their fondness for tobacco. "It took me forty years to quit!" she said, laughing. "Why on earth should they listen to me?"

Instead, Camilla turned her attention to another project: the renovation of her new home at Clarence House, for half a century home to the Queen Mother and now the London residence of Charles, William, Harry and Camilla. A royal palace for over 170 years, Clarence House boasted dozens of rooms spread out over four floors and housed the Queen Mother's extensive collection of twentieth-century English paintings. It had also not been painted for over fifty years.

Camilla had already hired noted British interior designer Robert Kime to rejuvenate some of the mustier rooms at Highgrove and her own home in Wiltshire, Raymill House. Now she gave Kime the task of spiffing up Clarence House, where the curtains were shredded and the upholstery worn, without erasing the memory of Charles's beloved grandmother altogether.

Toward that end, the Morning Room, with its eighteenth-century Chippendale giltwood furniture and Walter Sickert's romantic painting *A Lady in a Pink Ballgown* hanging over the fire-place, wound up looking much as it had when the Queen Mother was in residence. So too did chandeliered Main Hall, hung with massive portraits of previous royal occupants; the Horse Corridor, still lined with some of the Queen Mum's favorite equestrian paintings; the book-lined Lancaster Room, with its overstuffed sofa, and the sunlit, scarlet-draped ground-floor Garden Room used for formal receptions.

Camilla did feel free, however, to design from scratch the couple's adjoining suites on the second floor and the boys' rooms one floor up. For the Prince of Wales's bedroom, Camilla selected a soft pink fabric for the walls and a huge, carved mahogany four-poster bed with drapes that can be drawn on all sides. Clarence House now employed a permanent staff of ninety, but only a handful of those closest to Charles and Camilla would be permitted access to the royal boudoir. Total cost for Camilla's redo of Clarence House: $10 million.

No sooner had Camilla moved into Clarence House that summer of 2003, bringing her father Major Shand with her, than there were squeals of protest in the press about the cost of renovation. Since Camilla still possessed no official status, critics questioned whether British taxpayers should foot the bill for remodeling the rooms Mrs. Parker Bowles was to occupy. To settle the matter, Charles agreed to pay the $2 million cost of refurbishing Camilla's rooms out of his own pocket.

On the occasion of his twenty-first birthday, William took the opportunity to come to his father's defense. "He's been given quite a hard time recently," Wills said, "and I just wish people would give him a break. He does amazing things. I only wish people would see that more because he's had a very hard time and yet he's stuck it out and he's still very positive."

As for his younger brother, who delighted photographers on his last day at Eton when a girlfriend's pink G-string tumbled out of his dresser drawer as he packed to leave, William waxed sentimental. "We've grown up together and we have to go through a lot of things together," Wills said of Harry. "We will always have that common bond."

One thing they did not have in common was academic achievement. Harry was now taking two gap years off before entering Sandhurst Academy and a career in the military. Despite a D in geography—the lowest grade given any member of his graduating class—Harry had distinguished himself as a member of the Combined Cadet Corps and was a runner-up for the coveted Sword of Honor that William had won three years earlier. Harry would take two gap years off instead of one because Sandhurst was reluctant to accept cadets under age twenty. "My brother," William hastened to add, "is a very nice guy and extremely caring."

Wills also gave Diana her due. Instead of pursuing any of his father's various charitable causes, William announced that he intended to focus on helping Britain's homeless. "I was influenced a lot by my visits to shelters with my mother when I was younger," he recalled. "It's an important issue that needs to be highlighted. My mother used her position to help other people, as does my father, and I hope to do the same."

Still, William once again asserted his desire to be his own man—even if it meant bucking Buckingham Palace. "I'm not an overdominant person," he insisted. "I don't go around and expect everyone to listen to me the whole time. But," he added, "I like to be in control of my life because I have so many people around me, I can get pulled in one direction and then the other. If I don't have any say in it then I end up losing complete control and I don't like the idea of that. I could actually lose my identity.

"A lot of people think I am hugely stubborn about the whole thing," he went on. "But you have to be slightly stubborn because everybody wants you for one reason or another. If you don't stick to your guns, then you lose control."

True to form, Wills determined how, where, and with whom he would celebrate his coming-of-age. Before the official festivities at Windsor Castle, the Heir cut loose at Ma Bells in St. Andrews. Sitting on a sofa in a corner with his pals, the Prince knocked back an astonishing ten pints of hard cider over the course of a few hours. "Wills managed to stay on his feet at the end," said bartender Nick Philpott. "He seemed to be able to take the drink easily. He is very polite even when he gets tanked up."

For his Windsor party, William, still in the thrall of Africa after his gap-year stint on a big game preserve in Kenya, decided on an "Out of Africa" theme. The Queen approved—but only if William agreed to warn his three hundred guests to avoid any "racial overtones" in their costumes as well as overt references to colonies or the British Empire.

Satisfied that any potential diplomatic incidents had been averted, Her Majesty showed up dressed as the Queen of Swaziland in a white sheath, a white fur wrap, and an African headdress. William opted for a yellow-and-black-striped loincloth and nothing else. Charles slipped into a striped kaftan for the event, while Harry, Prince Philip, Prince Andrew, and Earl Spencer all opted for some variation of safari wear. Others came dressed as Foreign Legionnaires, witch doctors, bush pilots, even characters from *The Lion King*.

While several female guests wore grass skirts, most of the younger women—like the boys' cousins Princess Beatrice and Princess Eugenie—wore leopard-print minidresses. Slipping in after Prince Charles, Camilla wore a blue and red tribal costume topped off with a red feathered headdress.

There were elephant rides for the guests, and monkeys swung among palm trees imported for the event. At one point William jumped onstage and played African drums with the Botswanan band Shakarimba.

Throughout the evening all eyes were on the young, dark-haired woman who had a place of honor next to the future King and who appeared to have William's undivided attention the entire evening. With Kate Middleton's blessing, William had invited his old flame Jecca Craig to be his guest of honor.

Those who knew how deeply Wills had felt for Middleton were

also aware that Craig had been more than a friend to the Prince in Africa. Given the fact that he was now teaching himself Swahili—and that he had chosen Out of Africa as the theme for his party—obviously his African interlude had had a lasting effect.

Yet St. James's Palace, quick to quash any notion that the glamorous brunette from Kenya was anything more than "just a friend," took the extraordinary step of issuing a public denial "that there is or ever has been any romantic liaison between Prince William and Jessica Craig." Moreover, when Wills's handlers realized that Craig's own on-again, off-again boyfriend Henry Ropner had been omitted from the guest list, Ropner—heir to a shipping fortune—was hastily offered a last-minute invitation.

Middleton, meanwhile, managed to keep a low profile at the party. Just six months earlier, William had slipped quietly and unannounced into Kate's twenty-first birthday dinner at the Middletons' house in Berkshire. Now she was being just as discreet, keeping her distance from William and mingling mainly with the rest of the St. Andrews contingent.

Amid all the speculation regarding William's romantic life, few noticed that the occasion marked a rapprochement of sorts between the Windsor and Spencer clans. For the first time since Diana's funeral, all of Diana's siblings—Lady Sarah McCorquodale, Lady Jane Fellowes, and Earl Spencer—were together with the Royal Family (and Camilla) under the same roof. William, longing to heal the rift between the two sides of his family, had insisted that the Spencers not only be invited to the party, but that they also be asked to spend the night at Windsor Castle. The only Spencer to decline William's invitation was his other granny, Frances Shand Kydd, who by now was ill with Parkinson's disease and living as a virtual recluse on the remote Scottish island of Seil.

For all the attention to detail in planning the Prince's $800,000 birthday bash, no one could have anticipated what was to take place when William took the stage just before midnight to thank everyone for coming. The Prince was in the middle of his speech when a man disguised as Osama Bin Laden in drag—complete with beard, turban, sunglasses, strapless pink satin evening gown, and red high-heeled shoes—bounded onto the stage and grabbed the microphone out of his hand. As the stunned Prince tried to get the attention of his bodyguards, gate-crashing "Comedy Ter-rorist" Aaron Barschak began singing, "A beard on my cheek would be quite fundamental . . ." to the tune of "Diamonds Are a Girl's Best Friend."

The Queen, convinced that William's mischievous brother was playing another one of his practical jokes, turned to her husband. "That will be Harry," she said as she watched Barschak kiss William on both cheeks and shout "We all love you!"

It was a full minute before the royal bodyguards—suddenly aware that this was not part of the planned festivities—intercepted Barschak as he left the stage. Aware that many in the audience still mistakenly believed the intruder was Harry, Wills quipped, "I didn't know that my brother could do an accent like that!"

Her Majesty, according to one guest, was "positively livid" at this latest in a long series of security lapses. As it turned out, Barschak had crashed the party by simply climbing up a tree and over a stone wall—all the while lugging a backpack that contained his street clothes. Moreover, prior to the party he had marched up and down outside the entrance to Windsor Castle in full drag and fake beard, shouting "Happy birthday! Out of Africa, I am out of this world!" Periodically, he would raise his dress to reveal a second black beard covering his genitals. "I present," he then declared to shocked onlookers, "the real *hair* to the throne!" At one point, Barschak was even photographed chatting amiably with a uniformed police officer.

William, apparently unfazed by the incident, continued partying until 4 A.M. But Charles wasted no time demanding to know how an intruder could, in front of a small army of uniformed and armed undercover officers, talk his way to within a few feet of his son. "My God! What if he had been a suicide bomber?" Charles later asked Camilla when they returned to Clarence House. "He could have wiped us all out." Every member of the Royal Family, in fact, could have been killed, with the exception of Prince Edward, who was on an official visit to Canada. "Can you imagine?" asked an incredulous Prince of Wales. "Edward would have become king. *Edward!* Just incredible . . ."

At the Queen's urging, an embarrassed Scotland Yard chief Sir John Stevens and David Veness, the assistant commissioner in charge of Royal Protection and the security squads, launched an immediate investigation into the incident. In a masterpiece of understatement, one senior Scotland Yard official conceded, "Although Barschak may have been mingling among other guests as he moved to his 'target,' dressed as he was in pink, with a turban and false beard, he should have struck a discordant note."

No one was more surprised at how easy it had been to get past security than Barschak himself. Pretending to be a guest who had had too much to drink and lost his way, the intruder had no trouble convincing police that he belonged there. "It was unbelievably simple. I'm amazed I got in," he later recalled. "Royal security is not at all what I expected. . . . I didn't have to say anything. The police immediately started giving me directions. I was astounded that no one asked for my name or any ID, or why, if I had just popped out from the party, was I carrying a bulging rucksack [backpack]. I could have had anything in it."

There was nothing left for Sir John Stevens to do but apologize to the Royal Family for the "appalling breach of security . . . which should not have happened whatever the circumstances." There would be other appalling breaches of security, but the day after his party William was more concerned with overcoming the effects of a serious hangover. Astride his new $165,000 Argentine polo pony—a birthday gift from Papa—at the Beaufort Polo Club, Wills somehow managed to score within seconds of joining his father and brother on the field.

The pony was in lieu of the gift William had been angling for all year—a high-powered 750 cc off-roader motorcycle or a new Triumph 600 cc Daytona to replace his comparatively tame Yamaha 600 trail bike. "I've dropped many hints to my father about pretty much everything," Wills said before his birthday. "He'll do the paternal thing and decide what he thinks is best."

Although Papa had given William the Yamaha to replace his Kawasaki, he viewed Wills's passion for speed in general and powerful motorcycles in particular with growing concern. "Riding a motorbike can be dangerous," William conceded, "but so can lots of things. It is a risk, but as long as you've had sufficient and thorough training, you should be OK. You've just got to be aware of what you're doing. My father is concerned about the fact that I'm into motorbikes but he doesn't want to keep me wrapped up in cotton wool. So you might as well live if you're going to live. I don't know what it is about bikes, but I've always had a passion about them since I was small."

What appealed to Wills most about owning a motorcycle was

that it enabled him to maintain some degree of anonymity while at the same time experiencing a bond with other bikers. "It does help being anonymous with my motorcycle helmet on— it enables me to relax," William mused. "I just enjoy everything about motorbikes and the camaraderie that comes with them."

Most important, it allowed the Prince to indulge his passion for speed. Riding alone on the grounds at Highgrove or along Gloucestershire's winding country roads, William especially enjoyed pulling up alongside cars at intersections and, while waiting for the light to change, looking over at the other drivers. "They have absolutely no idea it's me beneath the helmet, so they just behave naturally," he said. "It's a great feeling for someone like me—not being recognized." There were also times when Wills pulled up along other bikers and, if there was no one else around and there was a clear stretch of road ahead, raced them head-to-head.

Wills's penchant for driving fast extended to cars. His bodyguards often found themselves struggling to keep up as the Prince, singing along to Eminem at the top of his lungs, tore through the English countryside in his VW Golf. "I imagine my father would go absolutely bananas," William allowed, "if he saw me driving, blaring music out the windows."

One aristocrat who did indeed go "absolutely bananas" when he encountered William was Charles's friend and Highgrove neighbor Earl Bathurst. The seventy-six-year-old earl was driving his white Land Rover along a narrow gravel road on his estate when suddenly William roared past him on the left at more than double the speed limit.

"He went on the grass to overtake me," Bathurst recalled. "I didn't know who the hell it was. I thought he was just a young yob [hooligan] driving a rather crummy VW Golf which anybody might have. I was very annoyed."

When the earl blared his horn and flashed his lights, William floored the VW and zoomed past. Bathurst, enraged, gave chase. "There were clouds of dust," the earl recalled. "I thought he was bound to stop—but not a bit of it." Taking a shortcut through the trees, Bathurst managed to pull up in front of William, blocking his path.

It was then that a Vauxhall Omega pulled up and two men—William's bodyguards—jumped out to confront the earl. A shouting match ensued. "They thought I was trying to take him out," Bathurst said. "I could have been shot."

While Bathurst stood outside his vehicle arguing with William's bodyguards, William sped off. "He just drove on round us," the earl said. "It wasn't very civil, to be honest."

The Prince of Wales had long worried about William's lead foot, but he drew the line at road rage—particularly when a fellow member of the aristocracy was involved. The next morning, Charles called Bathurst to apologize. "Young will be young, but I'm afraid they've got to learn," sputtered the earl. Charles, he continued, "Must tell his son to abide by the rules like everybody else. What would have happened if I had driven like that on Windsor Park? I would have ended up in the Tower!"

For his part, William was upset at his father for apologizing on his behalf. "No one apologizes for me," the young Prince angrily told an old Eton buddy. "I would have apologized if I felt what I did warranted an apology—but it didn't." Privately, he dismissed the incident as "silly."

Over the next few months, however, both William and Harry continued to push the proverbial envelope. In September 2003, both Princes attended a wild twenty-fifth birthday party for British TV sports broadcaster Natalie Pinkham at Purple, the notoriously hedonistic nightclub on Fulham Road in London's Chelsea district. While a soused William chatted up several girls at the same time, the birthday girl sat in Harry's lap. Within full view of everyone, Harry cupped Pinkham's right breast in his hand as he nuzzled her. It would be three years before photographs of the tawdry scene taken by another partygoer would be leaked to the press, causing yet another in a seemingly endless stream of royal scandals.

For the time being, however, the young Princes came to view Purple as a kind of safe haven. The night before he was to em- bark on a three-month gap-year stint working on an Australian cattle ranch, Harry was treated by his brother to a night of drink- ing—first at London's trendy Sofa So Bar (owned by the Princes' former friend and minder Captain Mark Dyer of the Welsh Guards) before moving on to Purple shortly before midnight. While Harry seemed uncharacteristically in control, nursing a sin- gle bottle of beer, William spent four hours straight drinking and dancing with a succession of girls on the main stage.

"At one point," said club patron Sue Thompson, William "was going flat out for about an hour, dancing like a lunatic with this arms flailing . . . doing his sexy moves and sweating so much his light blue shirt was dark." According to Thompson, William was "so wiped out by the end of the night" that he lay slumped in a corner with his friends desperately trying to get him to his feet. "He had to be literally carried off."

After Harry's departure for Down Under, William continued to frequent Purple, paying the fifteen-pound entrance fee at the door before spending the rest of the night partying with his friends in the club's roped-off VIP area. "Whenever the club had its 'Dirty

Disco' theme nights, you could find Prince William there," said one Purple regular. "Sometimes he would sit in a corner and just drink, but most of the time he'd get up on the dance floor with some half-dressed girl and just go crazy."

Not all of the young women he hooked up with at Purple and other London clubs were as discreet as Kate Middleton. After William spent one evening in September dancing and "snogging" (necking) with Elouise Blair, the nineteen-year-old model's mother went public with the story. "She would like to see him again because she really, really enjoyed his company," Blair's mom pleaded. "And if it happens, well, we'll just see. . . ." Needless to say, it didn't.

The following month, a twenty-nine-year-old single mother named Solange Jacobs spent a similar night at the club with William. When she learned a week later that William and Kate Middleton were purportedly a couple, Jacobs told one tabloid that "William has too much of a roving eye to ever settle down. The way he acted with me he didn't seem to be in love with anyone else," she sniped. "He also chatted with a dancer and eyed up a girl in the VIP area. You wouldn't have guessed he was seeing Kate. Wills looked very much on the prowl, so Kate better watch out if she doesn't want to be made a fool of."

Jacobs also claimed that William took her number and joked that he was going to take her to a party at Buckingham Palace. "Wills made no mention of a girlfriend," Jacobs claimed. "I don't think Kate will be too pleased that he chatted me up. Anyway, I wish Kate the best of luck. She might need it."

Jacobs's warning, as well as the other stories of Wills's overtly flirtatious behavior, did not fall on deaf ears. The next time he showed up at Purple, Kate made sure to tag along. "I believe William loves me and would never do anything to intentionally hurt me," she told one of her closest childhood friends. "But it's that family. . . ."

"That family" would come in for criticism from an unlikely quarter in late October 2003 when Charles's former spinmeister, Mark Bolland, publicly predicted the monarchy would fall unless the royals changed their ways. The warning came just after the final collapse of the Burrell case, and a direct plea to the butler from William and Harry to halt any more revelations about their mother. "They are blissfully unaware of real people's problems," Bolland wrote in the *Daily Mail*. "The Royal Family will at last reap the bitter harvest from the seeds their courtiers are now sowing with their 'do nothing, say nothing' strategy. The line between invisibility and irrelevance is no line at all."

The key to survival, Bolland argued, was to "learn lessons from Diana—it is still not too late. Why don't they build their own memorial to her? Encourage William to honor his mother's memory in a public way? Why not just embrace what good she represented and her dynamic force for change? To do that," he went on, "would require . . . an understanding of the way a modern, democratic society works in an age of global communication—all forces they are frightened of. Almost as much as they are frightened of the ghost of Diana."

Ten days after Bolland's public attack on his former bosses, scandal—and the ghost of Diana—struck again. When he returned from an official trip to India in early November, the Prince of Wales was forced to confront more damaging revelations from below-stairs. A year after George Smith charged that he had been raped by one of Charles's senior servants and had witnessed "a member of the Royal Family" in a compromising position, a newspaper was about to expose Charles as the royal in question.

Before the *Mail on Sunday* could go to press with the story, however, the Prince's former aide Michael Fawcett obtained a court
order blocking publication. In a secret videotaped interview,
Diana had complained that Charles and Fawcett were "too close.
What can one do when your husband is in an unhealthy relationship with a servant?" She also claimed the two men appeared
"uncomfortable" and "uneasy" when she disturbed them unexpectedly one evening in the Prince's room at St. James's Palace.
A decade younger than Charles and married with two children,
Fawcett had quit his $150,000 job as the Prince's valet eight
months earlier over the scandal involving the sale of royal gifts.
Fawcett's reported $800,000 severance package—plus a $160,000
freelance contract and assistance to purchase a house that added up
to another $750,000—had provoked outrage when it was leaked
to the press. Now a party planner, Fawcett was still frequently employed by Charles to arrange royal events.

Fawcett's court injunction did little to stop other publications
from running with their version of the story. IS CHARLES BISEXUAL?
asked the front-page *News of the World* headline. Mark Bolland's
reply—"Emphatically NOT"—was in smaller type. Unfortunately, in making his denial, Bolland revealed for the first time that
none other than Charles's private secretary, Sir Michael Peat, had
once asked him if he thought Charles was indeed bisexual.

Rushing back to Highgrove, Charles met with his advisors—
the most important of these being his mistress—to devise a strategy to salvage his reputation. Over strong objections from Camilla,
who suggested ignoring the rumors altogether, Charles took the
initiative and issued a statement conceding he was indeed the un-
named royal at the center of the scandal. "In recent days, there have
been media reports concerning an allegation that a former royal

household employee witnessed an incident some years ago involving a senior member of the Royal Family," Sir Michael Peat said. "I just want to make it entirely clear, even though I can't refer to the specifics of the allegation, that it's totally untrue and without a shred of substance. The speculation needs to come to an end. The incident which the former employee claims to have witnessed did not take place."

One of Charles's aides explained that Charles authorized the statement to offset the "drip, drip of innuendo, rumor, gossip. That's why we went on the offensive. We were sitting with a sword over our heads." But the bizarre admission had turned the steady drip into a torrent of sordid headlines. ME AND THE SERVANT . . . IT'S ALL LIES—CHARLES' ASTONISHING DENIAL screamed the *Mirror*. CHARLES ON THE RACK—CRISIS GROWS OVER "WHAT THE SERVANT SAW" read the headline in the *Daily Mail*.

Ironically, just as the rumors concerning Charles's sexuality reached a crescendo, the royal most widely suspected of being gay— Prince Edward—became a father for the first time. Edward was on a state visit to Mauritius when his wife, Sophie, the Countess of Wessex, was rushed to the hospital for an emergency Caesarean one month early. The baby girl, weighing just four pounds nine ounces, would later be christened Lady Louise Mountbatten-Windsor.

Once again, Charles watched as his standing with the British public spiraled downward in the wake of another sordid sex scandal. A poll taken after the slew of headlines speculating about his sexuality showed that only 39 percent of Britons now wanted Charles to succeed his mother; a majority wanted William as their next monarch.

No one would have been more pleased than Diana, who had often said she wanted William and not Charles to be next on the throne. Since this latest royal scandal had, like so many of the others, originated with something Diana had either written down or recorded, it seemed to some as if the Princess was orchestrating her ex-husband's downfall from the grave. Charles, described by one former servant as a "first-class whinger [whiner]," cried on his mistress's shoulder about the impact Diana was still having on his life. "My God," Charles complained to Camilla within earshot of the staff, "will it never end? Will I ever be free of her?"

For Camilla, the notion that Charles was anything but heterosexual seemed, in her words, "laughable." This was, after all, the same Charles who had slept with dozens of would-be princesses before presumably settling once and for all on her. "She had to deal with Diana and Kanga Tryon and that Canadian girl [Janet Jenkins] and a few others," observed a fellow member of the Beaufort Hunt Club who had known Camilla for over thirty years. "Camilla is still jealous of other women, and not entirely convinced that he is entirely trustworthy when it comes to the opposite sex. But men? I doubt if the possibility ever crossed her mind."

Charles persevered. On November 14, 2003—the day he turned fifty-five—the Prince was touring a retirement community near Highgrove when staff members and residents appeared with a cake and began singing "Happy Birthday." Charles could only manage a wan smile. "We wanted," said National Benevolent Trust president Lady Emily Blatch, "to cheer him up on his birthday." That night, Charles holed up at Highgrove with Camilla and William.

Purchased in 1980 from Member of Parliament Maurice Macmillan, son of former Prime Minister Harold Macmillan, Highgrove was now a world unto itself. Behind its walls, Charles had created an environment that served as both sanctuary and laboratory. It was here that he dabbled in animal husbandry and experimented with organic gardening. The Prince took special pride in his herd of black sheep and his organically grown onions, lettuce, and brussels sprouts.

The house itself—a three-story, stone-walled Georgian manse shaded by an ancient cedar of Lebanon—boasted four art-filled reception rooms, nine bedrooms, eight bathrooms, and the nursery wing, once occupied by William and Harry. Yet Charles was proudest of Highgrove's gardens, which he personally designed.

"I had absolutely no experience of gardening or farming," Charles recalled, "and the only trees I had planted had been official ones in very official holes." By the time he finished, the gardens covered twenty-five acres and were divided into "rooms": the Tulip Walk, the Southern Hemisphere Garden, the Sundial Garden, Thyme Walk, the Terrace Garden, the Wild Flower Meadow, the Stumpery, the Autumn Walk, the Walled Garden, and the Carpet Garden inspired by a Turkish carpet.

A tree house built for William and Harry in 1988 could be seen from the Stumpery, an arched pathway that led to two small Greek temples. In the Arboretum stood the Sanctuary, a small private chapel Charles had constructed to mark the millennium. It was here that the Prince came every day to meditate and pray before a large stone with a cross carved into it. Forced to contend with yet another sordid scandal, Charles was spending quite a lot of time alone in his tiny garden chapel. No one else, not even Camilla, was permitted to enter the Sanctuary. "Otherwise," Charles explained half-jokingly to a weekend guest, "it wouldn't be a sanctuary, now, would it?"

Blissfully unaware of the tumult at home, Harry was in Sydney, ecstatically cheering England's narrow victory over Wales in the Rugby World Cup. It was pointed out by resentful Welshmen that

Harry had apparently forgotten that his father was in fact the Prince of Wales and that it was simply bad manners to root for one side over the other. "This silly young man," said journalist Stephen Glover, "thinks it's right to celebrate an English victory over Wales. How would you feel if you were Welsh? Disgusted? Broken-hearted?" Harry came in for more criticism when he later cheered England's defeat of Australia. "Harry is a Prince of the United Kingdom and of the Commonwealth," Glover added, "and some-one should tell him that includes Australia too."

Harry spent most of his days Down Under working as a "jacka-roo"—one of Australia's famous ranch hands—on Tooloombilla Station, the 40,000-acre Queensland spread owned by Diana's friends Annie and Noel Hill. At first, Harry was so upset by the throng of reporters who swarmed around him that he threatened to cut short his trip and return to England. But once the press agreed to back off, Harry quickly settled into outback life, work-ing from sunup until sundown rounding up cattle and mending fences in the blistering 100-degree heat—a job for which he was paid $160 a week.

Once his three-month stint at Tooloombilla Station was over, Harry headed for Queensland's Sunshine coast to frolic on the beach with several bikini-clad locals. "He was having the time of his life," said a local surfer, twenty-one-year-old Robin Mayes. "He was a handsome, well-toned young bloke and full of energy—just the type the girls go for."

Nor was Harry wanting for female companionship on his so-journs to Sydney, where he partied until dawn at nightspots like the London Tavern Hotel and Hugo's Lounge, a celebrity haunt located above a strip club. While his ever-present bodyguards kept their distance, Harry, in the words of one club-goer, "flirted with every pretty girl in sight. When I went outside for a smoke he had this beautiful blonde pressed up against a wall and they were getting carried away. . . . It was too embarrassing to watch so I went back inside."

At least one of the women who had been the object of Harry's advances worried about what was really behind all the carousing. "I get the sense that he feels awfully insignificant—that he believes his brother is more important than he is and he is sad about it," said Suzannah Harvey, the model he had pursued so avidly at the Beaufort Christmas Ball. "Partying is perhaps some kind of escape for Harry. I feel quite sorry for him."

Several senior aides at Buckingham Palace shared Harvey's concern. "He needs to be properly guided," one said, "otherwise he could go off the rails. Prince Harry has simple tastes and a low boredom threshold, and when he is not being committed to something serious, his thoughts turn to drink and girls and he smokes endlessly."

Amid all the talk of gay rapes at Highgrove and princely hijinks in the outback, few were aware that two members of the Royal Family were facing serious health crises. William, who had spent two days whitewater rafting down the Nile during another month-long adventure in Africa, returned to St. Andrews in late October complaining of severe stomach pains. Blood tests revealed that he was suffering from bilharzia, a parasitic disease that can lead to seizures, paralysis, and fatal liver damage. William was promptly treated with massive doses of the drug praziquantel, which is also marketed as a veterinary medicine, and would be given a clean bill of health by the end of the year.

Meanwhile, Granny was in the throes of a cancer scare at Buckingham Palace. Just after Christmas 2003, the Queen quietly slipped into a London hospital for routine knee surgery and to have suspicious lesions removed from her face. The operation to remove cartilage from her knee went smoothly, but the procedure on her face left the Queen with deep scars above and below her left eye and along her nose.

The Queen was, in fact, diagnosed with a highly curable, non-life-threatening form of skin cancer. But when she hobbled out of King Edward VII hospital with the help of a cane, onlookers were shocked at her appearance. "The Queen looked all of her seventy-seven years," said a reporter for the *Mail on Sunday.* "She gazed around, rheumy eyed, as if disoriented. All at once, it seems, the Queen has become a frail, vulnerable old lady."

As it turned out, Her Majesty would completely recover within a matter of two weeks. The same could not be said for the monarchy's reputation. Even as Charles waited for the gossip concerning his sexual orientation to cool down, French authorities released six thousand pages of documents backing up their conclusion that Diana and Dodi Fayed were the victims of a simple drunk-driving accident. Yet, given the fact that Diana herself had predicted in writing that her assassination would be made to look like a car crash, doubts persisted. In late December 2003—six years after the accident that took the life of the world's most celebrated woman and her lover—Michael Burgess, now Coroner to the Queen, finally announced that he would be opening his own formal inquest into Diana's death.

If there had been any hope of putting an end to the conspiracy theories, it vanished with Burgess's announcement of a formal inquest. Scotland Yard investigators would plod along for the next four years, reviewing evidence and interviewing witnesses—all the while keeping alive the possibility that a smoking gun was about to be uncovered.

At their father's urging, William focused on his studies at St. Andrews while royal strategists tried to come up with productive ways for Harry to spend his two gap years before entering Sandhurst. In hopes of forging a new image for the party boy prince, St. James's Palace announced that Harry would be traveling in Diana's footsteps by working with young African mothers and children suffering from AIDS. His destination: the southern African nation of Lesotho, where 30 percent of the population—more than 360,000 people—suffered from AIDS and the average life expectancy was thirty-six.

But first, of course, Harry joined William at China White, a London nightclub popular with footballers, pop stars, and fashionistas. More cautious in the wake of the scandal plaguing Papa, William ducked out early and asked his brother to join him. True to form, Harry stayed until 3 A.M. drinking vodka, dancing, and necking with a buxom blonde who managed to run the gauntlet of bodyguards and deposit herself on the Prince's lap. As it turned out, Lauren Pope had posed topless for a British tabloid and was once mentioned in passing during a rape scandal involving several professional soccer players. (The alleged rape supposedly occurred in the hotel room of Pope's then boyfriend, and the charges were eventually dropped.)

Even the slightest whiff of scandal regarding Harry was enough to send his handlers into a panic. As they weighed how to counter stories about his most recent antics with a topless model, Harry embarked on a brief liaison that, even by the standards of this generation of royals, defied imagination. Her name was Camilla Simon, and her mother, Kate Simon, was the on-again, off-again mistress of the man perhaps most responsible for Harry's inner torment. His name: James Hewitt.

After all these years, they're just
happy to breathe the same air.
—Charles's friend
Patti Palmer-Tomkinson,
on his affair with Camilla

Rottweiler here!
—Camilla, jokingly
answering the phone

7

It was just after 1 A.M. on February 10, 2004, at Boujis, another smart South Kensington club owned by the young Princes' former aide and longtime friend Captain Mark "Marco" Dyer of the Welsh Guards. Downstairs in the VIP section, Harry sat in a booth, downing his fifth cranberry-flavored vodka. Nestled beside him was twenty-three-year-old Camilla Simon, lithesome blond daughter of Monsoon fashion mogul Peter Simon and his ex-wife Kate. For two years, Kate Simon had had a steamy relationship with Diana's former lover James Hewitt and reportedly bankrolled his lavish lifestyle to the tune of $800,000.

Simon and Hewitt had split a year earlier, but Harry was nonetheless curious about the riding instructor who stole his mother's heart and then betrayed her with a tell-all book. Over the course of the evening, said one member of their party, "Harry asked Camilla [Simon] what she thought about Hewitt, how he treated her mother and her, if she knew what he was up to now."

Harry's two bodyguards sat separately—one at a table and the other at the bar—sipping water and lemonade and, according to one waitress, "looking very much out of place." At one point, an increasingly soused Harry blurted out that all the rumors about Hewitt being his biological father were "total shit." Still, said one of Simon's friends, "It seemed obvious that he must have his own doubts—or why would he bring it up when no one else did, and why would he become so angry? No one else takes it seriously. Why does Prince Harry?"

Shortly after 2:30 A.M., Harry's Royal Protection guards helped him up the stairs of the club, out the front door, and into a waiting car. Camilla Simon, who seemed more subdued after speaking with Harry, stayed another hour before leaving. "They have a rather special bond," said her friend. "Both of their mothers fell for Hewitt. Quite a sad little club they belong to. . . ."

Harry was still licking his wounds the following week when journalist Carol Sarler issued a blistering attack on his behavior in the *Daily Express*. Under the headline SPOILED AND LAZY HARRY IS ONE OF A KIND, Sarler described him as a "national disgrace" for the "drinking, drugging, the yobbing [hooliganism]." She also claimed Harry "rarely lifted a finger unless it's to feel up a cheap tart in a nightclub." As for Harry's plans to help AIDS victims in Africa, Sarler said he only "reluctantly agreed to spend a bit of the trip staring at poor people. He has never," she continued, "done anything because it was the right thing to do."

Described by one aide as "apoplectic with rage," Charles ordered his new communications secretary, Patrick Harverson, to launch an unprecedented counterattack. Sarler's comments were, Harverson complained, "beyond the pale. This is very strong stuff and completely wrong—an unfair and unfounded attack on

Prince Harry's character that shows very little understanding of him as a person."

Once again, Harry was deeply humiliated by the growing public perception of him as spoiled, self-indulgent, and out of control. The next eight weeks doing volunteer work in the South African enclave of Lesotho would, he hoped, repair at least some of the damage. Why Lesotho? "Before this, it wasn't even on the map," he said. "I never heard of it, anyway."

An ITV documentary crew accompanied the Prince to Africa and recorded him digging ditches, helping to build a bridge, laying the foundation for a health clinic, hauling water, and—most movingly—playing with AIDS–infected orphans. At one point, Harry's eyes welled with tears as he cradled a ten-month-old girl who had been raped by her HIV-positive stepfather. (Witch doctors tell men infected with the virus that they will be cured if they have sex with a child—the younger the better.)

"I've always wanted to do this," Harry said, recalling the days when Diana took her sons to AIDS clinics late at night and without media fanfare. "I believe I've got a lot of my mother in me, basically, and I just think she'd want us to do this—me and my brother. . . . I want to carry on my mother's legacy as much as I can. I don't want to take over from her because I never will, I don't think anyone can, but I want to try and carry on to make her proud." One African who believed Harry had done just that was Lesotho's Prince Seeiso. "When he is old and gray," Prince Seeiso said, "he can look back and say he had an impact."

Even as Harry cradled AIDS babies in Africa, more royal bombshells were exploding at home. For the first time, journalist Andrew

Morton released the secret recordings Diana had made in 1991 for his landmark book *Diana: Her True Story*. In the tapes, Diana talked for the first time about Charles's adulterous affair with Camilla and the torment that drove her to bulimia and several suicide attempts.

At the same time, videotapes made by Diana's voice coach Peter Settelen in 1992 and 1993—tapes in which she talked frankly about, among other things, her sex life with Charles—were about to be broadcast on American television. "There was never quite a requirement for it from him," she said. "Once every three weeks about, and I kept thinking it followed a pattern. He used to see his lady [Camilla] once every three weeks before we got married."

As if that wasn't enough, photographs taken of Diana in the moments after her fatal crash in Paris were also broadcast on U.S. television. Earl Spencer claimed to be "shocked and sickened" by the airing of the photographs, which simply showed Diana slumped in the wreckage, her eyes closed. William and Harry did not see the grainy still photo of their dying mother, taken by a paparazzo inside the Alma Tunnel. But they were, in Charles's words, "deeply upset" that the photos had been shown publicly. Earl Spencer, speaking on behalf of Diana's family, said the airing of the pictures left them "shocked and sickened."

Harry, finishing up his work in Africa, was happy to be out of the line of fire. "Luckily, I've been out here—but I feel bad because my father and my brother have been taking the stick instead."

What clearly bothered Harry most was the salacious material on the newly released tapes. "It's just a shame, it's a shame that, after all the good she's done, even this far on, people can't bring out the good in her. They can't remember the good. All they want to bring out is the bad stuff. I mean, bad news sells."

As for those who believed that his trip to Africa was nothing more than a bald-faced attempt at an image makeover, Harry could only shrug his shoulders. "I've always been like this," he argued. "This is my side that no one gets to see. I am not going to take a camera with me when I am trying to help out in different countries. . . . Though I believe I am no one special, I can do things. . . .

"I'd love to let it wash over me, but I can't—I don't think anyone can," Harry said of the press accounts that depicted him as nothing more than a spoiled party animal. "It is hard. But I'm not out here for a sympathy vote."

Nor was he likely to get it. Just before returning home in late April, Harry was photographed cavorting, beer bottle in hand, on a beach at the exclusive Camps Bay resort near Cape Town, South Africa. "I can't control what other people think," he said after one tabloid ran the photos under the headline PRINCE FEELS NO PAIN— HARRY'S JUST WILD ABOUT PARTYING. "There are always going to be people who just want to make my family look bad."

Indeed, a week later Harry was again captured on film, this time kissing an old acquaintance, Cirencester Park Polo Club assistant manager Jo Davies. The photo ran in newspapers around the world alongside Davies holding polo balls over her exposed breasts. That shot, along with one of her dressed as a dominatrix about to crack the whip over two shirtless polo players, was for a calendar to benefit the club's cancer charity. Jo was Miss April.

For all his carrying-on, Harry was, in fact, a Prince in love. He had actually met Chelsy Davy two years earlier, when she was a student at Cheltenham Ladies College near Highgrove. Chelsy was the Zimbabwe-born daughter of a former Miss Rhodesia, Beverley Davy, and Charles Davy, wealthy part-owner of a 1,300-square-mile safari park that charged hunters over $1,000 a day to shoot at its wildlife. (In addition, there was a "trophy fee" of $3,700 for every bagged lion and $8,500 for every elephant.)

After graduating from Cheltenham, Chelsy returned home to study art at the University of Cape Town. It was there, while stopping off in Cape Town to visit Chelsy on the way to Lesotho, that, Harry would later tell friends, the two fell in love. While sitting by the fire during a camping trip in Botswana, Harry "couldn't stop talking about her," said fellow traveler Gary Robinson. "He was quite besotted."

No wonder. Blond, tanned, and curvaceous, Chelsy had a fondness for low-riding jeans, halter tops, and clunky African jewelry. She shared Harry's passion for the outdoors and his disdain for formality, and his fondness for Sex on the Beach—a concoction consisting of, among other things, peach schnapps, vodka, cranberry juice, and grapefruit juice. "Chelsy is the most down-to-earth person you will ever meet," said a Cheltenham classmate who was also a frequent visitor to "Club H," the boys' basement hangout at Highgrove. "The rest of us fantasized about marrying either William or Harry, but not her. Chelsy has no airs at all. She rides bareback and she loves animals. . . . she's just a country girl at heart."

William's romance with Kate Middleton, meanwhile, was becoming more and more serious even as he seemingly grew less and less obsessed about keeping it under wraps. When he went on his annual skiing vacation at Klosters with Papa, Kate was invited to tag along. Still, when Britain's *Sun* ran paparazzi shots of Wills and Kate cozying up on the slopes, Buckingham Palace issued a firm rebuke and banned the paper's photographers from official upcoming photo ops of both William and Harry.

Later that spring, both boys were out of the country—
William on a geography field trip in Norway and Harry performing gap-year duties in Botswana—when Charles called
them with the news that their grandmother had passed away.
William, thinking at first that the Queen had died, nearly passed
out—until he realized that it was Diana's mother, Frances Shand
Kydd, who had finally succumbed to degenerative brain disease
at the age of sixty-eight.

Both royal grandchildren rushed back to the United Kingdom
to attend the funeral in the Highlands town of Oban, near Shand
Kydd's Scottish home. Prince Charles and the Queen were pointedly excluded. Instead, only Spencers—the "blood family" that
Earl Spencer had spoken of in his moving eulogy for Diana—were
invited to attend.

The Princess and her mother were estranged at the time of
Diana's death, and it had been years since any of the Spencers—
Shand Kydd included—had really been a part of the boys' lives.
Yet William and Harry, who entered St. Columba's Church with
heads bowed in the pouring rain, were still shaken by the loss of
the grandmother they called "Gran Fran."

Inside St. Columba's, William gripped the lectern and faltered
slightly as he read a passage of Scripture. Later, they sat grim-
faced as their uncle Earl Spencer described his mother as "a woman
who was afraid of nothing and of nobody, somebody not interested in convention but in truth and fun. She believed in equal-
ity and decency and not time for self-pity." Conceding that there
had been "tensions" between Diana and Shand Kydd, Spencer
pointed out that "the true love Diana had for her mother was evident in her will. She left my mother executor and principal guardian
of her sons."

Indeed, Shand Kydd had also included the boys in her will, leaving them roughly one-quarter of her $4 million estate. Adding this to the roughly $35 million Diana had left them, William and Harry now each had a minimum of $18 million in the bank—this in addition to the hundreds of millions of dollars in assets William and, to a much smaller extent, Harry stood to share in as each assumed their royal duties.

In yet another odd twist for a woman who had lost two of her children—Shand Kydd gave birth to a son who died in infancy—the naked body of Diana's stepbrother, the forty-nine-year-old writer Adam Shand Kydd, was found that spring in a rented flat in Phnom Penh. Cambodian officials concluded that Adam, the eldest son of Frances's second husband, Peter Shand Kydd, had died of a Valium overdose.

The British coroner, however, remained unconvinced. Because Adam had no history of drug abuse and—once again—the embalming process done in Cambodia had made any conclusive test results impossible, no cause of death was determined. The verdict, rendered just weeks after Frances's funeral, merely added one more mystery to the growing Diana lore.

The funeral of Charles's former mother-in-law underscored the rift between the Windsors and the Spencers. Three weeks later, at the dedication of the Diana Fountain in Hyde Park, the Queen was determined not to let Earl Spencer once again claim the emotional high ground. "I believe," she told a senior palace aide, "we learned our lesson seven years ago." Knowing that the Spencers would attend in full force, the Queen insisted that this time Charles and the boys be there—regardless of whether William was studying for exams or Harry was eager to return to Africa. Only one de facto family member was explicitly barred from attending: Camilla.

With both families looking on, the Queen first defended the decision not to commemorate the Princess with a statue. "To present a likeness seemed at best unnecessary for someone whose image continues to exert such a fascination the world over," she said. "To find some other way to capture her spirit has been the challenge."

Acknowledging that "Diana's tragic death held the attention of the world," the Queen also recalled the days that followed when "we as a nation came to terms with the loss, united by an extraordinary sense of shock, grief, and sadness." Understandably, she omitted any reference to the anger resulting from her perceived indifference at the time, and the constitutional crisis she created by *not* publicly sharing in her countrymen's grief.

Praising Diana as a "remarkable human being," the Queen praised her "drive to empathize with those in difficulty, hardship, or distress, her willingness to embrace a new cause, her shrewd ability to size up all those she met"—all of which "allowed her not only to touch people's lives but also to change them." Her Majesty also conceded that, for those who knew Diana as "sister, wife, mother, or daughter-in-law" there "were difficult times. But memories mellow with the passing of the years. I remember especially," she added, turning to William and Harry, "the happiness she gave to my two grandsons."

Afterward, as Spencers and Windsors mingled amiably with one another, the Queen walked up to the man who had verbally eviscerated the Royal Family at Diana's funeral. "I hope," she said to Earl Spencer, "you feel satisfied by that."

"Yes, Ma'am," Spencer replied with a smile as he bowed his head. "More than satisfied."

While the Queen mended fences with her former in-laws, Harry and William worked the crowd like seasoned politicians.

When a middle-aged American tourist called him gorgeous, Wills shot back, "You're not bad yourself." Then, after a young mother took a photo of William chatting with her nine-year-old daughter, the woman shrieked, "I've got a photo of the future King of England!"

"Well," said William, turning to look behind him, "where is he, then?"

"Both boys have the same magic that their mother had," writer Peter Archer said. "It's amazing how they are able to so easily connect with people. You'd never suspect all the pressures to which they are almost constantly subjected."

The job had its compensations, however. That summer, the relationship between William and Kate continued to heat up as they vacationed together on the sun-drenched island of Rodrigues just east of Mauritius in the Indian Ocean. There the couple snorkeled and scuba dived among the island's spectacular coral reefs, explored Rodrigues's hilly terrain on motorbikes, and each evening joined a small circle of friends for drinks at the cabana bar. Kate and the Prince now had nicknames for each other: she was Kat, or sometimes Kitten. He was "Big Willy"—a not-so-subtle use of a British colloquialism for the male sex organ.

It was only a matter of weeks, however, before there was trouble in paradise. No sooner did they return home than Wills and Kate began squabbling about his planned trip to visit old flame Jecca Craig in Kenya. Despite his assurances to Kate that there was nothing between them, she begged him not to go. "She felt threatened and humiliated," said a member of their inner circle at St. Andrews. "It was one thing to never be publicly acknowledged, but quite another to have someone else bandied about in the press as the woman in his life. She knew that would happen all over again if he went to see Jecca Craig."

After Kate and William were spotted at St. Andrews screaming at each other in the front seat of his parked VW Golf, William relented and canceled his trip to Africa. But tongues began wagging when Jecca and William turned up at the wedding of Wills's old flame Davina Duckworth-Chad that September, and again two months later when Wills and Jecca were at the wedding of his old pal Edward van Cutsem and Lady Tamara Grosvenor. In both instances, Middleton was nowhere to be seen.

To further complicate matters, Wills was now also spending time with Anna Sloan, an American who had shared some of the Prince's classes at St. Andrews. Shortly after they met in the fall of 2001, Sloan's millionaire father was killed in a shooting accident— a loss that, in light of the violent death of William's mother, drew them closer together. Now, three years later in the late summer of 2004, he was accepting Sloan's long-standing invitation to stay at her family's 350-acre farm outside Nashville.

For a week, William lounged by the pool with Sloan—yet another dazzling blonde—went to the movies, and prowled the local mall like any American his age. Wills was delighted to be able to go wherever he wanted largely unrecognized. "Every so often I see someone's eyes sort of get big," he recalled, "and then that 'Oh, no, it's not him. . . . What on earth would he be doing here?' look."

The Prince also loved the nickname given to him by Anna Sloan's young Tennessee friends: the "Duke of Hazzard."

While William had made good his promise not to visit Jecca Craig in Africa for the time being, his Nashville interlude fueled more speculation that the Prince was about to call it quits with Kate. No matter. Gossip notwithstanding, Kate had already won over Prince Charles, and in addition to having spent several weekends with William at his "cottage" on the grounds of Balmoral, she had been invited to stay at Sandringham—a singular honor that had been accorded none of the Princes' other young women.

Oddly, the only chilly response came from Camilla. While Charles encouraged the romance, his mistress repeatedly muttered that William was "far too young" not to continue playing the field. "Camilla is very sort of rough hewn and down-to-earth," said a longtime friend of the Parker Bowles family. "But she also thinks that as Alice Keppel's great-granddaughter she was entitled to love the Prince of Wales. Camilla wants William to marry someone from another royal house, or at least an English girl with a title, and she has repeatedly said she doesn't think either William or Harry should marry before they are thirty-five."

At the time, William was more worried about Harry's state of mind than he was about the endless chatter concerning his own love life. In late July 2004, Harry was preparing for Sandhurst's grueling "Regular Commissions Board Test"—a combination of written exams, problem-solving tasks, interviews, and an assault course. It was then that more unsavory news broke concerning the man many believed to be Harry's biological father. James Hewitt had been arrested for cocaine possession outside a London bar where, according to one eyewitness, he had been "rolling drunk. He was out of it, almost on the floor." Hewitt spent the night in jail, but it appeared his luck had not yet run out. Instead of a fine or more jail time, Hewitt received a simple caution "for possession of a Class A drug—cocaine."

Despite the distracting headlines, Harry passed the Sandhurst fitness test but wound up injuring his knee in the process. As a result, his entrance into the military academy was delayed until the following spring—time Harry would devote for the most part to playing polo, club hopping with friends, and spending as much time as possible with Chelsy Davy in Cape Town.

Now that Harry was turning twenty, Charles and Camilla—neither of whom had ever shown Diana's natural knack for hands-on parenting—left the young Prince to his own devices as he waited to enter Sandhurst. It was a kind of parental neglect that Harry had suffered from ever since he was thirteen. "He was at a particularly vulnerable age when Diana died," said her old friend Vivienne Parry. Agreed a Highgrove neighbor, "When Harry went through all those teenage growing pains—hormones raging and the pressures of exams—that's when they need their folks around. During that period boundaries are set. I just don't think that happened for Harry."

What was the explanation for Charles's reluctance to take an active role in guiding his sons? One longtime friend of the Windsors believed that Charles simply does not "know how to get involved. So much of his life is done by other people."

As he had so often since their mother's death, William stepped into the breach, checking on his brother every day by phone and by e-mail. William paid even closer attention to his brother that October, when former Eton teacher Sarah Forsyth stepped forward to say that Harry had cheated two years earlier on his final art exam—a project that earned him the B he needed to balance the D he earned in geography. Forsyth claimed she had been pressured by a superior to write up Harry's coursework herself. To prove it, she produced a tape recording in which Harry appeared to admit that he had done only a "tiny, tiny bit—only about a sentence" of the exam. Forsyth claimed that another teacher actually painted the Expressionist paintings that had earned Harry his only high marks at Eton.

In the end, a special "employment tribunal" found in Forsyth's favor, while somehow managing to clear Harry of any wrongdoing. The panel concluded that the young Prince had not cheated, though on closer examination it was clear that his written work was riddled with factual and grammatical errors that had apparently gone unnoticed.

Over the next few days, Harry hit the club scene with a vengeance. Emerging from the London club Pangaea around three thirty the morning of October 21, 2004, the Prince was allegedly shoved as he made his way to a waiting car and fell into the backseat. "Then suddenly, he burst out of the car and lunged toward me as I was still taking pictures," recalled photographer Chris Uncle.

"Why are you doing this?" Harry screamed as he shoved the camera into Uncle's face, slicing open the photographer's lower lip. "Why the fuck don't you just leave me alone?" Harry never stopped yelling obscenities even as the club's bouncers and his own bodyguards held Harry back. Once back in his car, Harry buried his head in his hands. To another photographer on the scene, it looked as if Harry "regretted what he'd just done."

The next day, palace spokesmen would claim that Harry reacted only after one of the paparazzi hit him in the nose with a camera. Photographers there said no one was that close to the Prince. "Harry," said one, "just flipped."

So did the commandant of Sandhurst, Major-General Andrew Ritchie. "I view very dimly misbehaving over a weekend," General

Ritchie said, warning Prince Harry that he would have to clean up his act if he wanted to remain at the elite military academy. "I have removed certain cadets from Sandhurst as their behavior is not up to the standards of an office," he declared, "and I would do so again." Ritchie went on to stress that Harry should expect no special treatment merely because he was third in line to the throne. "He is the same as everyone else," the general huffed. "That is what he would expect and so would everyone else."

Yet Harry had his vocal defenders. "You wonder why he hasn't done this before," Diana's old friend Vivienne Parry said. "He doesn't have the maturity yet to be able to put a lid on it." Royal historian Robert Lacey suggested that Harry was merely behaving as Diana would have under the same circumstances. "When you saw Harry cradling an AIDS baby in Africa, you saw his mother," Lacey said. "When you saw him remonstrating with photographers, you saw his mother."

Harry apologized to his exasperated father the next day and promptly headed off on another jaunt—this time to spend two weeks in Argentina learning all the right moves from the man regarded as the world's top polo player, Adolfo Cambiaso. This time Chelsy Davy tagged along, sharing a suite with Harry at a ranch outside Buenos Aires called El Remanso ("The Backwater").

The local press promptly dubbed their royal guest El Principe Rebelde ("The Rebel Prince"), but Harry made a determined effort to stay out of the limelight—and out of trouble. Still, there were tales of drunken antics at a local bar that had purportedly left him vulnerable to being kidnapped by a band of local thugs. As it turned out, none of it was true.

"It doesn't really matter what I do," Harry complained of the stories that greeted him when he returned to London. "They'll say what they want to say about me. It's what sells, isn't it?"

"He is intensely frustrated," observed a senior aide at Clarence House. "He behaved himself perfectly, yet he comes home to face all of this."

Sadly, Harry was yet to face the toughest criticism of his life—and with good reason. In the meantime, his brother was busy at St. Andrews turning his summer idyll with Middleton into a geography dissertation on the coral reefs of Rodrigues Island. Now that he was in his final year at university, William once again gave an interview to the British Press Association and posed for pictures in exchange for being essentially left alone by reporters.

He made it clear that he had no intention of taking on royal ribbon-cutting duties as soon as he graduated. ("It's not that I never want to. It's just that I'm reluctant at such a young age to throw myself into the deep end.") William insisted that the prospect of someday becoming King did not keep him awake at night. "Frankly," he said with a shrug, "life is too short."

William also revealed his postgraduation plan to follow Harry into Sandhurst. "That's why I put my brother in," Wills joked. "As a guinea pig." With British troops now, in William's words, "fighting their hearts out" in Iraq, he claimed he wanted to join his comrades in arms on the battlefield. "Talks will happen before I went anywhere," he admitted. "But the last thing I want is to be mollycoddled or wrapped up in cotton wool, because if I was to join the army I'd want to go where my men went and I'd want to do what they did. I would not want to be kept back for being precious or whatever, that's the last thing I'd want. . . . It's the most humiliating thing and it would be something I'd find very awkward to live with, being told I couldn't go out there when these guys have got to go out there and do a tough job. . . ."

Memories of another war would be stirred up six weeks later, when William and Harry attended a costume party at the home of three-time Olympic gold-medal-winning equestrian Richard Meade. The affair was to celebrate the twenty-second birthday of Meade's son Harry, and many of those in attendance were, like the Meades and the Windsors, members of the Beaufort Hunt Club. All had been asked to dress in accordance with the evening's "colonials and natives" theme.

Immediately after the Royal Family's annual Christmas gathering at Sandringham, Charles and Camilla had rushed off to spend time alone at Balmoral, which, as usual, left Will and Harry to fend for themselves. The day before the party, the brothers headed for a local "fancy dress shop" to rent their costumes. Forgoing his customary loincloth, William opted this time for a lion costume. Harry wasted no time selecting his: the short-sleeved khaki uniform of Nazi tank commander Erwin Rommel's Afrika Korps, complete with the eagle badge of the Wehrmacht on the chest and a swastika armband.

"You look terrific, Harry," William said at the shop, never expressing any doubts about his brother's costume choice. In fact, the elder Prince took an active role in helping Harry pick it out.

That night when the Princes and their hell-raising friend Guy Pelly (who was dressed as the Queen) walked into the black and white tent set up on the lawn at the Meades' farm in Wiltshire, none of the 250 guests registered shock at Harry's Nazi getup. Several, in fact, clicked their heels and delivered a mock Nazi "*sieg heil*" salute to Harry. The lack of concern from this crowd should not have been that surprising; in keeping with the colonials and natives theme, a number of guests had actually come in blackface.

Only a few of the older guests murmured among themselves that, in the words of one, the Nazi uniform "might have been somewhat ill-advised for a member of the Royal Family." One man in a colonial-era white dinner jacket asked the Prince, who spent most of the party with a vodka in one hand and a cigarette in the other, what made him choose his costume.

"I guess it's a uniform the Germans wore in Africa," Harry said with a shrug, "but that's all I know about it. Do you have any idea," he said, pointing to the huge swastika on his left arm, "what this is?"

The guest looked at the Prince in disbelief. "It's a swastika," he replied. Harry, still clearly puzzled, shook his head. "You know," the guest continued in amazement, "Hitler . . . the *Nazis*?"

"It was fairly obvious," said a university student who overheard the exchange, "that Prince Harry did not have the slightest notion about swastikas or Nazis. Someone mentioned Rommel, the 'Desert Fox,' . . . Harry didn't know who he was. Frankly, I'm not entirely certain he could have told you who Hitler was."

Prince William, meanwhile, "seemed delighted with his brother's Nazi uniform. No one dared say anything to him about it, but he seemed just as clueless."

So clueless, in fact, that neither William nor Harry seemed bothered by the fact that snapshots of them were being taken at the party. The next morning, when the *Sun* ran a full-page photo of the Prince in costume alongside the heading HARRY THE NAZI, Harry still seemed unsure of what he had done wrong. "Was it that bad to wear a German uniform?" he asked a friend from Eton. "Are the Nazis really *that* terrible?"

Harry soon had his answer. Reaction was swift, brutal, and universal. Among those who immediately condemned Harry for wearing the Nazi uniform were several members of Parliament, the Israeli foreign minister, Holocaust survivors and their families, and several Jewish and World War II veterans' groups. For many, Harry's actions seemed particularly egregious because they came just ten days before ceremonies marking the sixtieth anniversary of the liberation of Auschwitz.

"He has let the country down," said Tony Blair's envoy to the Middle East, Lord Levy. "The royals are meant to be ambassadors to the world, but the Prince's behavior has sent shock waves through the international community. . . . It shows the Prince is clueless about the reality of what happened in the Holocaust. . . . It is appalling."

Rabbi Marvin Hier of the Simon Wiesenthal Center criticized Harry for "a shameful act," while Hitler biographer Sir Ian Kershaw accused him of "grotesquely bad taste." Even loyalists like former royals press spokesman Dickie Arbiter were furious with Harry. "Once again," Arbiter said, "Prince Charles has been let down by his wayward son. It can't go on."

As was his custom whenever he embarrassed the Royal Family, Harry's first act was to call his father and apologize. This time, Prince Charles was not so quick to forgive the second son. A bodyguard standing near Harry at Highgrove could hear the Prince of Wales "shouting at the top of his lungs" over the phone from Balmoral. "Prince Charles was apoplectic, and by the time he was finished poor Prince Harry was shaking."

Charles was not entirely without blame in the matter. He had distanced himself in recent years from both his sons' daily lives and had made it clear that he did not want servants or bodyguards "rising above their station" to offer the Princes advice. Basically, said a former bodyguard, "We were ordered not to overstep our bounds, to just do our jobs and mind our own business."

As a result, wiser heads did not prevail when it came to the way Harry and William comported themselves. "It's the sort of thing," a friend of Diana's said, "their mother never would have let happen."

Clarence House wasted no time issuing an immediate apology on Harry's behalf. "Prince Harry has apologized, for any offense or embarrassment he has caused," the carefully crafted statement read. "He realizes it was a poor choice of costume."

For some, a cautiously worded statement was not enough. "This young man," Arbiter said, "has got to be up front and be seen in person on television making an apology." The leader of the Conservatives in Parliament concurred. "Prince Harry should tell us himself," Michael Howard said, "just how contrite he now is."

Several Jewish leaders, pointing out that Harry's actions might well encourage neo-Nazi groups and a new wave of anti-Semitism, invited him to tour Auschwitz. When the invitation was relayed to Harry, he replied, "Auschwitz? Is that a ski resort?"

At Charles's insistence, Harry declined the invitation to visit the death camp where four million prisoners, mostly Jews, perished. Nor would he, or for that matter any member of the Royal Family, offer any additional comment on the matter. "Prince Harry has apologized immediately," Paddy Harverson reiterated, "and in a heartfelt fashion for making a very bad mistake."

That did not explain Harry's alarming lack of knowledge concerning World War II. Incredibly, Harry was patently unaware that his own family—in particular his great-grandfather King George

VI, the Queen Mother, and of course Granny the Queen—were international symbols of the struggle against fascism.

"Surely, even a complete thicko must have realized that there are a great many people alive today for whom the swastika revives memories of the most agonizing sort," said British commentator Tom Utley. "If Harry doesn't realize that, then what the hell did they teach him during his five years at Eton?" Utley, like many others, voiced the opinion that Harry's Nazi costume had less to do with insensitivity than sheer, unforgivable ignorance. "Prince Harry is a stupid young man who meant no harm," Utley concluded. "But . . . we are not talking about an average level of stupidity. We are talking about stupidity on an absolutely monumental scale. This is not the stupidity of a twenty-year-old who has gone through seventeen years of the best formal education money can buy. It is the stupidity of a rather backward child of twelve."

Before the dust settled, several members of Parliament demanded that Harry not be allowed to attend Sandhurst. "The young man," said Labor back bencher Doug Henderson, "is simply not suitable." Nevertheless, Sandhurst brass shrugged off the incident. "I am quite sure there are plenty of cadets who display lack of judgment," a senior officer said, "but we never hear of them because they do not end up on the front page of the *Sun*."

Among senior royals, the Queen was perhaps most sympathetic to Harry's plight. After all, she conceded that she herself was no intellectual and wondered aloud how much she would have known about World War II if she hadn't lived through it herself. She was now telling courtiers that she hoped Sandhurst would give direction to the wayward Prince. At least one editorial writer agreed.

The London *Daily Telegraph* called Sandhurst Prince Harry's "greatest hope of salvation."

The global outcry over Harry's latest gaffe was the last thing Charles needed in January 2005. Only two months earlier, a watershed event had occurred in his relationship with Camilla. During the wedding of Charles's godson Edward van Cutsem and Lady Tamara Grosvenor—the same affair at which William and Harry served as ushers—Charles and Camilla were asked to sit in separate pews and to arrive and leave in separate cars. The Queen and Prince Philip were there, but Charles and his mistress boycotted the event. Believing that he had suffered one indignity too many, Charles immediately met with his advisors to speed up plans for his marriage to Camilla.

There were other pressures as well. Camilla's son, Tom, now thirty, was planning to wed in September 2005. As William's romance with Kate Middleton deepened, there arose the real possibility that they might marry. Polls showed that the majority of Britons wanted William to be their next King. The sentiment, Charles's advisors pointed out, would be strengthened if William seemed settled in a marriage while his father was still dawdling with his mistress.

The Church of England was now leaning on Charles to put an end to his "sinful" liaison and marry Camilla. The Queen, who still resented all the damage Camilla had done to the monarchy, was now resigned to the inevitable. She now believed Charles and Camilla should marry long before he ascended to the throne, so the British people would have time to get used to the idea of them as their King and Queen.

There were also financial considerations. A special committee in the House of Commons had been poring over the Prince of

Wales's finances and discovered that each year he was spending $500,000—some of it taxpayer money—on Camilla. It was one thing for a royal to spend enormous sums from the public treasury on his wife, quite another to splurge it on his mistress.

Shortly before Christmas, Charles asked his sons for their blessing, and they gave it without hesitation. "Whatever resistance they may have had in the beginning just melted away," said a longtime friend of both Princes. "William and Harry always wanted their father to be happy, and by this time they were so used to Camilla being there, they didn't feel that they were betraying their mother any longer." In their official statement, both of Diana's boys later said they were "100 percent" behind the marriage. "We are both very happy for our father and Camilla," it read, "and we wish them all the luck in the future."

That same day at Highgrove, the Prince of Wales got down on bended knee ("Of course—what else?" she later joked) and at long last asked Camilla to be his wife. He then slipped the engagement ring on her finger. Weighing a total of eight carats, the emerald-cut diamond with three diamond baguettes on either side had belonged to the Queen Mother. Meeting promptly with the Queen and his private secretary Sir Michael Peat, Charles set the wedding date: April 8, 2005.

Astoundingly, the plans remained secret for weeks, thanks in large part to Fleet Street's preoccupation with "Nazi Harry." On February 9, in accordance with the Royal Marriages Act, the Queen formally consulted with Prime Minister Tony Blair during their weekly audience at Buckingham Palace. Details were leaked to the press within hours, forcing Clarence House to make the announcement a week earlier than planned—first in the series of glitches that would turn their wedding into a comedy of errors.

The couple hosted a charity gala at Windsor the night of the announcement, and Camilla made no effort to conceal her delight. "I'm just coming down to earth," she said. The Queen was somewhat more muted in her enthusiasm. "The Duke of Edinburgh and I," she said in a formal statement, "are very happy that the Prince of Wales and Mrs. Parker Bowles are to marry. We have given them our warmest good wishes for their future together."

The press, meanwhile, was not quite ready to let go of the last big royal brouhaha. One political cartoon showed two corgis sitting outside Windsor Castle. "I'm already panicking," says one, "about what Prince Harry will wear at the wedding."

With Operation PB—Parker Bowles—in its final stages, there would still be plenty of panicky moments over the next few months. First, the couple was forced to switch the wedding ceremony from Windsor to the Windsor Guildhall (town hall) because the castle wasn't a legal spot for a wedding. Then the Queen announced she would be skipping the civil ceremony altogether in favor of the subsequent blessing and reception at Windsor Castle. Charles pleaded with his mother to change her mind, but she said she did not want to interfere with the "low-key" nature of the civil ceremony—a decision that was rightly perceived to be a royal snub.

There was also a major challenge to the legality of the wedding itself. According to some experts, it was illegal for the future head of the Church of England to be married in anything other than an Anglican service. Eventually, the Lord Chancellor, Lord Falconer, ruled that the Human Rights Act of 1998 made it possible for Charles and Camilla to marry in a civil ceremony "like anyone else."

But there remained the dicey question of what to call Camilla.

To placate critics, the couple had agreed early on that Camilla would forgo using the Princess of Wales title, which was so closely associated in the public mind with Diana, and be known instead as the Duchess of Cornwall. Reacting to polls that showed only 7 percent of the public wanted Camilla as their Queen, Charles also promised that she would become England's first "Princess Consort"—not Queen—when he became King. But regardless of what she chose to be called, Camilla would by law and custom become Princess of Wales upon marrying Charles and Queen of England on his ascension to the throne.

Behind the scenes, there were more legal issues to be worked out—mainly, should Charles require his bride to sign a prenuptial agreement. The Prince was reminded that, because he and Diana had no such agreement, he was forced to pay her $22.5 million settlement out of his own pocket. "Princess Diana took every penny he had," recalled Geoffrey Bignell, the lawyer in charge of Charles's finances through 1996. "I was told to liquidate everything so he could give her cash. He was very unhappy about that."

Charles was willing to take the risk again. Against the advice of legal experts, he did not raise the issue of a prenuptial agreement with Camilla at all. "He was adamant," said a royal lawyer, "that the marriage has to be based from the start on trust and good faith."

Instead, Charles found another way to assuage whatever financial concerns his bride might have harbored. In early 2005 he set up a $20 million trust fund for Camilla that guaranteed her an annual income of $700,000. A key proviso: in the event of her death, the $20 million reverted to the royal estate.

The strain on Charles was beginning to show when he sat down with the BBC to discuss the wedding. "I thought the British people were supposed to be compassionate—I don't see much of it," he moaned, adding that for years he had been "tortured" over his relationship with Camilla. "I don't see any reason why I should define my private life," Charles went on. "All my life, people have been telling me what to do. I'm tired of it. My private life has become an industry. People are making money out of it. . . . I just," he pleaded, "want some peace."

The groom's frame of mind was not much improved by the time William and Harry took him, along with thirty friends, on a "stag week" ski trip to Klosters. Sitting on a wall to pose for a small army of photographers, Charles squirmed uneasily while his sons beamed away. With press microphones plainly visible in front of him and the press corps only a few feet away, Charles moaned about the press. "I can't bear that man," he said of the BBC's Nicholas Witchell as Witchell looked on in amazement. "He's so awful. He really is. . . . Bloody people," he went on. "I *hate* doing this."

Trying to calm his father down, William muttered, "Keep smiling, keep smiling." Actually, the boys looked genuinely happy to be there. When asked about his part as a witness at the wedding, Wills joked, "As long as I don't lose the rings, I'm all right!"

Charles's unprovoked rant stunned Britain's press corps, but it did nothing to spoil the young Princes' good time in the Swiss Alps. Just a few days before, William had told a reporter that he was "too young to marry" Kate Middleton. "I don't want to get married," he added, "until I'm at least twenty-eight or maybe thirty." Still, they made a cozy après ski couple, holding each other close on the dance floor and passing around a bottle of shared wine with friends.

Harry, downing a mixture of vodka mixed with Red Bull, spent much of the Klosters trip bemoaning the absence of his girlfriend,

Chelsy Davy. When a beaded necklace she had given him broke, Harry became upset. "It's really special," he tried to explain. As much as he may have missed Davy, Harry still boasted to any girl who would listen that he wore no underwear. One of the young women Harry zeroed in on, Emily Nash, thought he behaved "like an overgrown puppy."

There would be one unforeseeable hitch in the marriage of Prince Charles and Camilla Parker Bowles. The funeral of Pope John Paul II was scheduled for the same day as the wedding, forcing the couple at the last minute to push their ceremony back twenty-four hours while Charles represented the Queen in Rome.

Once the wedding was over and the happy couple had driven off to honeymoon at Balmoral, all the complications, legal challenges, snafus, and eleventh-hour delays did not seem to matter. After thirty-five years of deception, jealousy, passion, rage, tragedy, drama, and scandal, Charles and Camilla were at last lawful husband and wife.

Their marriage was, in fact, as much a stunning public relations achievement as it was a triumph of love. It had been exactly seven years since Camilla herself had enlisted Tony Blair's chief media man Peter Mandelson to counter Diana's popularity and make her more acceptable to the British people.

The result, said Diana's former private secretary Patrick Jephson, was a "sustained political-style spin that hijacked Charles's reputation to serve the needs of his true love's ambition." According to Jephson, Camilla's methods were "drawn from every shelf of the spin doctor's medicine cupboard, and from some pretty dark corners too."

Yet it was not enough that Camilla was now one giant step closer to becoming Queen. "Many of the friends who conspired in Charles and Camilla's extramarital affairs," suggested Jephson, "who conceived and executed their mission plan for public acceptability, would happily wish away Diana's achievements." Another Diana supporter, Mary Radcliffe, shared Jephson's concern. "It's as if," she said, "they were trying to airbrush Diana from history."

Theirs may have been one of history's most scandalous extramarital affairs, but those who knew the Prince and his lover never doubted they were destined for the altar. "How could it not be?" asked Santa Sebag Montefiore, a friend to both Diana and the woman she called "The Rottweiler." Charles and Camilla, Montefiore said, "fit together like two pieces of a jigsaw puzzle."

Yet there was a third jigsaw puzzle piece—one that, sadly, did not seem to fit anywhere. In the coming months, as Scotland Yard's long-delayed investigation into the events of August 31, 1997, forged ahead, the Royal Family would continue to be haunted by the specter of the woman who might have been Queen—Diana, Princess of Wales.

There are those inside the Palace and out,
myself among them, who say "God Save
the Queen" and really mean it. Perhaps
they are worried about what comes next.

—Dickie Arbiter, longtime royal aide

All my life people have been telling me
what to do. I'm tired of it.

—Charles

8

"A re you telling me there is still blood in the car?" he asked,
eyes wide with disbelief. As head of Operation Paget, the investigation into the death of Princess Diana, it seemed nothing
short of unfathomable to Lord Stevens that the black Mercedes
S280 at the center of the history's most famous car crash still contained untested forensic evidence, thanks to French authorities.

The twisted wreckage had been cut in two during the French
government's investigation in 1997, and the pieces had been
packed into two metal shipping containers. The containers were
then shipped to a junkyard southeast of Paris, where they remained
undisturbed for the next eight years—until Scotland Yard finally
asked to examine the car in which the Princess of Wales had died.

After the Mercedes arrived in London, it was uncrated, re-
assembled, and then left to decay even further in a police compound
for lost and stolen cars. "It's a very sad end to a tragic story," said
a spokesman for London's Metropolitan Police, "and the officers

involved have found it difficult to see the car just lying there rust-
ing away."

By the time Scotland Yard forensics experts would get around
to looking at it, they were astonished at the substantial amount
of dried blood still on the upholstery, floor, dashboard, steering
wheel, windshield, and even on the hood of the car—enough to
yield what Stevens would call "valuable information" in the crime
laboratory.

The Case of the Forgotten Car added just one more twist to
an investigation that seemed cursed from the very beginning. By
the summer of 2005, Operation Paget was investigating reports
that just hours after the crash, French officials had mixed up the
bodies of Dodi Fayed and the driver, Henri Paul, assigning Paul
the identification number 2416 after it had already been given to
Dodi (ID numbers were written in ink on bracelets attached to
the right wrist of each body).

That, along with the inexplicable fact that Paul's blood contained
an unusually high amount of carbon monoxide, added to suspicions
that the samples might have been inadvertently switched. Scotland
Yard was also looking into the possibility that the specimen showing Paul with a blood alcohol level over three times the legal limit
in France may not have come from either man, but from the corpse
of someone not even connected to the case. (For years Jean and
Giselle Paul had waged a court battle in France to prove that their
son, who did not have a history of alcoholism, was not intoxicated
the night of the accident; they argued that his blood was either con-
taminated or mixed up with someone else's.)

The partial embalming of Diana in Paris continued to perplex
investigators. Mohamed Al Fayed was now proclaiming more
loudly than ever that Dodi was to marry Diana, that she was car-

rying his child, and that Prince Philip had ordered British intelligence to assassinate them both before that could happen.

One eyewitness to the British autopsy, Robert Thompson of the Hammersmith and Fulham Mortuary in West London, would later say in a sworn affidavit that uniformed and plainclothes officers ("men in suits") were given special access to photograph the body and take samples from her corpse. When the autopsy was carried out, he testified that Diana's body gave off a strong smell of alcohol, but when the mortuary blood tests came back they reported no alcohol present. "I find this unbelievable," Thompson testified, "and it leads me to the conclusion that the blood sample had either been corrupted, or a false statement made."

At the very least, the partial embalming would cast doubt on subsequent tests—had there been any pregnancy tests on Diana's body at all. "The only concern of the medical staff was emergency treatment to save her life," Lord Stevens would ultimately conclude. "After the Princess was pronounced dead there was no need for further tests." Neither were any pregnancy tests done in Britain "because it was not relevant to the cause of death."

By the spring of 2005, Coroner to the Queen Michael Burgess had to concede that, depending on what Operation Paget uncovered, exhuming the Princess's body was not out of the question. "I will take that action," Burgess stated, "if I believe there is some serious criminal allegation requiring access to the body."

William and Harry were, in the words of a cousin, "horrified" at the prospect and asked their father if there wasn't something he could do to prevent it. But in light of the letter in which Diana accused Charles of a plot to kill her, there was no way the Prince

of Wales—or for that matter any member of the Royal Family—
could risk interfering with the investigation.

By this time, Lord Stevens no longer viewed the death of Diana
as an open-and-shut drunk-driving case. As early as 1995, the
Princess had met with her solicitor, Lord Mishcon, and told him
that "reliable sources" had warned her efforts were under way to
get rid of her, probably by arranging a car accident. "The Princess
apparently believed that there was a conspiracy," Lord Mishcon
told investigators, "and that *both* she and Camilla Parker Bowles
were to be 'put aside.'" In yet another strange turn of events,
Diana reportedly believed that both she and Camilla stood in the
way of Charles's marrying another woman—the woman Diana
was convinced he truly loved at the time: the boys' nanny, Tiggy
Legge-Bourke.

Even the notion that Prince Philip may have had a hand in
Diana's death no longer seemed impossible. In addition to the harsh
notes Philip had written to Diana, the Princess had told her friend
Roberto Devorik that she had a premonition that she would be
murdered. "They, the machinery," she insisted, "are going to blow
me up."

Diana also told Devorik that she feared three people: Charles's
chum Nicholas Soames, her brother-in-law and the Queen's
longtime private secretary Sir Robert Fellowes, and Prince Philip.
"He hates me," she said of Fellowes. "He will do anything to get
me out of the royals. He cost me the friendship with my sister."
Diana then added, "Prince Philip wants to see me dead." After she
gave the *Panorama* television interview that so angered the Queen,
Diana told Devorik, "I am sure Prince Philip is involved with the
security services. After this they are going to get rid of me."

After the divorce was finalized and she was stripped of her royal status, Diana was in the VIP lounge at Heathrow waiting to board a flight to Italy when she looked up at a portrait of Prince Philip. "He really hates me," she said, "and would like to see me disappear. He blames me for everything."

As she prepared to board her flight, Diana turned to Devorik. "Well, cross your fingers," she told him. "Any minute they will blow me up." When Devorik laughed, she replied, "You are *so* naive. Don't you see they took my HRH title and now they are slowly taking my kids? They are now letting me know when I can have the children."

In the face of such testimony, Lord Stevens conceded that "some of the issues that have been raised by Mr. Fayed have been right to be raised. We are pursuing those. It is a far more complex inquiry than any of us thought." So complex that Stevens now knew there was no way to avoid interviewing Charles, William, and Harry. "It's not part of the job," he told one detective, "that I am particularly relishing."

Prince Philip did not make Lord Stevens's job any easier. Asked about his sometimes brutally worded letters to Diana and her fear that he wanted her dead, Philip angrily refused to comment.

The Princes had other things to do while they waited their turn with Lord Stevens. The same week Operation Paget detectives quizzed Britain's two top spies—MI5 Director General Eliza Manningham-Buller and MI6 chief John Scarlett—Harry reported for forty-four weeks of officer training at Sandhurst. Before he did, Harry did some last-minute partying with friends. "They kept telling me don't change, don't change, don't change," he recalled. "Well, I'm not going to."

Accompanied by Papa, Harry arrived for boot camp with the mandatory ironing board Sandhurst required all new cadets to bring with them. Yet while the other cadets lugged theirs across a parking lot to their new quarters, William and Harry's new private secretary, Jamie Lowther-Pinkerton, did the lugging.

Still, Harry claimed he was "treated like a piece of dirt" at Sandhurst and laughed about the drill sergeants who shouted "You 'orrible little prince!" in his ear as he scrambled through obstacle courses and crawled through mud on his belly. "Nobody's really supposed to love it. I was shocked at first, but I'd prepared myself for the worst."

For the first five weeks at Sandhurst—actually described by the academy in its literature as "five weeks of hell"—cadets got up at dawn and were put through their paces by obscenity-spewing drill sergeants until midnight. "Expect," the commandant told Prince Charles and the other parents, "the odd anguished phone call."

In the course of his training, Harry lost weight ("I didn't think it was possible, but I have") and wound up in the infirmary three times, suffering from blisters and the flu, leading one British tabloid to dub him the "Prince of Ails."

There were a few isolated instances when Harry felt as if he was being singled out for harsh treatment. "In the sense that 'he is who he is, let's treat him even worse to make him feel really where he's at,'" he said. "It did me good." Besides, Harry added, "I do enjoy running down a ditch full of mud, firing bullets. It's the way I am. I love it."

His intention now was to join the infantry and, like his brother, fight on the front lines with his comrades. "If they said to me, 'No, you can't do front line duties,' then I wouldn't drag my sorry ass around Sandhurst," Harry declared. "The last thing I would want to do is have my soldiers sent away to Iraq and for me to be held back twiddling my thumbs.

"There's no way I'm going to put myself through Sandhurst," he went on, "and then sit on my ass back home while my boys are out there fighting for their country. I want to fight for my country too."

Harry looked forward to his brother arriving at Sandhurst the following year, when as an incoming cadet, William would be required to salute his little brother. "I'm really looking forward to that," cracked Harry.

The Spare took his customary backseat, however, when William graduated from St. Andrews on June 23, 2005. While the Queen (who was recovering from the flu but came anyway), Prince Philip, Harry, Charles, and Camilla watched from the best seats in Younger Hall—front row center of the mezzanine— William sat downstairs with his fellow graduates. Five rows and eighty graduates ahead of him was Catherine Middleton. As Kate, who wore high heels and a black miniskirt beneath her academic robes, walked back to her seat with her degree in the history of art in hand, she glanced over at William, and the two exchanged broad smiles. The Queen, who had been favorably impressed by Kate when they met for the first time at Windsor, smiled over to her husband and whispered "nice girl."

Then it was the Prince's turn. He sat nervously, biting his lower lip when Dean of Arts Christopher Smith called out "William Wales." The room exploded with flashing cameras and thunderous applause as William strode toward the stage. Kneeling before St. Andrews chancellor, Sir Kenneth Dover, William was tapped lightly on the head with the seventeenth-century cap that contained a scrap of cloth believed to be from the pants of the great Protestant Reform leader John Knox. A red and black academic hood signifying his Master of Arts status was then affixed to his collar, and William was finally handed his diploma.

"You will have made lifelong friends," university Vice Chancellor Brian Lang told the assembled graduates and their families. "I say this every year to all new graduates: you may have met your husband or wife. Our title as 'Top Matchmaking University in Britain' signifies so much that is good about St. Andrews, so we can rely on you to go forth and multiply."

In an instant, all eyes seemed to be on the couple Fleet Street had been speculating about for months. The Queen and Camilla both chortled, William grimaced, and Kate raised her eyebrows in mock horror. Afterward, William joined the rest of the graduates and their families outside. Kate was reluctant at first, but at Wills's insistence he introduced her parents to the Queen. "They lit up, and of course Kate's mother curtsied," said another graduate standing a few feet away. "Her Majesty was so warm toward them, and she treated Kate just like family."

The easy rapport between the Queen and her favorite grandson's girlfriend had much to do with the simple fact that Kate had by now been an important part of William's life for nearly four years. The Queen had learned something from the marital calamities of her own children. The brief courtships of Charles and Diana and Andrew and Sarah Ferguson had led to marriages that could only be described as calamitous. Her Majesty was now of the firm opinion that no royal should date for less than five years before heading for the altar. In Kate, the Queen noted, William had obviously found someone who had stood the test of time.

It remained to be seen how well Kate might cope with the endless walkabouts, ribbon cuttings, ground breakings, and wreath layings that make up the day-to-day life of a working royal. Within a matter of days, William was on board a royal jet bound for New Zealand to meet the touring British and Irish Lions rugby team.

While there, the Prince carried out his first solo engagements as the Queen's representative at ceremonies in Auckland and Wellington marking the sixtieth anniversary of the end of World War II.

Privately, Harry often complained that people did not understand the pressures on his brother. "How would you like it," he'd ask friends, "if you had your entire life planned out for you?" Even though it would be six months before he could join his brother at Sandhurst, the palace had arranged for Wills to spend the time working at not one but three separate jobs—an occupational smorgasbord intended to give the future monarch a range of work experience.

First, William learned land management skills working on the Chatsworth Estate in Derbyshire. Wearing a straw boater and apron, the future King served customers from behind a counter in the Chatsworth Farm store. After that, William was to roll up his shirtsleeves working for HSBC Investments, one of the UK's largest financial institutions—something he was "particularly keen to do" because it would make him more savvy at raising money for charity.

Later that year, William would join an RAF Mountain Rescue Team at Holyhead Mountain in North Wales. With the press looking on, William rappelled down the face of a two-hundred-foot cliff while steadying a stretcher filled with ballast to simulate an injured climber. Before he leapt into action, Wills joked with the assembled photographers. "You're just waiting for me to fall over," he shouted down to them, "aren't you?"

While publicly expressing enthusiasm for the agenda mapped out by his handlers, William complained to his father that he felt he was losing control of his own life. "I have so many things I want to do," he said. "I'm scared, really scared, that I won't have time."

Before he started any of the jobs that had been assigned to him, William decided to spend some time with his old friend Jecca Craig at her family's sprawling big-game preserve at the foot of snowcapped Mount Kenya. This time, Kate and a dozen friends went along, camping out in six *bandas*—thatched cottages—on a hill next to the Ngare Ndare River. Apparently Middleton needn't have worried about William rekindling his romance with Jecca; William's former girlfriend was now involved with financier Hugh Crossley.

Once back in London, Kate found herself increasingly drawn into the world of the Windsors. The Queen, eager to get to know Middleton, arranged several private meetings without William present. Kate also dined three times during the summer of 2005 with the Queen and William. It was significant that one of these dinners took place at Her Majesty's favorite royal residence, Windsor Castle.

While Granny was busy sizing up his brother's girlfriend, Harry and Chelsy—who had yet to dine privately with the Queen—conferred on how best to celebrate his upcoming twenty-first birthday. After the hijacking two years earlier of William's birthday bash by a self-proclaimed "comedy terrorist" and Harry's Nazi uniform debacle, the Spare had no interest in marking his coming-of-age with a costume party of any kind. Instead Harry, still in the thick of officer training, would celebrate comparatively quietly with family and friends at Highgrove.

There would, however, be other opportunities for "Haz," as Chelsy nearly always called Harry these days, to cut loose with friends. The first week in September, Harry took his girlfriend and a dozen pals on a cruise of Botswana's remote Okavango Delta aboard a two-story houseboat, the *Kubu Queen*. "These guys were having a pretty wild time up and down this river," said Harry's fishing guide. Between the smoking and the drinking and blaring of loud rap music into the early morning hours, some of the locals were not too pleased. "It's bad," said one. "It disturbs the hippos and the elephants."

Harry cleaned up his act once he returned home, donning a morning suit for the wedding of his stepbrother, Tom Parker Bowles, to Sara Buys in Oxfordshire. In Chelsy's absence, Harry still drank and smoked—but apparently in moderation. He was, said Buys's friend Oliver Jones, "in good form and well behaved. He just blended in."

Now that he was no longer a minor, Harry seized the opportunity to let fly on a variety of subjects, starting with his own behavior. Insisting that he was misunderstood by the public, Harry described himself unapologetically as both a "party prince" and a "caring prince" and vowed to keep his "child streak. Everyone has to have a beer now and then. Cigarettes—trying to give them up."

Prince Harry also complained about not being able to fight back against an often hostile press. "There's truth and there's lies," he said, "and unfortunately I can't get the truth across because I don't have my own column in the paper, which I'm thinking about getting."

The one person who fully understood Harry's predicament was his big brother. "It's amazing how close we've become," Harry said of William. "Ever since our mother died, obviously we were close, but he is the one person on this earth who I can actually really . . . we can talk about *anything*. If I find myself in really hard times, then at least I can turn to him, and vice versa, and we can look after each other."

But for the first time, the Spare also confessed to having nightmares about succeeding to the throne instead of his brother. "He assures me," Harry said, laughing nervously, "that he's not going to do that. I've had dreams. . . ."

For the woman who now stood to one day become Queen in Diana's stead, Harry had only kind words. "To be honest," he said, "she's always been close to me and William. But no, she's not the wicked stepmother. I'll say that right now." Acknowledging that Camilla was perhaps showing signs of strain in her new role as royal wife, Harry urged people to "understand that it's very hard for her. Look at the position she's coming into. Don't always feel sorry for me and William, feel sorry for her."

Married life with Camilla, the Prince observed, had left Papa "much more relaxed"—in stark contrast to the tempestuous relationship with Diana. Camilla, Harry went on, "is a wonderful woman and she's made our father very, very happy, which is the most important thing. William and I love her to bits."

There was one figure—arguably one of the most significant people in his life—about whom Harry had never spoken publicly. Years earlier, when William turned eighteen, a financially strapped James Hewitt was paid $8,000 to tell one publication that he did not meet Diana until 1986 and therefore could not possibly be Harry's father. Now he was preparing to be hypnotized on national television for a standard $1,500 performer's fee, apparently confident that he would not divulge anything that he did not fully intend to reveal to well-known hypnotist Tony Rae.

Over the course of two days in a West London house, Rae, chairman of the British Council of Professional Hypnotists, joined broadcaster Rob Butler in grilling Hewitt—before and after putting him under. This time, Hewitt stated that he first spotted Lady Diana Spencer at a polo match in Tidworth, Hampshire, in June of 1981, six weeks before she married Charles. The Prince was playing on the navy team, Hewitt for the army.

Hewitt claimed that he spoke to Diana that day, that he "found her to be a very attractive woman" and was instantly drawn to her. But he also said it was she who initiated the affair, calling him a few days later and inviting him to join her for dinner at the London home of mutual friends. It was on the sofa of that house, Hewitt said, that they kissed for the first time. He realized that she loved Charles but already knew that "Charles didn't love her."

Over the course of the next year, they grew increasingly close. A few months after William was born in June 1982, Diana invited the young cavalry officer to Kensington Palace. It was then, Hewitt said, that they made love for the first time.

Describing Diana as "lonely" and "sad," Hewitt also remembered that she wanted to "settle down" with him. "Diana thought she'd make a very good army wife," he said. "It wasn't possible to do that. I think it was a dream." He also seemed "amazed" that they managed to conduct their affair for years "without anything appearing in the papers," but also recalled receiving an anonymous phone call saying it would be "healthier for me not to see her anymore."

Several months into their affair Diana summoned Hewitt to Kensington Palace. "I'm pregnant, James," she told him, in a manner Hewitt described to a friend as "part anxious and part matter-of-fact."

After Diana became pregnant a second time, Hewitt said they "stopped having a full sexual relationship, as it seemed more respectful," but they still continued to see each other regularly. Shortly after she gave birth to Harry in 1984, Diana called Hewitt from the hospital to say it was a boy. "I told her," Hewitt recalled, "that it was wonderful, absolutely lovely and happy news."

They resumed their relationship with renewed passion. When a panicky Hewitt consulted the well-known British publicist Max Clifford in 1984 asking how to keep the affair under wraps, Clifford suggested that he should simply start giving the boys riding lessons as a cover. Their trysts continued for another eight years until Diana abruptly and inexplicably ended it in 1992. "I'd served my purpose," Hewitt told the hypnotist.

Hewitt insisted that he had "always tried to protect" Diana's family by claiming that he could not possibly have fathered Harry. Even under hypnosis, Hewitt admitted that part of him still did not want to "reignite any smoldering embers" over the question of whether or not he could be Harry's father. "I don't want to talk about that," Hewitt snapped at Butler. "I think that's out of line."

Nor did he talk about continuing speculation that in one of the love letters Hewitt burned—or perhaps didn't—Diana had told Hewitt that the "rusty-haired" infant whose arrival spelled the beginning of the end of the royal marriage was in fact his son. "You can't hide the truth forever," he said cryptically, "nor should you."

"In the past, James has always been very careful to stick to the story that they didn't meet until 1986," said an associate of Clifford's. "It was a brilliant answer—the kind of flat statement that nipped all conversation in the bud. The only problem with that is, it simply wasn't true."

At Clarence House and Buckingham Palace, there was once again spirited debate about how to handle the ongoing "Hewitt Problem." Any thought of removing doubt by simply doing genetic testing to prove that Harry was a Windsor met with firm resistance from the Queen, Prince Philip, and from Charles. No royal had ever been asked to submit to such an indignity, protested the Crown. Poor benighted Harry, who had endured so much, was not about to be the first.

The "Men in Gray" who ran the monarchy were in full agreement. The precedent set by such an action would, in the words of one courtier, "weaken the monarchy in the eyes of the people beyond all imagining." Another former palace official with strong ties to the Queen's advisors believed that was only half the story. "No one really knows the answer to the question, do they?" he said. "Diana and Hewitt were lovers for years. However slim the possibility, it would be an absolute catastrophe if it proved to be true."

There was little doubt that, even if DNA tests proved Harry was not a Windsor, he would continue to be regarded as such by Charles and the rest of the Royal Family. Yet he would no longer be in line for the throne (his third-place position would be assumed by Prince Andrew).

The heartbreaking possibility that he might not be Charles's biological son still gnawed away at Harry, and more so now that Hewitt seemed to be hinting at paternity. The pubs and bars where Harry usually found solace were no longer an option. Instead, he hunkered down at Sandhurst, determined to impress his superiors. Sandhurst's commandant, Major-General Andrew Ritchie, believed Harry shared in his fellow cadets' desire to put "meaning in their lives. They want excitement and danger and sex, like most young men and women, but they also want to do something worthwhile."

For Harry, that now meant forgoing the infantry for life as a soldier on horseback in the Household Cavalry—either with the Life Guards or the Blues and Royals. The Windsor-based Household

Cavalry was the most glamorous of the Guards regiments, in part because of the flashy ceremonial uniforms consisting of gleaming breastplates, thigh-high black leather boots, and plumed helmets. Harry had reasons of his own for wanting to join: in addition to taking part in military operations, the unit's links to the equestrian community would make it possible for him to keep playing polo. (Harry and William were now the only Waleses on the polo field; by this time Charles, plagued by back trouble and fearing injury, had retired from the game.)

Coincidentally, James Hewitt and Camilla's ex-husband, Andrew Parker Bowles, both served with distinction in the Household Cavalry. Another royal who had long been highly regarded in the equestrian world actually held the rank of colonel in the Blues and Royals: Harry's Auntie Anne, the Princess Royal.

William commiserated with his brother about Hewitt, now better known to most Britons by such sobriquets as "The Cad" and "The Love Rat." But the Princes devoted more time to talking about their respective girlfriends. Harry was "desperate" for Chelsy Davy, who was in her final year at the University of Cape Town studying economics, politics, and philosophy. Wills would later tell friends Harry was "madly in love" with the girl he now called "Chedda" (street slang for money). Davy's pet names for Harry: "Haz" and "Spike."

As accustomed as he was to apologizing for his own behavior, Harry was not prepared to see his girlfriend and her family come under intense media scrutiny. Soon Chelsy's father, one of Zimbabwe's largest landowners, was being widely criticized for his alleged ties to the regime of that country's dictator, Robert Mugabe. "No one," said a friend of Chelsy's, "is allowed to say a word against Charles Davy in Prince Harry's presence. He gets very angry when they do because he knows the only reason anybody cares is because he and Chelsy are a couple."

The Heir, meantime, was in the midst of what friends called "a bit of a rocky patch" in his romance with Kate Middleton. Kate was nowhere to be seen that October when William showed up at Falmouth harbor and sounded an airhorn to celebrate the return to dry land of his friend Oliver Hicks.

The bearded adventurer, a friend of both Middleton and the Prince, had spent four months rowing from North America to the Isles of Scilly—a feat that earned him a place in the record books as the youngest person ever to row solo across the Atlantic. After celebrating with cake and champagne at Falmouth's Chain Locker pub, the raucous group moved on to the Hicks family home nearby. Middleton, to the dismay of Wills's friends, never showed up among the thirty revelers.

The next day, Kate did attend a charity ball at Whitehall to benefit the Institute for Cancer Research, but she was not seated at William's table. While she was left to her own devices, the Prince openly flirted and danced with other young women. At one point, Kate was spotted glowering in a hallway, clearly upset over being neglected by William. "It was one of those strange things," said another guest. "He was obviously ignoring her for some reason, and it was just as obvious that she did not have a clue what that reason was."

It was no coincidence that at the same time, William was undergoing the strain of being interviewed at length by Lord Stevens's team as part of Operation Paget's probe into Diana's death. Among other things, William told Scotland Yard that he had no knowledge of any plan for his mother to become engaged to Dodi, as Mohamed Al Fayed had repeatedly claimed.

Prince Charles had also agreed to answer Lord Stevens's questions—once he returned from his first official trip abroad with his new wife. It was important that Camilla make the right impression; they had been man and wife a few days when, while performing her first walkabout as a member of the Royal Family, it was pointed out that Camilla had worn the same outfit—a tartan-trimmed red coat, tartan wrap, and pearl choker—for the third time in less than a week.

Leaving nothing to chance, the royal couple departed November 2, 2005, for their six-day U.S. tour in a chartered jet (cost: $370,000) loaded down with a wardrobe of fifty dresses for Camilla, more than a dozen double-breasted blazers and suits for Charles, and a sixteen-member entourage that included a butler, a valet, a dresser, a hairdresser, makeup artist, several private secretaries, and a physician. Also on board: fifty British reporters who, the palace prayed, would report back that the new Princess of Wales was a worthy successor to the wildly popular Diana.

Charles, more than anyone, realized that Camilla had her work cut out for her. He often referred to the United States as "Diana territory" and lamented that most Americans clung to a "completely unrealistic view" of what his late wife was really like. He also worried that there were "Diana fanatics" who might do them both harm in the wake of a marriage that they might see as a betrayal of the Princess's memory. At Charles's insistence, security for the trip was doubled.

Arriving in New York on the first leg of their tour, Charles and Camilla went straight to Ground Zero for the dedication of a memorial stone at the nearby British Memorial Garden. That night, the couple attended a luminary-packed gala at the Museum of Modern Art. A *New York Times* reporter pointed out that Camilla's blond coif was styled with so much hairspray and her bangs were so long over her eyes that she had to look sideways to see who she was talking to. The Duchess, wearing a blue velvet dress, black stilettos ("really, really trying," sniped the *Times*) toted a Union Jack clutch purse and periodically waved it around, saying "I'm flying the flag!"

Outside in the cold, diehard Diana fan Muriel Hartwick waved a sign that read CAMILLA IS NOT WELCOME IN THE USA. "I think Charles has nerve bringing her over here," said Hartwick, who was joined by a small group of protesters. "She's not Princess Diana and she never will be."

The New York press, yearning for some of the old Diana dazzle, was also less than welcoming. FRUMP TOWER! was the *New York Post* headline used to describe Camilla's wardrobe. "Charles got it backward," cracked one columnist. "He married his first wife second and his trophy wife first." One of those who disagreed was actress Elaine Stritch. "I don't care what other people say," Stritch bellowed when she met Camilla in New York, "you look terrific. No bullshit, you look great!"

"Well," replied the Duchess, "you must be wearing the wrong spectacles."

In Washington, Charles and Camilla were treated to not one but two meals at the White House on the same day—lunch (lemon sole, petite asparagus, golden pea tendrils) followed by a black tie dinner (celery-and-shrimp soup, buffalo, Chartreuse ice cream). Twenty years earlier, Diana had caused a sensation swirling around the White House dance floor with John Travolta in a daring blue velvet gown that was later auctioned off at Christie's for $222,500. This time Camilla struck a decidedly more matronly note in a black cashmere jacket worn over a black floor-length pleated silk skirt.

In his exchange of toasts with President Bush, Charles recalled his first visit to the White House in 1970 "when the media were busy trying to marry me off to Tricia Nixon. And it's very interesting to see," he added wryly, "the same sort of thing happening to my eldest son. So it seems to be an entirely hereditary feature."

In between their dining sessions at the White House, the Prince of Wales and his new wife accompanied the first lady, Laura Bush, on a tour of a charter school in Southeast Washington. As their motorcade departed the White House, they spotted an animal rights activist in a bear suit protesting the use of Canadian bear fur to make hats for the Queen's ceremonial guards. His placard read: GOD SAVE THE BEARS. When they arrived at the school, they again encountered protester Muriel Hartwick and her anti-Camilla sign; the forty-six-year-old Upstate New York bed-and-breakfast owner had followed the royal couple down from New York. "I am," she said slyly, "their little pain in the butt."

The next day, wearing a navy blue suit and pearls, the Duchess of Cornwall arrived with Charles to meet with physicians and patients at the National Institutes of Health in Bethesda, Maryland. U.S. Surgeon General Richard Carmona greeted them, and then came perilously close to leading Camilla straight through a glass door. Pulling back, a startled Camilla touched her nose, as if she had bumped into the glass, prompting a laugh from Charles and the hospital staff. As patron of Britain's National Osteoporosis Society, she gave a speech on the devastating illness that had taken the lives of both her grandmother and her mother. Charles looked on proudly and gave her a reassuring smile when she finished.

After Charles accepted the prestigious Vincent Scully architecture prize for his commitment to urban planning, the couple then attended a Georgetown University conference on "Faith and Social Responsibility" before boarding a plane for New Orleans. In the Big Easy, Charles and Camilla chatted with relief workers and were visibly shaken by the scene of total devastation left by Hurricane Katrina. At one point Camilla, who toted around a shopping bag filled with Mardi Gras decorations that had been given to her by a survivor, clambered up the side of a patched-up levee in a skirt and high heels to survey the damage.

In San Francisco, they visited a homeless shelter where Prince Charles was repeatedly addressed as "Your Honor," then moved on to an open-air market in Marin, where Camilla devoured everything from green beans and blue cheese to smoked salmon, butternut squash soup, and organic wine. She did not offer to pay for any of it—something Princess Diana had always made a point of doing in similar circumstances. At one point, Camilla snatched up an apple from a vendor's stall, took two big bites out of it, and then handed the pulpy remains to her Royal Protection officer.

The purpose of the trip had been crystal clear from the outset: "To make Camilla's first tour a PR success," admitted a palace official, "and nothing else really matters." From the American standpoint, Charles and Camilla seemed like a gracious enough couple, though they failed to generate the kind of excitement that Diana always had stateside. "Princess Diana was everybody's favorite movie star," observed Letitia Baldrige, Jackie Kennedy's former press secretary and close pal. "Camilla is no movie star."

Back home in the U.K., however, the trip was being trumpeted as a resounding success. Even in Diana territory, Charles observed, it seemed that the press—and by extension, the public—were beginning to warm to the Duchess. And, it was duly noted in Palace circles, unlike her predecessor, Camilla had never tried to overshadow her husband. After decades watching from the shadows,

Camilla was now so familiar with royal protocol that she never strayed from the "four steps back" rule: When arriving at a venue, one must always lag four paces behind the more senior royal—in this case the Prince of Wales.

Nevertheless, there were rumblings at Clarence House that Charles was already envious of the amount of attention being paid to Camilla. "He was jealous of Diana and at times he is jealous of Camilla," Richard Kay said. "Prince Charles does not like being eclipsed by anyone—including his own sons."

Given Camilla's rave reviews in the British press, it came as something of a shock when the Queen ruled that the Duchess of Cornwall should be specifically excluded from the state prayers for the Royal Family that are recited, after a separate prayer for the monarch, at all Church of England Sunday services. "Almighty God, the fountain of all goodness," the prayer reads, "we humbly beseech thee to bless Philip, Duke of Edinburgh, Charles, Prince of Wales, and all the Royal Family." Diana, the Princess of Wales, had been included by name and title in the prayers until she was stripped of her royal status following her divorce in 1996.

Charles angrily demanded to know why his mother was snubbing Camilla, but the Queen stood firm. "Too many people are still unhappy with the marriage, Charles," she explained, citing polls that showed that showed three out of four Britons still did not want Camilla as Queen. "I don't wish to appear insensitive."

Charles would face other indignities that December, not the least of which was a lengthy grilling by Operation Paget chief Lord Stevens. Stepping into the Main Hall of Clarence House, Stevens was immediately struck by how dark it was, despite the Brobdingnagian chandeliers that hung overhead. The Queen Mother's presence was still very much felt here, thanks to her adoring grandson. Her favorite Dick Francis novels were still in the bookcases, paintings of her favorite Thoroughbreds occupied a place of honor in the Horse Corridor, and Lord Stevens smiled when he spotted a watercolor of two of the Queen Mum's beloved corgis, Billy and Bee, on a table in the Morning Room.

Lord Stevens and two members of the Operation Paget team were ushered to the Lancaster Room, where he was greeted by a surprisingly relaxed-looking Prince of Wales. For the next two and a half hours, the veteran detective politely but firmly questioned Prince Charles about the events leading up to and immediately following the death of his former wife. Had Princess Diana ever indicated to him that she believed she was under surveillance, or that she feared for her life? Did he have any reason to believe that she intended to marry Dodi Fayed? Was he aware of the letter that she had written, eerily predicting her death in a car crash—the note in which Diana allegedly named Tiggy Legge-Bourke as the woman she believed he really wanted to marry?

Not surprisingly, Charles grew increasingly impatient as the session wore on. He seemed on the verge of calling a halt to the proceedings when Lord Stevens nervously cleared his throat and asked, "Did you, Your Highness, plot to murder the Princess or have anything to do with her death?"

Charles was clearly taken aback. He knew that in some form or other the question would be posed, but not so bluntly. He paused for a moment and shook his head in disgust. "No," Charles shot back, "I did not." Later, he complained bitterly to Camilla about having to be subjected to such questions. "Really," he told her. "The *impertinence.*"

Camilla agreed with her husband that the investigation had dragged on too long, and with no end in sight. After all, Lord Stevens's report would only serve as the basis for the coroner's inquest, which in and of itself could drag on for a year or more.

With every passing development and rumored finding in the case, the public in general and the Royal Family in particular were reminded of Diana's status at one time as the most famous—and most relentlessly hunted—person on the planet.

Against this backdrop, William fretted over how to protect the woman he loved from a similar fate. During their time together at St. Andrews, Kate and William were more or less left alone as part of the palace's ongoing privacy agreement with Fleet Street. The gloves had come off since graduation, but as long as Kate was with William, his security detail provided something of a shield against intrusions by the press.

William and Kate had essentially lived together for three years at St. Andrews, but now he could only stay over the occasional night at her stucco-fronted flat across from a bus stop in Chelsea. Kate's apartment was repeatedly checked over by Scotland Yard because of William's presence there. But there was nothing police were obligated to do to protect Kate when she ventured outside without the Prince.

Now an average of six or seven photographers dogged her every move, tailing Kate whenever she went out shopping or to meet friends. They crouched between cars and lunged from behind bushes, snapping away as Kate loaded groceries into the back of her car or fumbled with her apartment keys.

For the moment, Kate was able to smile gamely back. But William worried that she would, like his mother, begin to feel like a "hunted animal." The issue came to a head when a German magazine, *Das Neue*, published photographs showing William leaving Kate's apartment after spending the night. A large red arrow pointed to the flat with the caption "The Love Nest."

In the wake of the July 7, 2005, terrorist bombings that had ripped through London killing fifty-two commuters, William

fumed at the "sheer irresponsibility" of pinpointing the exact location of Kate's flat. Rather than simply wait for the next crisis,
William asked his senior advisors at Clarence House to make some
sort of preemptive strike.

In October, the royal law firm of Harbottle & Lewis sent a letter to newspaper editors warning them to stay away from Kate
and suggesting that some of the photographers who had been
hounding Kate had done so in violation of the Press Complaints
Commission.

Against his father's advice, William pushed for even tougher legal action. After decades of being pursued by the press, Monaco's
Princess Caroline had managed to get a court order banning the
German tabloid press from publishing photos of Caroline or her
children. Now William wanted to see if the ruling might apply to
Kate. He asked his lawyers to be prepared to take Kate's case for
privacy to the European Court of Human Rights—but only if the
situation worsened.

Papa disagreed with his son's combative stance toward the media
and warned him that any court action might backfire. Once again,
he hewed to the family's tried-and-true "say nothing, do nothing"
approach until the whole thing blew over.

By the end of 2005, it was painfully clear that that was not
about to happen. Kate was still being pursued by paparazzi, although she lessened her exposure to the outside world somewhat
by choosing to work at home with her parents on her own children's clothing line.

Now gushing stories about the young commoner who might
someday be a royal bride—perhaps even Queen—were filling the
mainstream as well as the tabloid press. Hearkening back to the "Shy
Di" days, the *Independent on Sunday* dubbed Kate "Her Royal Shy-
ness." The *Independent* went so far as to predict that "the People's

Princess may be replaced, in Kate, by a real princess of the people: a non-blueblood."

St. James's Palace, with William's blessing, peppered Fleet Street editors with reprimands and warnings. The result: a working press that had always been overwhelmingly fond of Diana's elder son was now growing tired of being scolded by his minions. Moreover, some editors who were reluctant to concede William's self-confessed need for control, began to blame Kate. "Kate Middleton wants the privacy of a nun," objected the *Sun*'s deputy editor Fergus Shanahan, "yet she chooses to go out with Prince William. . . . She can't have it both ways."

No one understood that better than the Duchess of Cornwall. After decades of living on the periphery of the Royal Family—being at once part of it and apart from it—Camilla was now savoring the benefits of full membership. December 25, 2005, would mark another milestone in her metamorphosis from mistress to royal wife—her royal Christmas at Sandringham *as* a royal.

Following the usual schedule, everyone had arrived at Sandringham by Christmas Eve; Charles, William, and Harry, as predicted, straggled in last. That afternoon, everyone helped the Queen put the finishing touches on the twenty-foot tree that had been cut down on the grounds of the estate and set up in Sandringham House's White Drawing Room.

Family members then placed gifts for one another on several trestle tables covered in white linen; name cards made it clear where each person's gifts were to be left. Tea was served around five, and an hour later everyone returned to the tree and awaited permission from the Queen to begin opening gifts. Following the German tradition of their ancestors, the Windsors always opened their presents on Christmas Eve.

For the family that has everything, Yuletide gift giving centered on who could buy the least extravagant— and often most tacky— gift. The Queen would always insist that the casserole dish or the teapot she was given was "just what I always wanted," while everyone tried to top Charles's all-time favorite Christmas gift: a white leather toilet seat.

After exchanging gifts to howls of laughter, everyone changed into formal attire—gowns for the women, black tie for the men— for predinner cocktails and then a lavish banquet. To signal her complete acceptance by the family and acknowledge her rank among royal women as second only to the Queen, Camilla was seated next to Prince Philip. After dinner was over at ten, the women withdrew to another room while the royal menfolk stayed behind with Grandpapa for port, brandy, and cigars.

The following morning, everyone awoke to find stockings stuffed with small gifts and fruit tied to their bedposts. Once they had indulged in a full English breakfast, it was off on foot—except for the Queen—to the church on Sandringham's grounds, St. Mary Magdalene. This time, more than two thousand well-wishers turned out at the church to welcome the newest member of the family. Charles beamed as Camilla, struggling to carry several bouquets that had been thrust at her, thanked the crowd.

Still hewing to tradition, they ate again—this time a traditional Christmas lunch served promptly at 1 P.M. and consisting of turkey raised on the estate. Two hours later, Camilla huddled with the family around the TV to watch Her Majesty's taped Christmas broadcast to the nation. Afterward, the Queen bundled up to take her corgis for a stroll on the estate grounds while Camilla and Charles retired to their rooms to read.

The day after Christmas, celebrated in England as Boxing Day,

Prince Philip organized a shooting party. Camilla, never one to miss an opportunity to tromp through the countryside in boots, tagged along.

Following her separation from Charles, Diana had felt the sting of ostracism most keenly during the holidays. While her sons celebrated with the Windsor relatives at Sandringham, the Princess spent her last Christmas on Barbuda, in the British West Indies. Relegated to the sidelines for years, Camilla understood what it was like to spend Christmas apart from someone she loved. The trappings, she told a friend from Wiltshire, meant little to her. "As long as I'm with Charles," Camilla, "it's a happy Christmas."

William was also missing his mate. Like Harry's girlfriend, Chelsy Davy, Kate Middleton was being slowly being wrapped in the Royal Family's embrace. But neither young woman yet warranted the coveted invitation to a Sandringham Christmas; for the time being, Kate would have to settle for spending New Year's with her Prince Charming.

For all the paparazzi's undeniable persistence, no one up to this point had actually photographed William and Kate kissing. The palace had led reporters to believe they would celebrate the arrival of 2006—and William's last few days of freedom before entering Sandhurst—at one of their favorite holiday spots, Verbier in Switzerland. Instead, they quietly headed for Klosters. While reporters searched for them two hundred miles to the southwest, William and Kate spent the days skiing and nights holed up alone in a small chalet.

Both accomplished skiers, William and Kate went off-trail to try the powder atop Casanna Alp—a risk that Royal Protection officers present apparently thought was acceptable. Had he known, Charles almost certainly would not have approved; it was while skiing here at Klosters that the Prince of Wales was nearly killed in the 1987 avalanche that took the life of his close friend Hugh Lindsay.

Once they had made their run, the young couple paused to take in the view. Then William put his arm around Kate, looked into her sapphire blue eyes and, as she caught her breath, pulled her close for a lingering kiss. "It was very romantic," said an onlooker, "and lasted several moments."

What they had not realized was that the press had finally caught up with them. The next day, the first photo of William and his girlfriend kissing was everywhere, alongside the inevitable KISS ME KATE headlines.

Before Wills headed for Sandhurst, he joined Kate for a quiet dinner at her apartment in Chelsea. When she flung the door open, thirty of the Prince's friends who had crowded into Kate's small flat yelled "surprise." Wills "had no idea what was up," said one of the guests. "He walked in and beamed a big smile when he realized Kate had surprised him."

On January 8, 2005, William arrived at Sandhurst with his father, his ironing board, and 268 other officer cadets to begin forty-four weeks of military training. Wills would not be there to help Kate celebrate turning twenty-four the following day; in fact, he would not be allowed to see her for the next five weeks as he adjusted to military life.

With Harry on the verge of completing his training to become an army officer, pressure had been brought to bear on William to follow in Papa's footsteps and join the British Navy. But the Heir's brief stint training with the Welsh Guards on Belize five years earlier had left their mark. William's military game plan had changed a bit, however. Now his stated goal was to sign up for

flight training and eventually serve in the Army Air Corps as a helicopter pilot.

Just as they had with Harry, officers at Sandhurst were determined to make it clear that William would be shown no fa-
voritism. "Although Prince William is the future head of the
armed forces," Major General Ritchie said, "he will be treated
the same as every other cadet." Less diplomatic was Lieutenant
Colonel Roy Parkinson. "We receive people from all back-
grounds," Parkinson stressed, "but background goes right out the
window once training begins. It's a team effort here. If someone steps out of line, they're stamped on, whether they're a
prince or not."

As if to underscore the point, William was immediately given
a close-cropped military haircut that, to his horror, exposed the
bald spot inherited from Papa. After the endless inspections,
marches, and drills that characterized the first phase of instruction,
Officer Cadet Wales faced Sandhurst's most daunting physical
challenge: the "Long Reach"—a twenty-four-hour, forty-mile
trek with full battle gear across the snow-covered Welsh hills.
Nearly a third of the 269 cadets failed to finish; for William, whose
Uncle Edward had been pilloried for washing out of training to
become a Royal Marine, failure was not an option.

Nor was it an option for Kate, who now had to hold on to
her place at the royal table in William's absence. On March 17,
2006, Camilla was set to present the winner's trophy at the prestigious Cheltenham Gold Cup Thoroughbred races. Wearing a
fawn-colored coat, gloves, and a striking mink hat, Kate entered
the grounds with a girlfriend and mixed among the other spectators before making her first appearance by herself with the
Prince of Wales and Camilla in the royal box.

The level of familiarity between Kate and Charles surprised on-lookers, as did the obvious rapport between Kate and Camilla. If anything, the Duchess of Cornwall, outwardly nervous at having to present the trophy, was relieved to have another woman sharing the spotlight. Just two weeks earlier, Camilla had received her own seal of approval of sorts when, during opening ceremonies for the new home of the Welsh Assembly, the Queen exchanged a peck on the cheek with her new daughter-in-law.

William was back in the picture the following week, when he showed up at Eton to play on an "old boys" alumni team competing in something called "The Field Game"—a soccer-rugby hybrid. This time, the jeans-clad Kate and William made no effort to conceal their feelings for each other. They hugged and kissed openly, and he laughed when she reached up to check out his new military buzz cut.

Over the next few months, Middleton's place within the family grew more and more secure. By late March, Prince Charles heeded his son's pleas and hired a bodyguard to protect her. He also gave his explicit permission for Kate and William to occupy the same room whenever she visited Highgrove—which was often. The Queen, meanwhile, decided the house William had shared with Harry at Balmoral for years did not afford either brother the privacy they now required. At a cost of $150,000, she ordered the renovation of a 120-year-old, three-bedroom hideaway in a section of the Balmoral estate called Brochdhu—her gift to William and, she now hoped, the woman who would become his bride.

Camilla, so often accused in the press of resenting the competition, actually joined the Queen in championing Kate as a potential royal bride. "Camilla is very sweet to me," Middleton told a close friend since childhood. "She is very warm and very funny, and she doesn't take herself too seriously. But," Kate noted, "she still gets nervous about the job she's got to do."

Before she embarked on a two-week tour of Egypt, India, and Saudi Arabia, the Duchess did something more in keeping with her English country roots: she joined the Tetbury chapter of the Women's Institute, a volunteer organization whose middle-aged members famously shed their clothes for charity and inspired the 2003 hit film *Calendar Girls* starring Helen Mirren. In doing so, Camilla, who was assured by the president of her local WI chapter that she would not "have to worry about starring in any calendars," joined Princess Anne and the Queen. In fact, Her Majesty was president of the WI's Sandringham chapter.

Perhaps remembering Sharon Osbourne's comment about Camilla's "gorgeous old tits," the Duchess almost seemed disappointed that her chapter would not be doing a calendar of their own. "I loved the movie," said Camilla, who with Charles had actually invited several of the original Calendar Girls portrayed in the film to tea at Clarence House. "It was the movie that inspired me to join." Roger Hallett, whose wife, Heather, is also a member, was not at all surprised. "I always said," he smirked, "that *Calendar Girls* would attract *that* kind of woman to the WI."

That kind of woman was more determined than ever to fulfill her "spousing duties," as she jokingly called them. While she was the first to admit she lacked Diana's glamour, Camilla insisted that she could still be a helpmate to her husband as he traveled abroad.

In Cairo, she removed her shoes and put on a veil to enter the 1,000-year-old Al Azhar temple. While visiting ruins in the town of Siwa, her devoutly Muslim hosts were less than amused when the dress she was wearing swirled up in the wind à la Marilyn Monroe's subway grate scene in *The Seven Year Itch*.

The mood was more somber at El Alamein, when, in honoring a promise made to her own war hero father, she visited the graves of two of his fallen comrades in the Commonwealth War Graves Cemetery. "I've a huge lump in my throat," she said as she knelt down at the graves. "It's quite hard to speak."

Saudi King Abdullah also seemed at a loss for words when, in violation of strict Wahhabite Islamic law, Camilla chose not to wear a headscarf during their formal introduction. She did manage a deep curtsy, however. Charles, the first non-Muslim allowed to speak at Imam Muhammad bin Saud University, began his comments with "Your Excellencies, ladies and gentlemen"—apparently oblivious to the fact that strict Islamic law also saw to it that there was not a single female in sight.

The 108-degree temperatures in India, Camilla would later recall, "almost did me in." She was forced to stop and rest in the shade several times, and at one point a physician treated her after she complained of stomach pains. "Please," she asked her Indian hosts as she walked through the village of Artiya, "turn the thermostat down!"

At a Sikh shrine in Punjab, things got even worse when, while signing a guest book, Camilla went to sit down and someone inadvertently pulled the chair out from under her. Crashing to the floor, Camilla was then helped to her feet by Charles and several officials. Amid a flurry of profound apologies, she graciously laughed it off. "How she managed to keep smiling all the way down as she hit the floor," said the *Telegraph*'s Caroline Davies, "is a marvel."

Fleet Street concurred, to the extent it cared. While the Prince of Wales and his wife battled heat, flies, sand, wind, and stomach cramps, the press was more interested in the escapades of the next generation of royals.

Prince Harry was more than willing to oblige. The week before he was scheduled to "pass out" (graduate) from Sandhurst, the Spare and several of his cadet chums made a 3 A.M. visit to the nearby Spearmint Rhino strip club in Berkshire. Harry whooped his approval at the strippers, but politely declined a private lap dance. "Sorry," he told dancer Mariella Butkute, "but I love my girlfriend too much."

The next day, Harry picked up the phone to hear a woman screeching at him in a distinct South African accent. "It's Chelsy. How *could* you? I see you had a lovely time without me. But I miss you so much, you big ginger," she went on, "and I want you to know that I love you." By this time, it had begun to dawn on Harry that the hysterical girl on the other end of the line was actually William.

Still, when Chelsy flew in from South Africa four days later, the beautiful blonde in jeans and knee-high boots looked anything but pleased. Escorted by five armed guards, she ignored reporters' questions about Harry's strip club adventure as she made her way through the passenger terminal at Heathrow.

Davy was not, according to friends, angry with Harry for celebrating with friends at a strip club. She was used to this sort of thing. "The phone will ring at 3 A.M. or 4 A.M. and it's him swearing how much he loves her," said a friend of the Davys. "It would be more convincing if there weren't music, clinking glasses, and girls' voices in the background."

Davy was, said friends of the couple, more distraught over having to cope with Britain's voracious tabloid press. "I can see how upset she gets," Harry said, who allowed that he made a point of reading everything written about him. The stories "still upset me," he explained, "and I still read them. Why, I do not know, but I have to read them—to see who wrote the articles and who took the pictures. . . . I write the names all down," he joked, as if he were making an enemies list, "for later."

Ostensibly, Chelsy had made the trip from Cape Town to see him graduate from Sandhurst on April 14, 2006—or, more accurately, to celebrate at the lavish ball that followed. Like the other cadets, Harry was permitted to invite only ten guests to the actual graduation ceremony, the Sovereign's Parade. Charles and Camilla were there, along with Prince Philip, longtime friends Hugh and Emilie van Cutsem, William, and the nanny Diana and Camilla both viewed as a rival: Tiggy Legge-Bourke Pettifer. (Kate Middleton had also been invited but, determined not to eclipse Chelsy on the day she rightfully shared with Harry, chose not to attend. The point was moot, since Chelsy, preferring to spend her time getting ready for the formal ball, opted out as well.)

Tiggy, who had also been one of the guests at Windsor for the blessing of Charles's marriage to Camilla, was apparently no longer regarded as a threat by the Duchess of Cornwall. The woman Diana at one time believed would marry Charles after both she and Camilla were put "out of the way" and who Camilla used to refer to as the "Hired Help" and "Big Ass" was now a smiling presence at most major events involving William and Harry.

Of course, the most important figure present that day was Granny, who was attending the Sandhurst graduation ceremonies for the first time in fifteen years. Standing for inspection with their ceremonial swords raised, more than four hundred cadets remained stern-faced as the Queen passed before them—with one exception. Blushing, Harry could not suppress an ear-to-ear grin. Speaking to freshly minted army officers—her own grandson among them— who might soon be sent to fight in Iraq, the Queen said, "My congratulations, my prayers, and my trust go with you all."

Harry's grandparents, his father, and the rest of the royal party stayed long enough to tell him how proud they were. Rank and protocol then led to a bewildering family display. Prince Charles, wearing the uniform of a lieutenant general, saluted Prince Philip, who was decked out in full field marshal regalia and scores of medals. Prince Philip then saluted back. Then cadet Prince William and Second Lieutenant Harry saluted them both. As Harry left with his fellow officers, William saluted again.

Meanwhile, Camilla followed protocol with a deep curtsy to the Queen. When William and Harry approached their stepmother, they removed their caps before kissing her on the cheek. Mercifully, the group departed early so Harry and his chums could get down to celebrating.

As the sun began to set, Harry donned the crimson jacket of his dress uniform for the first time and, after drinks with his fellow platoon members, went looking for his girlfriend. To his obvious delight, Chelsy showed up at the black tie gala with an upswept hairdo and her tanned back exposed in a plunging blue-green satin sheath. Not surprisingly, for the rest of the evening Harry seldom left her side.

While his Royal Protection detail hovered not far away, Harry and Chelsy drank and smoked and laughed and talked, breaking occasionally to exchange knowing looks and languid kisses. Not that this deterred female admirers. When one slightly inebriated girl walked up and pinched his derriere, a delighted Harry responded by pinching her back.

Playfulness aside, Harry was determined not to repeat the mistakes of his past—at least not tonight. After years of being viewed as a "national disgrace," he was no longer Harry Pothead or Harry the Nazi. He was Second Lieutenant Wales, and while he was clearly enjoying the party, Harry was careful not to embarrass his family or his superiors.

The same, sadly, could not be said for William. At midnight he congratulated his brother when, like the rest of the cadets, Harry followed time-honored tradition by ripping black tape off his uniform to reveal his new rank. But as the night progressed, the Heir became louder and steadily more obnoxious, lurching about the dance floor and then joining in when one of his fellow cadets started impersonating a general—a send-up that several senior officers present found offensive. Wills screamed with laughter at the off-color stories of another pal, and by 2 A.M. he seemed so out of control that a senior officer ordered him to go home. The next morning, a furious Commandant Ritchie phoned Prince Charles's offices at Clarence House to make it clear that William's crude behavior indicated that he was obviously neither an officer nor a gentleman.

If he was at all remorseful, William certainly did not let on. The next night, the two Princes continued celebrating with Kate and Chelsy at Boujis in South Kensington. Photos of the bleary-eyed foursome, taken after they had boozed it up for hours, were splashed across Britain's tabloids the following morning.

The future King, one of his Eton buddies observed, "can be a very moody guy. He starts breaking all the rules when he's feeling trapped." Trapped by what? Sandhurst? Kate Middleton and the prospect of marriage? The burden of monarchy? A life and a future over which he has no control?

"Yes," his friend replied.

Another sign that William's spirits were sagging under the lorry-load of responsibilities he now faced was his growing obsession with speed. His motorcycles had always offered him the sense of freedom mixed with anonymity that he craved. Concealed beneath his helmet, he could hit the open road like any other person his age without being pestered or stared at.

But William's new superbikes—a Yamaha RI and a Honda CBR 1100XX Blackbird—were among the most powerful on the road, capable of reaching speeds in excess of 160 miles per hour. After watching him tear across the countryside with his four Royal Protection officers trying to keep up, Kate begged Wills to be more careful. The Queen shared Middleton's concern and asked Charles if he couldn't persuade William to give up motorcycles altogether. "I understand they can be terribly difficult to control," she told one motorbike enthusiast during a walkabout. "Prince William rides them but it frightens me. . . ."

The young man's need for speed would have given any doting grandmother cause for alarm. So too was William's continued insistence—not to mention Harry's—on fighting alongside his comrades. As the situation in both Afghanistan and Iraq grew more dire and terrorist threats to her country increased, the Queen realized that she could not prevent her grandsons—or at least not *both* William and Harry—from putting their lives on the line.

The decision would ultimately have to be left up to the military and the government. Much to Her Majesty's relief, there was a general consensus that the heir to the throne could not be put in harm's way, no matter how strenuously he objected.

Harry was another matter. Once he completed his training, Second Lieutenant Wales would be put in charge of four light tanks and eleven men. Yet senior military officials feared that Harry would be, in the words of one general, "a fat prize" for terrorists. They also worried that the Prince would be an obvious target wherever he went in Iraq or Afghanistan, thus putting his fellow soldiers in greater jeopardy.

Like his brother, Harry left no doubt that he intended to fight. In making his case, he pointed to Uncle Andrew, who saw combat as a helicopter pilot attached to the aircraft carrier HMS *Invincible* during the Falklands War. At the time, the British government, faced with the distinct possibility that the then second in line to the throne might be killed in action, wanted Prince Andrew reassigned to a desk job. But the Queen, remembering how many of her fellow Britons put their lives on the line in World War II, personally intervened on her son's behalf. She insisted that he be allowed to perform combat missions like any other naval officer. However, she was later surprised to learn that, in addition to engaging in antisubmarine warfare, Andrew had piloted a helicopter that deployed an Exocet missile decoy—a particularly hazardous mission.

Military experts were quick to point out, however, that this time Britain and its allies were facing a very different kind of enemy—one who kidnapped Westerners and then beheaded them. "Can you imagine capturing or abducting a member of the Royal Family, and then getting that on videotape?" asked one member of Britain's foreign intelligence agency MI6. "It would be a nightmare."

Still, Harry was counting on Granny to back him up, and those who had known her since girlhood were confident she would. "Like other people of her generation," observed her cousin Margaret Rhodes, "the Queen is a great believer in duty—and sacrifice."

It's as if Diana has been reincarnated.

—*Peter Archer,*

about Prince William

It's not a question of wanting to be King.
It's something I was born into and
it's my duty.

—*William*

9

The band of the Irish Guards struck up "Happy Birthday" and a flag-waving crowd of 25,000 cheered wildly as she emerged from Windsor Castle into the sunlight. For the next forty-five minutes, Her Majesty Queen Elizabeth II mingled with Britons who had come to wish her a happy eightieth birthday on April 21, 2006. A familiar figure in a pink wool coat with matching hat—the trademark handbag dangling on her forearm—the Queen appeared, Countess Mountbatten observed, "as happy as I have ever seen her."

She seemed equally ebullient when she was shown an aerial photo of five hundred crew members spelling out "Happy 80th" on the deck of the aircraft carrier HMS *Illustrious*, and when she played host at Buckingham Palace to "my ninety-nine twins"—Britons who just happened to share her birthday.

Not even Charles's characteristically stiff video tribute to the woman he called "my mama" could dampen her spirits. Having already widely complained that his mother was cold and aloof, Charles chose to remember the eve of her coronation and vivid memories "of my mother coming to say good night to my sister and me while wearing the crown so that she could get used to its weight." He also recalled his mother's long absences when he was a small boy—particularly her six-month-long coronation tour, and the frustration of trying to talk to her long-distance when all one heard was "the faintest of voices" over an incessant "crackle and static."

Nothing seemed to buoy the Queen's mood quite so much as the birthday dinner attended by twenty-five members of her family at the newly refurbished Kew Palace, once home to George III. Before the dinner began, everyone stepped outside to watch fireworks explode overhead while the Royal Marine band played Beatles, Elvis, and even some show tunes. Wearing a pale blue gown and a spectacular diamond necklace that had belonged to her grandmother Queen Mary, the Queen could not contain a mile-wide smile as she gazed skyward.

Inside, a twelve-piece string ensemble played selections from Handel's *Water Music* while guests dined by candlelight on Hebridean smoked salmon and shrimp, juniper-roast loin of Sandringham Estate venison, and chocolate sponge birthday cake with fresh fruit from Highgrove's organic gardens. Seated before the fireplace in Kew Palace's white-paneled dining room, the Queen was flanked by William and Charles. "Mama" talked animatedly with her children, grandchildren, and cousins for ninety minutes before Charles rose to end the meal with a toast—to a "wonderful" queen and "darling mama and grandmother."

Predictably, the Queen's birthday gave rise to speculation that she might retire. After all, Charles was now fifty-six—just three years younger than Edward VII when he succeeded Queen Victoria on the throne. Like Edward, Charles had grown impatient—even bitter—during a lifetime spent playing the waiting game. Such questions regarding the future of the monarchy were not left to chance—far from it. In 1992 Lord Airlie, a particular favorite of the Queen's and at the time Lord Chamberlain, set up the Way Ahead Group to steer the monarchy into the next century. Presided over by the Queen, the group was made up of senior members of the Royal Family and a handful of key advisors whose identities remained a closely guarded secret. The details of their discussions were not disclosed to anyone; even the prime minister was kept out of the loop.

During their twice-yearly, closed-door meetings, this powerful clique grappled with issues ranging from whether the Crown should pay taxes (in one of its first actions, the group decided that it should), to scrapping the royal yacht *Britannia*, to ending male primogeniture, the existing rule in Britain giving male heirs precedence. Starting in 2006, Prince William was permitted to sit in on meetings of the Way Ahead Group.

William's active participation in the decision-making process underscored Granny's desire for the monarchy to begin a seamless transition to the next generation. The Queen was, in fact, gradually turning over more responsibility to her son. She now intended to take more four-day weekends away from Buckingham Palace, and for the first time Charles would begin to hold his own regular audiences with the prime minister and Commonwealth leaders. The Prince of Wales was also being given more access to government papers and was presiding over more investitures. He was also standing for his mother more frequently when ambassadors presented their credentials to the Court of St. James's.

Still, those closest to the Queen insisted she would never step aside—in part because, for the first time, she regarded herself as the true head of the Royal Family. "I think in a funny way, perhaps, the death of the Queen Mother had quite a huge effect on the Queen," said her cousin Margaret Rhodes. "Not only of sadness, but in a way that she could come into her own as the head of the family and as the senior royal lady." As a result, Rhodes continued, "I'm perfectly certain she will never retire as such. Because it's not like a normal job, and to the Queen the vows she made on Coronation Day are something so deep and so special that she wouldn't consider not continuing to fulfill those vows until she dies. I am sure she will never abdicate." Prince Philip's cousin the Countess Mountbatten agreed: "She regards the job as a job for life."

Even if she were willing to step aside, the Queen took note of the polls that showed the public's reticence about seeing Charles on the throne and their unalloyed affection for her and for William. Charles's marriage to Camilla had complicated things even more; those same polls still showed that three out of four Britons were vehemently opposed to the Duchess of Cornwall becoming Queen.

It did not help matters that Camilla, who had begun wearing Diana's jewelry as early as 2000, angered many fans of the late Princess by wearing a particularly recognizable piece to a movie premiere. Originally given to Edward VII to celebrate his 1863 wedding to Princess Alexandra of Denmark, the royal heirloom consisted of a dazzling emerald pendant attached to a diamond circle, the gold three feathers insignia of the Prince of Wales. Diana always wore the brooch on a diamond necklace, along with matching diamond and emerald drop earrings Charles had given her as a wedding present. Now Camilla was wearing the brooch alone, pinned to the shoulder of her jacket. "Prince William did not say anything," a Clarence House staff member observed, "but when he saw the photos of her wearing it in the papers, you could tell he was surprised."

Ironically, the sons who were now so devoted to Charles were part of the problem. They served as a constant reminder of the rebel Princess whose glamour, style, openness, and generosity had changed the monarchy. They also made it impossible to forget that Camilla had once been her sworn enemy, and that Charles's infidelity had sparked the chain of events ultimately leading to Diana's destruction.

No less than his brother, who had adopted several of Diana's pet charities, Harry was intent on following in her footsteps. One week after wishing Granny happy birthday at the lavish royal dinner, Harry was on leave from the army and back in Lesotho—this time to join with Lesotho's Prince Seeiso in formally announcing their new charity for children orphaned by AIDS, Sentebale ("Forget Me Not"). Like Diana, Seeiso's late mother, Queen MaMohato, was a beloved figure in her country. Both Princes dedicated Sentebale in honor of their mothers.

On this visit, Harry was particularly interested in reconnecting with Mutsu Potsane, a six-year-old boy he had befriended on his last visit a year earlier. "Where is he?" Harry asked as soon as his truck rumbled up to the entrance of the Mants'ase Children's Home. The shy boy emerged from the crowd, and Harry knelt down to give him a bear hug before scooping him and swinging him in the air.

"How are you?" Harry asked the boy. "Do you remember me?" Harry had given Mutsu a pair of boots on his last visit and noticed the boy wasn't wearing them. "Where are your wellies?" he asked.

Harry held the boy's hand and affectionately stroked his head as he was brought up to date on changes at the children's home, but the child seemed to shrink from the attention. "I've never seen him so quiet," Harry said of the once-mischievous child.

A staff member, Anne Bothma, explained that Mutsu was overwhelmed. "He's been waiting for you," Bothma said.

Mutsu took a place of honor on Harry's lap as all the children gathered around the Prince for a photo op. "You'll be surprised," Harry promised. "Come back in twenty-five years. You'll see a massive difference. As far as I'm concerned, I'm committed to this for the rest of my life." Would his mother be proud? someone asked. Harry paused for a moment and smiled broadly. "I hope so," he said.

William was also taking advantage of a two-week break from his military training at Sandhurst, vacationing with Kate on a Caribbean island he hoped would provide a modicum of privacy. Part of the Grenadines, Mustique (from *moustique,* French for *mosquito*) was acquired in 1958 by British developer Colin Tennant. Later given the title Lord Glenconner, Tennant built a scaled-down version of the Taj Mahal for himself and gave his friend Princess Margaret property on which to build her own hideaway. She called it Les Jolie Eaux—"The Beautiful Waters."

The high-living Princess Margaret, whose affair on the island with the seventeen-years-younger Roddy Llewellyn would effectively end her marriage to Lord Snowden, invited her friend Mick Jagger to build his own "cottage" there in 1971. For the next thirty years, the Queen's sister, Jagger, and the seventy-odd homeowners (including Margaret's son Lord Linley, advertising mogul Mary Wells Lawrence, Lord Litchfield, and David Bowie) fought to keep outsiders to a minimum. They succeeded: despite its fame, the island boasted only one small hotel, the Cotton Club, a small guest-house called Firefly, and one restaurant, Basil's Bar.

For eight days William and Kate strolled Macaroni Beach hand in hand, splashed in the turquoise surf, and spent evenings sipping tropical drinks as they gazed at taffy pink sunsets. As was so often the case for members of the Royal Family, William had been given the use of Villa Hibiscus, the spectacular hilltop estate of Jigsaw fashion mogul John Robertson, gratis. By way of thanks, the Prince offered to make a donation to a hospital on nearby St. Vincent.

With no sign of paparazzi, they began to relax. The couple swam off a yacht that had also been lent to them, and afterward a bikini-clad Kate wrung out her hair as Wills hosed himself off. By the time they landed at Basil's Bar that evening with a group of friends, the Prince had loosened up enough to belt out his own renditions of Elvis's "Suspicious Minds" and the Frank Sinatra anthem "My Way." (Not surprisingly, Wills and his brother were both huge fans of television's *American Idol* and shared an intense dislike of the show's dyspeptic judge, Simon Cowell.)

William felt his holiday with Kate had gone his way—until he returned home to find London's newspapers filled with pictures of their afternoon aboard the yacht. Understandably frustrated, the Prince once again consulted with the Crown's solicitors to see what could be done to protect Kate's privacy. "I have to put up with this because it's the world I was born into," William told the lawyers, "but why should Kate? She shouldn't have to give up her privacy just because of me."

Just a few days after returning from Mustique, Kate and William showed off their Caribbean tans at the wedding of Camilla's daughter, Laura Parker Bowles, and Harry Lopes, a former Calvin

Klein underwear model and grandson of the late Lord Astor of Hever. For Kate, the invitation to a Royal Family wedding was just one more "significant step forward," as the *Sunday Telegraph* put it, in her romance with William. That Harry came alone sent an equally strong signal that Chelsy Davy might not have progressed quite as far.

An audible gasp went up from the thousand-plus spectators gathered outside St. Cyriac's Church in the tiny Wiltshire village of Lacock when the golden couple appeared. Once again, Kate seemed an elegant addition to the family in a striking golden-and-cream embroidered coat and ostrich-plumed hat. "There was," said St. Cyriac's Reverend Sally Wheeler, "a terrific buzz as they came in."

From St. Cyriac's everyone moved on to the reception at Raymill House, the country home Camilla purchased after her divorce from Andrew Parker Bowles. Her fourth home after Clarence House, Highgrove, and Birkhall in Scotland, Raymill House was now costing the British taxpayers $3 million yearly in security expenditures alone. Here, where Camilla and Charles had trysted so many times during his marriage to their mother, William and Harry mingled happily with the extended Parker Bowles clan.

Scarcely a month later, the royals joined the Parker Bowleses again—this time for the funeral of Camilla's father, dead at age eighty-nine. Camilla was, in Charles's words, "absolutely devastated by the loss."

Major Bruce Shand, who had the P.G. Wodehouse penchant for ending every sentence with "what?" had always stood steadfastly behind his daughter—even when, after Diana's death, Camilla was the most hated woman in England. But he had also reportedly blasted Prince Charles in private for not marrying his daughter more quickly. The lack of a marriage license, however, did not dissuade Shand from moving into Clarence House even when Camilla was still only mistress to the Prince of Wales. Major Shand's typically understated response to the news that Charles and Camilla were finally to wed: "Being Prince Charles's father-in-law," he said, "will be fine."

"He was the perfect English gentleman," claimed Shand's friend John Keegan. Camilla's father didn't care for being called "well connected," though, Keegan added, "through the marriage of his daughter to the Prince of Wales he became quite as well connected as it is possible to be."

In burying her father, Camilla closed an important chapter in her life. There was another chapter, however—the chapter titled "Diana"—that looked as if it would never end.

Four years after he launched the official investigation into Diana's death, Royal Coroner Michael Burgess withdrew from the case, claiming the strains of a "heavy and constant workload." Burgess's announcement threw the investigation into turmoil and ignited a firestorm of conjecture. Was the royal coroner worried that Operation Paget may have uncovered a plot to murder Diana? Was he pressured to quit for getting too close to the truth? Or did he simply see the inquest as a no-win situation?

In truth, Burgess's withdrawal from the case came only hours after the government admitted that he had no jurisdiction in the case. Burgess's predecessor as Coroner of the Queen's Household, Dr. John Burton, had initially been told by St. James's Palace that Princess Diana's body would be interred at Windsor Castle. "The body of Diana, Princess of Wales, was taken after the postmortem examination to lie in the Chapel Royal, St. James Palace within the jurisdiction of the Coroner for the Queen's Household," said Judith Bernstein of Britain's Department for Constitutional Affairs. "At that time, Dr. Burton understood the body of Diana, Princess of Wales, would be buried in Windsor Castle or its grounds, which are also part of the district for the Coroner of the Queen's Household." It was on this basis that Dr. Burton assumed control of the inquest.

Diana was buried not at Windsor, but at Althorp. Nor, since the divorce, had she even technically been a member of the Royal Family. Moreover, there was belated concern that any investigation headed by the Queen's Coroner could hardly be viewed as impartial. Among other things, in the event a coroner's jury were selected, its members could conceivably all be royal staff members.

That the wrong person had been heading up the inquest from the outset simply added to the comedy of errors. Six weeks after Burgess's stunning announcement, the job would be handed to a retired judge who had spent thirty-five years on the bench. Lady Elizabeth Butler-Sloss, Britain's most senior woman jurist, was the sister of Britain's Lord Chancellor, Lord Havers, and the daughter of the high court judge who sentenced to death the last woman to be hanged in England. Without ever having attended college, much less law school, the well-connected Butler-Sloss managed to get admitted to the bar in 1955 at the age of twenty-two.

Now, a half-century later, Butler-Sloss began her stint as head of the inquest into Diana's death by announcing that she would hold preliminary hearings behind closed doors. Reaction was swift and almost universally negative; Butler-Sloss reversed herself within the month.

With the inquest into their mother's death once again front-page news, William and Harry tried to keep up each other's spirits over the phone. But Harry, again separated from Chelsy for months as he learned to drive a tank at the Bovington training camp in Dorset, appeared to be reverting to old habits.

At the London home of a mutual friend, Harry cornered blond beauty Catherine Davies, who also happened to be thirty-four and the mother of two, in the bathroom. "I was up against the wall," Davies recalled, "and he literally lifted me off the floor and gave me a lovely kiss. I was stunned by it. It was long and lovely." Harry kissed her a second time, and, Davies insisted, she ended things right there.

Maya French, another blonde who was closer to Harry's age, had a somewhat different experience. Harry kissed the twenty-four-year-old masseuse in the VIP room at Boujis and asked her to meet up with him later. When she returned, French said, Harry "was lying on a sofa in a drunken stupor. All he had to do was give me the nod, but he was too drunk for anything."

Then there was his old friend, the TV sports personality Natalie Pinkham. Harry was spotted kissing the stunning blonde as they left a party together at 5 A.M.

Harry's relapse extended to the polo grounds, where at one point he unzipped his riding pants and relieved himself in full view of female spectators. Unfortunately for the Prince, an enterprising photographer was there to record the public urination incident for posterity.

Not even the Queen, who shrugged off most tabloid stories about her grandchildren's carousing, was prepared for the photo that ran on the front page of the *Sun*'s August 16, 2006 edition. Accompanied by the headline DIRTY HARRY, the color photo showed Harry kissing TV personality Natalie Pinkham as he fondled her right breast. Seated directly behind them in the photo was a red-faced, bleary-eyed William, evidently about to down yet another drink. The inside spread headed "The Booze Brothers" showed William and Harry drinking, dancing, and chatting up an assortment of attractive young women.

This time, Clarence House could at least argue that the photo had not been taken during that summer, as the *Sun* had stated, but actually dated back to 2003. Harry was on the phone instantly to Chelsy, pointing out that the photo of him fondling another woman was taken before they began dating.

The *Sun* story, which succeeded in humiliating Harry and William regardless of when the pictures were taken, was only the latest skirmish in the ongoing war between the Windsors and Fleet Street. Months earlier, William began to suspect that his phone was being tapped when details about a minor knee injury suffered at Sandhurst found their way into the press. Around the same time the *Sun* printed its salacious photos of the Princes, Scotland Yard acted on William's tip, arresting three men on charges of not only bugging the Prince's phone, but of plotting to eavesdrop on the phone conversations of Charles and Camilla as well. Among those arrested: the *News of the World*'s well-known royals editor, Clive Goodman. (Later, Goodman would apologize to William, Harry, and Charles and plead guilty to intercepting their phone messages.)

By September, William and Kate were under no illusions about maintaining their privacy when they took off for another sun-drenched holiday—this time for an end-of-summer week on the Mediterranean island of Ibiza. Once again accompanied by a dozen friends and their Royal Protection officers, the couple relaxed by the pool of their rented mansion and boarded a yacht bound for the healing mud baths of nearby Espalmador. While bikini-clad Kate hung back, Wills and his pals covered themselves in mud for the recommended thirty minutes, then washed off in the sea. Nights were spent at Ibiza's Pacha club where, said a long-time patron, Kate "seemed perfectly happy talking with friends while Prince William was going crazy dancing to techno music."

Now, as William and Kate eased into their fifth year together, it no longer seemed a question of *if*, but *when*. Prince Charles quietly went ahead with plans to build an environmentally friendly, 8,500-square-foot neoclassical stone mansion complete with stables and a chapel on the Duchy of Cornwall's Harewood Park Estate. The property, with six reception rooms on the ground floor, six bedroom suites upstairs, and sweeping views in all directions, was intended to be a "starter palace" for William once he married. The Queen had already set aside royal titles for William and his bride—whether it was Kate or someone else. The royal couple, according to senior courtiers, would become the Duke and Duchess of Cambridge.

On September 20, William showed up at St. Mary's Hospital in London to preside over the reopening of the Winnicott Baby Unit where he was born. The Prince cradled a three-week-old in his arms, and it was hard not to notice that her T-shirt read LIT-TLE PRINCESS. Did all this cuddling and cooing make him feel "broody?" a reporter asked.

"I don't know about that," William said, abruptly bringing a halt to any talk of royal fatherhood. "Not yet."

In the meantime, they behaved like any young couple in love. When she locked herself out of her apartment, the first person Kate called for help was William. They continued to send text messages to each other several times a day, and on weekends away from Sandhurst Wills would take his girlfriend to trendy restaurants like London's Archipelago (where she dined on wild boar and he tried the crocodile) or, more often, order takeout to eat at her flat.

The rest of the time, Middleton still managed to get out to parties and clubs, often chaperoned by Wills's best pal, Guy Pelly. Whenever she did, she could count on being ambushed throughout the evening by paparazzi. By this time, the lawyers at Harbottle & Lewis hired by William to represent Kate were secretly videotaping photographers as they accosted her—evidence they threatened to use in court unless the tabloids backed off.

Wills, said a palace official, "never stopped complaining" about the way Kate was being hassled by the press. There was an understandable reason for William's mounting sense of panic: he was now having nightmares about Kate meeting the same fate as his mother, behind the wheel of her small car as she was being pursued through the streets by paparazzi. "Pure terror" were the words William chose to describe the recurring dream to one of his closest Eton chums. "I wake up shaking."

Notwithstanding William's disturbing premonition, Granny was no longer quite as sympathetic as she once had been. "When my sister and I were young," the Queen said, "our friends would arrange parties in their homes and we had quite a lot of fun. We did not," she added, "go to West End nightclubs." Her Majesty's growing impatience was understandable; after all, she was only twenty-five—Kate Middleton's age now—when she succeeded her father on the throne.

Indeed, if any royal girlfriend deserved the monarch's sympathy that fall it was Chelsy Davy. In early September she was having a drink with a fellow coed at Cape Town's Cubana Latino Cafe when five men seated at a table nearby suddenly leapt to their feet, pulled out knives and guns, and herded everyone into the kitchen. Chelsy, along with the rest of the patrons and restaurant staff, was ordered to lie on the floor while the robbers demanded that the manager give them the keys to the safe. When he told them the keys were not kept at the restaurant, the robbers kicked him in the face and stole everyone's keys, wallets, and cell phones.

As soon as the ordeal was over, a shaken Chelsy called Harry. She was less concerned about her safety than the fact that her stolen cell phone contained his private numbers and several text messages.

Such considerations had already come to dominate the lives of both Davy and Middleton as each waited dutifully for the next formal sign of acceptance. If Kate was expected to bide her time, she decided she might as well do it as a working woman. In December 2006 she went to work for Jigsaw as an assistant buyer for their junior accessories line. Middleton soon discovered that she didn't have to be in a West End nightclub to make news. When she quarreled with a parking warden who was about to give her a ticket in front of her apartment, photos of the confrontation were splashed across the front pages of several British papers.

The one woman who would have understood Kate Middleton's plight reclaimed center stage on December 14 with the release of the ominously titled, 832-page *Operation Paget Inquiry Report into the Allegation of Conspiracy to Murder*. In the end, Stevens reached the same conclusion French investigators had reached in 1999— that driver Henri Paul was drunk, and that Diana was simply the victim of a "tragic accident." Conspiracy theories, Stevens declared, were "completely unjustified."

Calling Mohamed Al Fayed "a genuine grieving parent," Lord Stevens nonetheless added "there are other people who are grieving too. This has been a traumatic event which is why at some stage you have to draw a line under it and move on. There was no conspiracy to murder any of the occupants of that car."

An angry Al Fayed, who had left Britain and now resided in Monaco, wasted no time blasting the report. "This is just another cover-up, a whitewash," he said. "I feel sorry for the taxpayers and the money that has been wasted on such garbage."

For the most part, the Operation Paget report aimed at killing off one assassination theory after another. On the question of Diana's supposed pregnancy, for example, the tests that were not done at the time were at long last done in 2005 using samples of blood taken from the wreckage of the car. The sample showed no trace of the pregnancy hormone HCG. In addition to her friend Rosa Monckton's claim that Diana had her period in mid-August, there was new testimony from holistic healer Myriah Daniels, who was traveling with Diana and Dodi on board the yacht *Jonikal*. "I know for a fact Diana wasn't pregnant," Daniels testified, "because she told me she wasn't, and throughout the course of my work on her body I found no indications to show me that she was."

Was Henri Paul moonlighting for British intelligence? The chauffeur's salary at the time was in the neighborhood of $30,000, and yet he somehow managed to stash away over $200,000 in fourteen bank accounts and another $70,000 in stocks. While claiming there was not enough evidence to support the charge that Paul may have been involved in some "clandestine" activity, the Operation Paget report acknowledged that Paul's "cash flow could not be accounted for solely from known income sources." Investigators claimed Paul's bank balances "neither prove or disprove" that he received payments from intelligence or security services.

Scotland Yard also spent three weeks going over MI6 records—

none of which indicated that the spy agency conducted any operations at the Ritz Hotel—and interviewed all MI6 agents posted in Paris in 1997. No one admitted to knowing Henri Paul. The report's conclusion: "There is no evidence that Paul was a paid informer of MI6." Nor was there any evidence, the report went on, "that any Secret Intelligence Service (MI6) officer of any designation was involved in the events surrounding the crash."

As for the autopsy on Henri Paul that inexplicably showed lethal levels of carbon monoxide in his blood, the report had no definitive answer. Some of the procedures relating to the first autopsy on Paul in France were, Lord Stevens's report conceded, "not to the highest standard."

Nor was there any definitive answer concerning the role of the mysterious white Fiat Uno that, moments before the crash, allegedly collided with Diana's Mercedes. After checking 4,668 cars, French police stopped hunting for the white Fiat Uno in 1998. It was unlikely, Scotland Yard investigators admitted, that it would ever be found.

Operation Paget had dragged on for so long that no one could accuse Lord Stevens of rushing to judgment. But there were those close to the investigation who felt that the report left too many loose ends. "You got the feeling from the beginning," said one, "that Operation Paget's main job was to disprove any conspiracy so that the Royal Family could just put the whole mess behind them. The longer it took, the more pages in the report, the more it looked as if every stone had been unturned. That just wasn't the case."

The night before the report was released, Lord Stevens met with William and Harry to brief them on Operation Paget's findings. According to one Scotland Yard detective, "They did not really ask detailed questions and seemed very relieved to be told it was just an accident." As had been expected, Clarence House wasted no time issuing a statement saying William and Harry hoped the "conclusive findings" of the report—which neither of them had yet read—would put an end to speculation surrounding their mother's death.

At Buckingham Palace, the Queen, accustomed to plowing through mountains of files virtually every day, studied the report carefully. She would be the only member of the Royal Family, according to one aide, to actually read the document in full.

"Well," she said as she took off her reading glasses and placed them on the desk, "Lord Stevens seems to have done an exhaustive job. But of course nothing will ever satisfy Mr. Al Fayed, I'm afraid."

Indeed, if he held out hope that the formal inquest would take his allegations more seriously, they seemed dashed by the early rulings of Lady Butler-Sloss. After backing down on her decision to hear evidence in private, Butler-Sloss would rule out appointing a jury altogether. Instead, she would insist that she hear the case alone.

Al Fayed branded Lady Butler-Sloss's ruling "shocking but predictable," and went on to say she was merely "continuing the Establishment policy of cover-up. I am sure her next step will be to prevent most of the relevant evidence from even being heard at the inquest."

Weeks later, a three-judge panel would agree with Al Fayed, ruling that a jury—and not Lady Butler-Sloss alone—should hear the case. Referring to Al Fayed's repeated allegations that Prince Philip was behind a government plot to murder Diana and Dodi, London's High Court ruled that "a jury should be summoned in cases where the state, by its agents, may have had some responsibility for the death."

The day after Lord Stevens released Operation Paget's report on the death of his mother, William stood proudly at attention during the Sovereign's Parade at Sandhurst. And just as his brother had done eight months before, William beamed unabashedly as Granny passed by.

Her Majesty spent most of the parade seated in the VIP section with Prince Philip, Prince Charles, and Camilla. (Harry, on duty at Windsor Palace, was a no-show.) But all eyes were on the general stand, where Kate Middleton was not exactly difficult to spot in a scarlet coat and black hat. Palace aides emphasized that she was not there as a member of the royal party, but simply as Wills's girlfriend. "Wills and Kate were just tired of all the talk about their getting engaged," said a Middleton family friend, "so this time she agreed to sit apart from the Royal Family." (Kate had also decided to turn down the coveted invitation to Christmas Dinner at Sandringham that signaled her complete acceptance into the family. "Family dinner really should just be for family," insisted Middleton, who would wind up having Christmas dinner with her own clan instead.)

On this brisk December day at Sandhurst, a smiling Kate chatted brightly with her parents and pointed William out when he marched by carrying an SA80 rifle. Towering over the other cadets and wearing the red sash of the sovereign's banner holder, her boyfriend was not hard to spot, either. "I love the uniform," said Kate, turning toward her mother. "It's so, so sexy."

Once again, amid a dizzying display of gold-braided, medal-encrusted uniforms (William's, Papa's, Grandpapa's), salutes, bows, curtsies, and kisses, William was congratulated by his family on becoming a second lieutenant. It had been less than twenty-four hours since the Operation Paget report was released, and already there was yet another reminder that a changing of the guard had taken place.

Completed just in time for William's commissioning, a new family portrait that was to hang in the grand entrance hall at Sandhurst was unveiled. The Queen was clearly delighted with the painting—the first official portrait of the Royal Family to include Camilla. Unfortunately for the woman who stands to become England's next Queen, she was relegated to the background, her face partially obscured by an officer's hat. "Yes, yes," the Queen said as her gaze drifted to the left of the painting where the distinctly sidelined figure of Camilla stood. "Splendid!"

The day would, in fact, be fraught with symbolism. As she addressed Sandhurst's newest graduates, the Queen knew that Tony Blair's government was deciding whether her grandsons would be headed for duty in Afghanistan or Iraq. Both would soon be trained in desert warfare—specifically to become troop commanders in an armored reconnaissance unit—but there was a consensus among government officials that only Harry could conceivably be sent into harm's way. "William is the last best hope for the monarchy and the Queen knows it," said a veteran British diplomat with close ties to the Royal Family. "So does Tony Blair. There is simply no way they are going to put him at risk, no matter how much he wants to fight."

From here, William was to join his brother with the Household Cavalry's Blues and Royals. But unlike career officer Harry, William would follow up his tour of duty in the army with stints in both the Royal Air Force and the Royal Navy—all by way of preparing him for his role as King. In the meantime, the Princes' commanding officer, Major General Sebastian Roberts, insisted that it was entirely possible both could be deployed to a war zone. "Of course, there are special factors for William," General Roberts said, "but nothing should be ruled in or out."

Either way, it would not be a decision for Granny to make. On this frigid afternoon at Sandhurst, the Queen, wrapped in a crimson coat of her own, shivered slightly before making her remarks. "For those who are to be commissioned today," she told William and his fellow junior officers, "a great deal will be expected of you. You must be courageous yet selfless, leaders yet carers [sic], confident yet considerate. And you must be all these things," she added, pausing to ponder what it meant for her family, "in some of the most challenging environments around the world."

It soon appeared that Harry would be given the chance to serve in one of those "challenging environments." Shortly after New Year's 2007, Charles, the Queen, and the top brass of Britain's armed forces conferred on the wisdom of putting Harry on the front lines. On February 21, Harry was told that he had gotten his wish. Despite ongoing concerns that he would be an obvious target for terrorists, Prince Harry was ordered to ship out for Iraq with the rest of the Household Cavalry Regiment's A Squadron in May. Oddly, the official confirmation of Harry's deployment to Iraq came the day after Prime Minister Tony Blair announced that Britain would be withdrawing 1,600 of its troops from the region.

When he got the news, "Cornet Wales," as Harry was known in the army, jumped in the air, waved his arms, and cheered. "He was," said a fellow officer, "over the moon" at the news that he was headed for an area near the southern port city of Basra. Like any other troop commander, Harry was to lead twelve men in four Scimitar armored reconnaissance vehicles. Their likely assignment: to patrol Iraq's border with Iran.

"Diana would have been immensely proud of Harry," said her friend Richard Kay. As the patroness of several military units, the Princess had dressed her young sons up in uniforms and fatigues, helped them decorate their rooms with military paraphernalia, and taken them to bases to watch combat exercises and ride in tanks. "She would have been immensely proud—and sick with worry at the same time."

Diana would not have been alone. "Haz," an anxious Chelsy confided to a friend, "is off to war."

It would be, William promised, an event "full of energy, full of fun and happiness, which I know she would have wanted." The Princes had already planned a memorial for August 31, 2007 to mark the tenth anniversary of Diana's death—a church service that they stressed would bring together both sides of the family. But, as William pointed out, "the church service wasn't enough." To pay tribute to their mother, only a pop concert would suffice— "a *big* concert," stressed Wills.

The Concert for Diana promised to be that and more. Scheduled for July 1, which would have been Diana's forty-sixth birthday, the star-packed concert at London's new 60,000-seat Wembley Stadium would include a tribute prepared specially for the occasion by Andrew Lloyd Webber, and, most notably, a performance by Diana's old friend Elton John. Although the palace had objected to a rock star performing at Westminster Abbey, it was Sir Elton's moving tribute to his friend, "Candle in the Wind 1997 (Good-bye, England's Rose)" that had reduced a number of mourners, Harry included, to tears. Although it had become the biggest-selling single of all time, John never again performed the song in public—until the Concert for Diana.

Within minutes of going on sale, the first 22,000 tickets to the Concert for Diana had sold out. The total proceeds—conservatively estimated at $10 million—were to be divided up among Diana's favorite charities. To be sure, the Princes were determined to make this a fund-raising event like no other. "First and foremost, the evening is for her—it's all about remembering our mother," William said. "It's got to be the best birthday present she ever had."

In a chilling account given to Operation Paget investigators, Paris police officer Sebastien Dorzee described Diana's last conscious moments. The Princess was bleeding from her nose and her mouth, her head between the two front seats and facing Dodi's mangled body. "She moved, her eyes were open, speaking to me in a foreign language [English]," Dorzee recalled. "I think she said 'My God' on seeing her boyfriend. At the same time she was rubbing her stomach. She must have been in pain." Then, Dorzee said, Diana "turned her head toward the front of the car, saw the driver and then I think she had an even better realization of what was happening. She became quite agitated. A few seconds later she looked at me. Then she put her head down again and closed her eyes. . . ."

Diana never regained consciousness. But what would she have thought if, by some miracle, she could have opened her eyes ten years later? True, it would have been hard to see Camilla replace her as a Princess of Wales destined to become Queen—harder still to see Camilla step into the role of stepmother to her two boys.

There is much about the changed world of the royals, however, that almost certainly would have pleased Diana. The Princess had fought to humanize the monarchy, to replace frosty hauteur with self-deprecating laughter, aloofness with compassion, and soul-deadening inertia with change. As history's renegade Princess, she paid a heavy price for trying to drag the Royal Family, kicking and screaming, into the twenty-first century. Diana was betrayed by her husband, ostracized by the Royal Family, spied upon by powers both foreign and domestic, and hounded by the same voracious media that had made her the world's most idolized human being.

After the first year of shock and grief over her untimely death, Diana's enemies began chipping away at her iconic image. Now the People's Princess was vilified as dangerously neurotic, wantonly promiscuous, self-destructive, obsessively self-centered.

As Diana had feared, in the absence of their mother William and Harry had been thoroughly Windsorized—indoctrinated in the polo-playing, foxhunting, horse-loving ways of the Royal Family. Nevertheless, the seed she had planted in them at an early age took root and bloomed in a way she could hardly have imagined. The excesses of youth aside, both William and Harry were taking on many of the causes she had championed, and finding some of their own.

Tall, handsome, dynamic, and charismatic, Diana's sons seemed to represent the best of both worlds—steadfastly upholding the time-honored traditions of the monarchy while at the same time vowing to connect with their subjects in a way no Windsors ever had before. Nor would it have displeased Diana to know that both

William and Harry had experienced love. (Pointing to the fact that Charles's decision not to marry his first love—Camilla—had turned out to be catastrophic for the Royal Family, many hoped William's unexpected breakup with Kate Middleton in the spring of 2007 would turn out to be temporary.)

For such seismic shifts to occur, profound changes had to first take place in the heart of one person—the woman who had reigned over England for fifty-five of her eighty-one years. From the vantage point of 2007, even the Queen now conceded that the woman who so threatened the monarchy in life may in death have rescued it from oblivion. Yet the confounding truth remained that, after a full decade, neither the Queen nor Prince Charles had ever visited Diana's lonely grave on the tiny island at Althorp.

Ten years after Diana, the debate over what caused her death rages on. Ten years after Diana, whether Charles ever becomes King and Camilla his Queen remains uncertain. Ten years after Diana, the world is more captivated than ever by the lives and loves of Prince William and Prince Harry. Future generations may well simply divide the story of the British monarchy into two parts: the thousand years that went before and the years After Diana.

ACKNOWLEDGMENTS

When Scotland Yard first approached me in 2005 to assist Operation Paget, the official investigation into the death of Princess Diana, I was both flattered and surprised. Flattered because Great Britain's most seasoned investigators told me that my account of the events surrounding the Princess's death, *The Day Diana Died*, had proved to an important source of information and contacts for Operation Paget. Surprised because, *eight years* after that fateful crash in Paris, British authorities had *still* not sought answers to some of the most basic questions regarding Diana's death.

Even more surprising was how quickly the pendulum of public opinion swung from adoration for Diana as a humanitarian and larger-than-life figure to contempt for the "unbalanced" and "spoiled" young woman who "did not know her place" as a member of the Royal Family. Having written extensively about the Royal Family in two bestselling books and profiled Prince William for the cover of *Vanity Fair*'s landmark twentieth anniversary edition, I already knew that this was no accident. The trashing of Diana's memory had less to do with the fickleness of the British public or a handful of memoir-scribbling disgruntled former servants than it did with a highly orchestrated plot to replace the most beloved woman in the realm with the most reviled woman in the realm—and ultimately make Camilla Queen.

With Camilla as the new Princess of Wales (though she calls herself the Duchess of Cornwall), William flirting with marriage, Harry flirting with disaster, and Charles itching more than ever to wear the crown, the Royal Family has changed greatly over the last years—and in some ways, not at all.

After Diana was a joy to write—in no small part because it marked an opportunity for me to once again work with my old friend Will Schwalbe, Hyperion's talented editor in chief. Will is the whole publishing package—that special combination of insight, skill, imagination, humor, and passion that every author treasures in an editor. He is also quite simply one of the nicest people in the industry.

I also owe a debt of gratitude to the entire Hyperion family, especially Bob Miller, Ellen Archer, Brendan Duffy, Katie Wainwright, Beth Gebhard, Phil Rose, Fritz Metsch, David Lott, Navorn Johnson, Muriel Tebid, Rachelle Nashner, and Chisomo Kalinga. My thanks as well to Brad Foltz for his usual splendid cover design and to Camille McDuffie of Goldberg-McDuffie Communications.

Twenty-five years and as many books later, Ellen Levine is also an author's dream: both consummate agent and consummate friend. I also owe a debt of thanks to the Trident Media Group, and in particular to Ellen's associates Alanna Ramirez, Claire Roberts, and Melissa Flashman.

It goes without saying that I am grateful to my father, Cdr. Edward F. Andersen, and to my mother, Jeanette—to whom this book is dedicated. The beautiful, talented, and highly individual Andersen Sisters—Kate and Kelly—continue to make their father proud. This is no small feat; their mother, Valerie, like Diana, is a hard act to follow.

Additional thanks to Peter Archer, Beatrice Humbert, Richard Greene, Dr. Frederic Mailliez, Janet Jenkins, Andrew Gailey, the late Lady Elsa Bowker, Thierry Meresse, Richard Kay, Jeanne Lecorcher, the Countess of Romanones, Lord Bathurst, Alan Hamilton, the late Harold Brooks-Baker, Mark Butt, Elizabeth d'Erlanger, the late Hamish Barne, Andy Radford, Josy Duclos, Remi Gaston-Dreyfus, Natalie Symonds, the late Lord Mishcon, Penny Russell-Smith, Geoffrey Dignell, Lady Yolanda Joseph, Delissa Needham, Rachel Whitburn, Letitia Baldrige, Ezra Zilkha, Elizabeth Whiddett, Miriam Lefort, Penny Walker, Claude Garreck, Patrick Demarchelier, Peter Allen, Nicholas Musgrave, John Marion, Elizabeth DeLeeuw, Fred Hauptfuhrer, Jessica Hogan, Betty Kelly Sargent, Dudley Freeman, Tom Freeman, Laura Elston, Gered Mankowitz, Vivian Simon, Janet Allison, Michelle Lapautre, Alain-Phillipe Feutre, Mary Robertson, Tom Corby, Cecile Zilkha, Kevin Lemarque, Pierre Suu, Hazel Southam, Ray Whelan Jr., Vincent Martin, Everett Raymond Kinstler, Michelle Melliger, Ray Whelan Sr., Paula Dranov, Steve Stylandoudis, Marcel Turgot, Jeanette Peterson, Mary Beth Whelan, David McGough, Barrie Schenck, Yvette Reyes, Charles Furneaux, John Marion, Connie Erickson, Andy Rouvalis, Patrice Fitch, Francis Specker, Hilary Hard, Scott Burkhead, Jo Aldridge, Claudine Wykes, John

Stillwell, James Price, Elizabeth Loth, Ian Walde, Mary Skone
Roberts, Wolfgang Rattay, Richard Grant, Mick Magsino,
Lawrence R. Mulligan, Tasha Hanna, Jane Clucas, Paul White,
David Bergeron, Michelle Melliger, Gary Gunderson, the Press
Association, Kensington Palace, St. James's Palace, Clarence House,
Windsor Castle, Buckingham Palace, Eton, the Queen's Gate
School, Ludgrove, St. Andrews University, Sandhurst, the BBC,
Sky Television, Channel Four Television Ltd., the *Times* of London, the *Daily Mail*, the Litchfield Library, the Gunn Memorial
Library, the Brookfield Library, the New York Public Library, the
Boston Public Library, the Bancroft Library of the University of
California at Berkeley, the Silas Bronson Library, the Reform
Club, the Lansdowne Club, the *New York Times*, the Associated
Press, Reuters, AP/Wide World, and Globe Photos.

SOURCES AND CHAPTER NOTES

The following chapter notes have been compiled to give an overview of the sources drawn upon in preparing *After Diana*, but they are by no means all-inclusive. Certain key sources at Clarence House, St. James's Palace, Windsor Castle, Kensington Palace, Sandringham, Highgrove, Balmoral, Buckingham Palace, and inside Scotland Yard—not to mention friends, acquaintances, and employees of the Royal Family—agreed to cooperate in the writing of this book only if they were assured that their names would not be mentioned. Therefore, the author has respected the wishes of many interviewed sources who wished to remain anonymous, and accordingly has not listed them, either here or elsewhere in the text. Needless to say, there have also been thousands of news reports and articles concerning the Royal Family published in the decade since Diana's death. These reports appeared in such publications as the *New York Times*, the *Sunday Times* of London, the *Wall Street Journal*, the *Washington Post*, the *Guardian*, the *Boston Globe*, the *Los Angeles Times*, *The New Yorker*, the *Daily Mail*, *Vanity Fair*, *Time*, *Life*, *Newsweek*, *Paris Match*, *Le Monde*, *U.S. News and World Report*, the *Times* of London, and the *Economist*, and carried over the Associated Press, Knight-Ridder, Gannett, Bloomberg, and Reuters wires.

CHAPTERS 1 AND 2   Interview subjects included Beatrice Humbert, Alan Hamilton, Frederic Mailliez, Jeanne Lecorcher, Richard Kay, Thierry Meresse, Richard Greene, the late Lady Elsa Bowker, Peter Archer, Ezra Zilkha, Lord Bathurst, Harold Brooks-Baker, Andy Radford, Mark Butt, Claude Garreck, Elizabeth DeLeeuw, Josy Duclos, Remi Gaston-Dreyfus, Peter Allen, Miriam Lefort, Pierre Suu, Steve Stylandoudis.

Published sources included Lord Stevens of Kirkwhelpington, *The Operation Paget Inquiry Report Into the Allegation of Conspiracy to Murder Diana, Princess of Wales, and Emad El-Din Mohamed Abdel Moneim Fayed*, December 14, 2006; "The Nation Unites Against Tradition," *The Observer*, September 7, 1997; "The Princes' Final Farewell," *The Sunday Times* of London, September 7, 1997; "Farewell, Diana," *Newsweek*, September 15, 1997; Annick Cojean, "The Final Interview," *Le Monde*, August 27, 1997; Anthony Holden, "Why Royals Must Express Remorse," *The Express*, September 3, 1997; John Simpson, "Goodbye England's Rose: A Nation Says Farewell," *Sunday Telegraph*, September 7, 1997; "Diana, Princess of Wales 1961-1997," *The Week*, September 6, 1997; Joe Chidley, "From the Heart," *Macleans*, September 15, 1997; "Lady Dies," *Liberation*, September 1, 1997; "Driver Was Drunk," *Le Monde*, September 3, 1997; "Charles Escorts Diana Back to a Grieving Britain," the *New York Times*, September 1, 1997; Andrew Morton, *Diana: Her True Story*, (New York: Simon & Schuster, 1997); Pascal Palmer, "I Gave Diana Last Rites," *The Mirror*, October 23, 1997; Christopher Andersen, *The Day Diana Died* (New York: William Morrow, 1998); "Flashback to the Accident," *Liberation*, September 2, 1997; Howard Chua-Eoan, Steve Wulf, Jeffrey Kluger, Christopher Redman and David Van Biema, "A Death in Paris: The Passing of Diana," *Time*, September 8, 1997; "Diana, Investigation of the Investigation," *Le Point*, September 13, 1997;

Robert Hardman, "Princes' Last Minutes with Mother," *The Daily Telegraph*, September 3, 1997; Alan Hamilton, Andrew Pierce and Philip Webster, "Royal Family Is 'Deeply Touched' by Public Support," *The Times*, September 4, 1997; Thomas Sancton and Scott MacLeod, *Death of a Princess: The Investigation* (New York: St. Martin's Press, 1998); Marianne Macdonald, "A Rift Death Can't Heal," *The Observer*, September 14, 1997; Polly Toynbee, "Forever at Peace," *Radio Times*, September 13-19, 1997; Tess Rock and Natalie Symonds, "Our Diana Diaries," *Sunday Mirror*, November 16, 1997; Robert Jobson and Greg Swift, "Look After William and Harry," *Daily Express*, December 22, 1997; Hamish Bowles, "At Long Last Love," *Vogue*, April 2005; Alan Cowell, "Royal Wedding Put Off One Day for Funeral," *The New York Times*, April 5, 2005; Live converge by the BBC, CNN, Fox News (on which the author offered live commentary), and MSNBC of the wedding of Charles and Camilla Parker Bowles; Mark Oliver, "Charles and Camilla Wed," *The Guardian*, April 9, 2005; Andrew Alderson, "Husband and Wife—At Last," the *Sunday Telegraph*, April 10, 2005; Barbra Kantrowitz, "Legal at Last," *Newsweek,* April 18, 2005; Simon Freeman, "The Royal Wedding Day, Minute by Minute," *The Times*, April 9, 2005; Anne-Marie O'Neill, "Finally, Husband and Wife," *People*, April 25, 2005; Jasper Gerard, "Wed at Last After 34 Years," the *Sunday Times*, April 10, 2005.

CHAPTERS 3 – 5   For these chapters, the author drew on conversations with Peter Archer, Lady Elsa Bowker, Hamish Barne, Delissa Needham, Richard Greene, Alan Hamilton, Penny Walker, Geoffrey Bignell, Lady Yolanda Joseph, Lord Mishcon, Richard Kay, the Countess of Romanones, Fred Hauptfuhrer, David McGough, Hazel Southam, Charles Furneaux, Evelyn Phillips, Elizabeth Widdett, Janet Lizop, and Mary Robertson.

Among the published sources consulted: David Ward, "Prince's Pride in His Sons," *The Guardian*, September 20, 1997; Wendy Berry,

The Housekeeper's Diary (New York: Barricade Books, Inc., 1995; Sean O'Neill, "Lady 'Kanga' Tryon Is Detained Under Mental Health Act," *The Telegraph*, June 18, 1997; Stephen P. Barry, *Royal Service: My Twelve Years as Valet to Prince Charles* (New York: Macmillan, 1983); "Di's Son Injured," Associated Press, June 4, 1991; James Hewitt, *Love and War* (London: Blake Publishing Ltd., 1999); Sarah Bradford, *Elizabeth*, (London: William Heinemann, 1996); Sally Bedell Smith, *Diana In Search of Herself* (New York: Signet, 2000); David Leppard and Christopher Morgan, "Police Fears Over William's Friends," *Sunday Times*, February 27, 2000; Barbara Kantrowitz, "William: The Making of a Modern King," *Newsweek*, June 26, 2000; P.D. Jephson, *Shadows of a Princess* (New York: HarperCollins, 2000); Adam Sherwin, "Anti-Hunting Car Bombers Threaten Prince," *The Times* of London, October 23, 2000; Warren Hoge, "Queen Breaks the Ice: Camilla's Out of the Fridge," *The New York Times*, June 5, 2000; Rita Delfiner, "Camilla Finally Comes in from the Cold," the *New York Post*, June 6, 2000; Richard Kay, "William Stalked by His Uncle's TV Crew," the *Daily Mail,* September 27, 2001; Bob Colacello, "A Court of His Own," *Vanity Fair*, October 2001; Cowell, "Charles's Leaked Letters Land Him in Hot Water," *The New York Times*, September 26, 2002; J.F.O. McAllister, "Once Upon a Time, There Was a Pot-Smoking Prince," *Time*, January 28, 2002; Warren Hoge, "Charles's Response to Use of Drugs by Son is Praised," *The New York Times*, January 14, 2002; Ellen Tumposky and Corky Siemaszko, "Look to Put the Lid on Pot Prince," the New York *Daily News*, January 15, 2002; Antony Barnett, "Prince Taken to Drink and Drugs Rehab Clinic," *The Observer*, January 13, 2002; Ben Summerskill, "The Trouble with Harry," *The Observer*, January 13, 2002; Simone Simmons, *Diana: The Last Word* (New York: St. Martin's Press, 2005); Robert Hardman, "Birthday at School for Royal Highness Who Towers Over His Dad," the *Daily Telegraph*, September 15, 2000; Alan Hamilton, "Birthday Prince at Ease with Himself," the *Times*, September 15, 2000; Pico Iyer, "A Ma'am for All Seasons," *Time*, April 8, 2002.

CHAPTERS 6-9   Information for these chapters was based in part on conversations with Richard Greene, Peter Archer, Lord Mishcon, Alan Hamilton, Lady Elsa Bowker, Lord Bathurst, Grigori Rassinier, Ezra Zilkha, Kitty Carlisle Hart, Aileen Mehle, Janet Allison, Muriel Hartwick, Oleg Cassini, Letitia Baldrige, Gared Mankowitz, Nicolas Musgrave, Cecile Zilkha, Laura Elston, Vincent Martin, Natalie Symonds.

Published sources included Richard Price, "Hewitt Wanted 10 Million Pounds for Letters from Diana," *Daily Mail*, December 16, 2002; Warren Hoge, "Royal Palace Is Roiled Again by New Round of Revelations," *The New York Times*, November 11, 2002; Tom Rawstorne, "William: In His Own Words," the *Daily Mail*, May 30, 2003; Christopher Andersen, "The Divided Prince," *Vanity Fair*, September 2003; Richard Kay and Michael Seamark, "Charles on the Rack," the *Daily Mail*, November 8, 2003; Robert Jobson, "Why Charles Allegations Can't Be True," *Evening Standard*, November 10, 2003; Stephen Glove, "The Royals Must Change . . . or Die," the *Daily Mail*, November 11, 2003; Bob Colacello, "Charles and Camilla, Together at Last," *Vanity Fair*, December 2005; Warren Hoge, "As Royal Rumors Swirl in Britain, Charles Orders a Palace Inquiry," *The New York Times*, November 13, 2002; Paul Henderson, "I Was Raped by Charles' Servant," *The Mail on Sunday*, November 10, 2002; Dominick Dunne, "Diana's Secrets," *Vanity Fair*, January 2003; Joan Smith, "Prince Charles: What a Guy! What a Boss! What?," *The Independent*, March 12, 2003; "William The Young Yob: Charles Forced to Apologize for His Son's Road-Rage," the *Daily Mail*, June 16, 2003; Richard Kay and Mike Pflanz, "Prince Harry, a Stunning Heiress and the Hewitt Connection," the *Daily Mail*, February 12, 2004; Michael Dynes and Alan Hamilton, "Harry's Sobering Stay in the AIDS Kingdom," *The Times,* March 4, 2004; Samantha Miller, Simon Perry and Ellen Tumposky, "A Tale of Two Princes," *People*, November 8, 2004; Patrick Jephson, "Everyone Loves a Royal Wedding . . . Usually," *Sunday Telegraph*, March 27, 2005; "The Two Vital Questions," *People*, November 9, 1997; "It Was No Accident,"

The Mirror, February 12, 1998; Rosa Monckton, "Time to End False Rumors," *Newsweek*, March 2, 1998; Jerome Dupuis, "Diana: The Unpublished Report of Witnesses at the Ritz," *L'Express*, March 12, 1998; Henry Porter, "Her Last Summer," *Vanity Fair*, October 1997; Kate Snell, *Diana: Her Last Love* (London: Granada Media, 2000); "Diana: The Man She Really Loved," *Point de Vue, Images du Monde*, November 5–11, 1997; Daniel Waddell, "Diana's Mother Speaks of Her Concern Over Young Princes," *Daily Telegraph*, July 16, 1998; Charles Rae, "Wills and Harry Do Full Monty," the *Sun*, August 1, 1998; Judy Wade, "Marking a Milestone in Charles's and Camilla's Relationship," *Hello!*," August 15, 1998; Christopher Morgan and David Leppard, "Party Girl in William's Circle Snorted Cocaine," the *Sunday Times*, February 26, 2000; Richard Kay, "Willful Will," *Daily Mail*, December 23, 1999; Robert Hardman, "Just (Call Me) William," *The Daily Telegraph*, June 9, 2000; Alex O'Connell, "Prince Chases Adventure in Remotest Chile," September 30, 2000; Michelle Tauber, "Speaking His Mind," *People*, October 16, 2000; Andrew Pierce and Simon de Bruxelles, "Our Mother Was Betrayed," *The Times*, September 30, 2000; Trevor Gundy, "Mugabe's One Million Pound Party as Millions Face Starvation," *The Scotsman*, January 12, 2005; Matthew Bailey, Andrew Pierce, "'I'm Sorry for Wearing Nazi Swastika,' Says Prince Harry," *The Times*, January 13, 2005; Neil Tweedie and Michael Kallenbach, "Prince Harry Faces Outcry at Nazi Outfit," the *Daily Telegraph*, January 14, 2005; Jamie Turner, "Harry's Choice of Costume Was Lazy," *The Times*, January 15, 2005; Caroline Graham, *Camilla and Charles: The Love Story* (London: Blake Publishing Ltd., 2005); Roxanne Roberts, "Fairy Tale for Grown-Ups: Charles and Camilla Once Upon a Time," the *Washington Post*, Feb 11, 2005; Barbara Kantrowitz and Stryker McGuire, "Now You Ask Me?," *Newsweek*, February 21, 2005; Josh Tyrangiel, "The Prince Proposes," *Time*, February 21, 2005; Thomas Fields-Meyer and Pam Lambert, "Royal Stepmum," *People*, February 28, 2005; Heather Timmons, "The Once and Future Camilla," *The New York Times*, April 3, 2005; Susan Schindehette and Allison Adato, "Princes in Love," *People*, August 8, 2005; Nicola Methven, "Hypno-Di-Sed:

Hewitt Put in Trance," *The Mirror*, September 19, 2005; Michelle Green, "Is She the One?," *People*, October 17, 2005; Caroline Davies, "First Royal Sandringham Christmas for Camilla," *Daily Telegraph*, December 24, 2005; Paul Cheston, "Charles's Dicy Court Drama," *Evening Standard*, March 17, 2006; Caroline Davies, "Duchess Gets a Glimpse of Life Behind the Veil in Saudi Arabia," the *Daily Telegraph*, March 30, 2006; Robert Jobson, "Royals Out in Force as Camilla's Daughter Marries an Old Etonian," *Evening Standard*, May 5, 2006; Robert Stansfield, "Harry the Hangover," the *Mirror* June 16, 2006; Robert Jobson, *William's Princess* (London: Blake Publishing, Ltd., 2006); Richard Palmer and Lizzie Catt, "William and Kate on Ibiza 'Rave' Holiday," the *Daily Express*, September 2, 2006; Pia Nanny, "Davy Robbery Causes Uproar," News 24.com., November 9, 2006; Sandra Laville and Owen Gibson, "Scooped by His Own Mobile Phone," *The Guardian*, November 30, 2006; Emily Nash, "Diana: The Verdict," the *Mirror*, December 11, 2006; Alex Tresniowski and Ashley Williams, "Will & Kate: The Perfect Match," *People*, December 11, 2006; J.F.O. McAllister, "Debunking the Conspiracy Theories," *Time*, December 14, 2006; Lord Stevens of Kirkwhelpington, *The Operation Paget Inquiry Report into the Allegation of Conspiracy to Commit Murder*, December 14, 2006; "Prince William Graduates As an Officer," *The Guardian*, December 15, 2006; Chris Hughes, "Salutes You, Sir," *Mirror*, December 16, 2006; Frances Gibb, "Lawyers Planning Test Case to Stop Paparazzi Hounding Kate Middleton," *The Times*, January 9, 2007; "News of the World Journalist Jailed," Reuters, January 26, 2007; "Prince Harry Will Serve in Iraq," BBC News, February 22, 2007; Michael Evans, "Charles and the General Let Harry Join His Men in Iraq," *The Times*, February 23, 2007; Richard Norton-Taylor, "No Special Favors as Prince Gets His Iraq Orders," *The Guardian*, February 23, 2007.

BIBLIOGRAPHY

Allison, Ronald, and Sarah Riddell, editors. *The Royal Encyclopedia.* London: Macmillan, 1991.

Andersen, Christopher. *The Day Diana Died.* New York: William Morrow, 1998.

————. *The Day John Died.* New York: William Morrow, 2000.

————. *Diana's Boys.* New York: William Morrow, 2001.

Barry, Stephen P. *Royal Service: My Twelve Years as Valet to Prince Charles.* New York: Macmillan, 1983.

Berry, Wendy. *The Housekeeper's Diary.* New York: Barricade Books Inc., 1995.

Boca, Geoffrey. *Elizabeth and Philip.* New York: Henry Holt and Company, 1953.

Botham, Noel. *The Murder of Princess Diana.* New York: Pinnacle Books, 2004.

Bradford, Sarah. *Diana*. New York: Viking, 2006.

Brander, Michael. *The Making of the Highlands*. London: Constable and Company Ltd., 1980.

Bryan, J., III, and Charles J.V. Murphy. *The Windsor Story*. New York: William Morrow, 1979.

Burrell, Paul. *A Royal Duty*. New York: New American Library, 2004.

———. *The Way We Were*. New York: William Morrow, 2006.

Campbell, Lady Colin. *Diana in Private*. London: Smith Gryphon, 1993.

Cannadine, David. *The Decline and Fall of the British Aristocracy*. New Haven: Yale University Press, 1990.

Cannon, John, and Ralph Griffiths. *The Oxford Illustrated History of the British Monarchy*. Oxford and New York: Oxford University Press, 1992.

Cathcart, Helen. *The Queen Herself*. London: W.H. Allen, 1983.

———. *The Queen and Prince Philip: Forty Years of Happiness*. London: Hodder and Stoughton, 1987.

Clarke, Mary. *Diana Once Upon a Time*. London: Sidgwick & Jackson, 1994.

Clifford, Max, and Angela Levin. *Max Clifford: Read All About It*. London: Virgin, 2005.

Davies, Nicholas. *Diana: The Lonely Princess*. New York: Birch Lane, 1996.

———. *Queen Elizabeth II*. New York: Carol Publishing Group, 1996.

———. *William: The Inside Story of the Man Who Will Be King*. New York: St. Martin's Press, 1998.

Delderfield, Eric R. *Kings and Queen of England and Great Britain.* London: David & Charles, 1990.

Delorm, Rene. *Diana and Dodi: A Love Story.* Los Angeles: Tallfellow Press, 1998.

Dempster, Nigel, and Peter Evans. *Behind Palace Doors.* New York: Putnam, 1993.

Dimbleby, Jonathan. *The Prince of Wales: A Biography.* New York: William Morrow, 1994.

Edwards, Anne. *Diana and the Rise of the House of Spencer.* London: Hodder and Stoughton, 1999.

Ferguson, Ronald. *The Galloping Major: My Life and Singular Times.* London: Macmillan, 1994.

Fisher, Graham and Heather. *Elizabeth: Queen & Mother.* New York: Hawthorn Books, 1964.

Foreman, J.B., ed. *Scotland's Splendour.* Glasgow: William Collins Sons & Co. Ltd., 1961.

Fox, Mary Virginia. *Princess Diana.* Hillside, N.J.: Enslow, 1986.

Goldsmith, Lady Annabel. *Annabel: An Unconventional Life.* London: Phoenix, 2004.

Graham, Caroline. *Camilla—The King's Mistress.* London: John Blake Publishing Ltd., 1994.

———. *Camilla and Charles: The Love Story.* London: John Blake Publishing Ltd., 2005.

Graham, Tim. *Diana: HRH The Princess of Wales.* New York: Summit, 1988.

———. *The Royal Year 1993.* London: Michael O'Mara, 1993.

Gregory, Martyn. *The Diana Conspiracy Exposed*. London: Virgin Publishing, 1999.

Hewitt, James. *Love and War*. London: John Blake Publishing Ltd., 1999.

Hoey, Brian. *All the King's Men*. London: HarperCollins.1992.

Holden, Anthony. *Charles*. London: Weidenfeld and Nicolson, 1988.

————. *The Tarnished Crown*. New York: Random House, 1993.

Hough, Richard. *Born Royal: The Lives and Loves of the Young Windsors*. New York: Bantam, 1988.

Hutchins, Chris, and Peter Thompson. *Sarah's Story: The Duchess Who Defied the Royal House of Windsor*. London: Smith Gryphon, 1992.

Jephson, P.D. *Shadows of a Princess*. New York: HarperCollins Publishers, 2000.

Jobson, Robert. *William's Princess: The Love Story That Will Change the Royal Family Forever*. London: John Blake Publishing Ltd., 2006.

Junor, Penny. *Charles*. New York: St. Martin's Press, 1987.

————. *The Firm*. New York: Thomas Dunne Books, 2005.

Lacey, Robert. *Majesty*. New York: Harcourt Brace Jovanovich, 1977.

————. *Queen Mother*. Boston: Little, Brown, 1986.

Lathan, Caroline, and Jeannie Sakol. *The Royals*. New York: Congdon & Weed, 1987.

Maclean, Veronica. *Crowned Heads*. London: Hodder & Stoughton, 1993.

Martin, Ralph G. *Charles & Diana*. New York: Putnam, 1985.

Montgomery-Massingberd, Hugh. *Burke's Guide to the British Monarchy*. London: Burke's Peerage, 1977.

Morton, Andrew. *Diana: Her True Story*. New York: Simon & Schuster, 1997.

———. *Inside Buckingham Palace*. London: Michael O'Mara, 1991.

———. *Diana: In Pursuit of Love*. London: Michael O'Mara, 2004.

Pasternak, Anna. *Princess in Love*. London: Bloomsbury, 1994.

Pimlott, Ben. *The Queen: A Biography of Elizabeth II*. New York: John Wiley & Sons, Inc., 1996.

Reese-Jones, Trevor, with Moira Johnston. *The Bodyguard's Story*. New York: Warner Books, 2000.

Sancton, Thomas, and Scott Macleod. *Death of a Princess: The Investigation*. New York: St. Martin's Press, 1998.

Sarah, The Duchess of York, with Jeff Coplon. *My Story*. New York: Simon & Schuster, 1996.

Seward, Ingrid. *The Queen and Di*. New York: HarperCollins, 2000.

Simmons, Simone, with Susan Hill. *Diana: The Secret Years*. London: Michael O'Mara, 1998.

———. *The Last Word*. New York: St. Martin's Press, 2005.

Smith, Sally Bedell. *Diana in Search of Herself*. New York: Times Books, 1999.

Snell, Kate. *Diana: Her Last Love*. London: Granada Media, 2000.

Spencer, Charles. *The Spencers: A Personal History of an English Family*. New York: St. Martin's Press, 2000.

Spoto, Donald. *Diana: The Last Year*. New York: Harmony Books, 1997.

————. *The Decline and Fall of the House of Windsor*. New York: Simon & Schuster, 1995.

Lord Stevens of Kirkwhelpington. *The Operation Paget Inquiry Report into the Allegation of Conspiracy to Murder Diana, Princess of Wales, and Emad El-Din Mohamed Abdel Moneim Fayed*. London, December 14, 2006.

Thornton, Michael. *Royal Feud*. London: Michael Joseph, 1985.

Wade, Judy. *The Truth: The Friends of Diana, Princess of Wales, Tell Their Stories*. London: John Blake Publishing Ltd., 2001.

Wharfe, Ken, with Robert Jobson. *Diana: Closely Guarded Secret*. London: Michael O'Mara Books, 2003.

Whitaker, James. *Diana v. Charles*. London: Signet, 1993.

Wilson, Christopher. *The Windsor Knot*. New York: Citadel Press, 2002.

INDEX